Rather poor
Difficult to
read

Fundamentalism, *Jan 98*
Mythos, and
World Religions

Read the
"Conclusion"

Jan 2001

Niels C. Nielsen, Jr.

Fundamentalism, Mythos, and World Religions

STATE UNIVERSITY OF NEW YORK PRESS

Published by
State University of New York Press, Albany

© 1993 State University of New York

For information, address State University of New York
Press, State University Plaza, Albany, N.Y., 12246

Production by E. Moore
Marketing by Bernadette LaManna

Library of Congress Cataloging-in-Publication Data

Nielsen, Niels Christian, 1921-
    Fundamentalism, mythos, and world religions / Niels C. Nielsen,
Jr.
        p.   cm.
    Includes bibliographical references and index.
    ISBN 0-7914-1653-4 (acid-free). — ISBN 0-7914-1654-2 (pbk. : acid
-free)
    1. Fundamentalism—Comparative studies.   2. Myth.   I. Title.
BL238.N54   1993
200'.9'04—dc20   92-37601
                                                                    CIP

10 9 8 7 6 5 4 3 2 1

Contents

Preface

The terms *fundamentalism* and *fundamentalist* have been so widely used that they have become familiar to all who follow the news. Reports on "the new religious Right" have filled the media ever since the Moral Majority movement emerged in the United States, and today television evangelists continue to exemplify its stance for viewers nationwide. *Islamic fundamentalism* has become a standard media catchword for various right-wing Muslim parties that have gained political importance. By extension, the label *fundamentalist* is applied to Jewish, Hindu, Sikh, and Buddhist groups that represent similar positions within their own traditions.

Scholarly research, seeking some critical distance, increasingly has focused on a plurality of fundamentalisms rather than on one single form. Is there a single set of common characteristics by which fundamentalist phenomena can be identified and defined? Or is *fundamentalism* a word that only obscures the real diversity of piety and belief? Either alternative is too simple! The goal of this study is to appraise fundamentalisms against the background of the diverse outlooks of the major religions. Of course, questions of definition become more complex and probing, but also more revealing, in such a strategy.

Even if it is not possible to subsume all diverse manifestations under a single heading, fundamentalism may still be identified as a religious phenomenon. One must locate its social patterns and attitudes at a deeper historical and existential level. Both Christianity and Buddhism, for example, defy any simple empirical definition with their bewildering variety of branches, denominations, and sects. Still each has a defining common core with its basic symbols and mythos (e.g., monotheism and incarnation, or Enlightenment and emptiness). Paradoxically, social scientists and historians have researched fundamentalist phenomena often before theologians have taken note. Even if fundamentalism is not a religion, it has its own kind of coherence as a phenomenon in most religions in the modern world.

The term *mythos* is used in this study with the meaning that it has in the history of religions, as archetypal and paradigmatic, and not in its popular

reductionistic sense. Such an approach assumes that arguments and rationalizations are less basic, less primordial, than the symbols that sustain them and
that they in turn seek to sustain. Theological claims and interpretations develop out of a prior commitment to an underlying symbolism or mythos and
cannot be understood apart from that commitment.

This book is written by a nonfundamentalist who in his teaching has introduced students to the major world faiths in a variety of courses in religious
studies. Its premise is that religion has a many-sided and meaningful history of
its own that cannot be judged simply from any one tradition or culture. Each
of the major religions has its own distinctive symbolic paradigm or mythos.
What is too often lacking in the study of fundamentalism is an approach that
examines particular faiths in the inclusive setting of the history of religions.

All major faiths have been forced in one way or another to come to terms
with modernity. Fundamentalists characteristically take a defensive stance in
reaction against the modern world. The continuing strength of their position is
that it treats the religious symbolism of mythos with radical existential seriousness. This stance makes fundamentalism an appealing and powerful phenomenon in a time of social crisis and ideological change. Its great weakness,
I will argue, is its simplistic understanding of mythos. In short, fundamentalists
do not "demythologize"!

This study seeks to understand contemporary fundamentalist movements
by reference to paradigm theory as developed by Thomas Kuhn and used by
Hans Küng to periodicize the history of religions in different models. Major
religions exhibit diverse paradigms even within their own respective settings. A
critical approach to fundamentalism, combining Küng's periodization and historicism with Eliade's still highly debated analysis, supplies rich understanding
beyond the common stereotypes. Eliade was convinced that the dynamic of
religion lies in its mythos. He saw religions as symbol systems expressed in
narrative story and ritual; in his view, mythos has always been paradigmatic.

Of course, throughout much of the past, the truth of mythos has hardly
been challenged: Mythos has been accepted simply as true. The recognition of
myth as myth—I will argue—is an achievement of modernity. In the case of
fundamentalism, this distinction is not made. Its adherents characteristically es-
pouse a single literal paradigm or model.

The account presented in this book can be divided into two parts. The
first chapter begins with a general overview of the growth of fundamentalism
in the United States. It soon becomes evident that this development can be
better understood when it is related to phenomena in other religions and areas
and not viewed simply as standing alone. The second chapter examines the history of fundamentalism in North America in greater detail. Addressing the
question of comparative worldviews as well as the relation between modern

science and religion, it employs the paradigm theory that later is applied to other religions. The difference between fundamentalism and traditional ortho-doxies is emphasized; as compared to the latter, fundamentalism is significantly a twentieth-century revolt against modernity.

Chapters 3 and 5 define the book's use of the theme of mythos. Chapter 3 places mythos in the history of religion; chapter 5 is more generally philo-sophical. Chapter 4, between them, explores the impact of evolutionary theory and higher criticism on nineteenth-century evangelicalism. The reader may wonder how mythos figures in this chapter. The intention is to illustrate the relation between paradigm and mythos and to show the consequences of ne-glecting questions of symbolism in fundamentalist literalism. What was gen-erally accepted as common sense is revealed as actually being a matter of mythos, it is argued.

The more interesting long-term issue, in studying the emergence of fun-damentalism, is how religious paradigms from different eras relate to each other cross-culturally. This is the topic of the second part of the book. Chapters 6 through 10 apply the perspectives developed in the first section to major world religions. These chapters treating fundamentalism in major world religions can be read and judged independently of the first part, if the reader wishes. They focus less on the epistemological and ontological aspects of symbolism than on changes of mythos in the contemporary setting. In so doing, they provide a phenomenological historical account of this fascinating development and un-cover dimensions previously overlooked by both fundamentalists and their crit-ics. The concluding summary chapter includes reflections on the limits and future of the so-called new religious Right.

I am grateful to a variety of friends who have critically commented on my writing. They include David G. Bradley (Duke University), Norvin Hein (Yale University), and Thomas J. Hopkins (Franklin and Marshall College), all of whom are fellow members of the American Society for the Study of Religion; Rabbi David Hartman of the Shalom Hartman Institute in Jerusalem; and Father J. Rosaario Narchison of the Indian School of Ecumenical Theology in Bagelore, India. None of them are responsible for, or necessarily in agree-ment with, my conclusions; all have made helpful suggestions and corrections of the text.

Chapter 1

The Problematic

DELIMITATION AND DEFINITION—WHAT IS FUNDAMENTALISM?

"Fundamentalism has become an evocative image *in* our time," observes Lionel Caplan, of the School of Oriental and African Studies in London, in his *Studies in Religious Fundamentalism*.[1] "There can be few terms which have, of late, obtruded on popular consciousness in the West as persistently."

Fundamentalism "is not one revolt but a series of revolts by those who uphold deep-seated religious values"—in this way Bruce B. Lawrence characterizes "the new religious Right" in a variety of religions.[2] Pointing to the notoriety that fundamentalism has received in the media, he calls it "a blue-chip stock" for journalists and notes that its advocates are "marketable symbols."[3]

Fundamentalist symbols and myth, more than the arguments used in the defense or refutation of the position they represent, deserve much greater attention than they have received. Analysis is not easy here, given the fact that there are a number of fundamentalisms and not just one. The outlook seldom has taken the form of a single unified movement in any major religion; yet there are repeated symbolic patterns and themes that continue to reappear in fundamentalist ideology. For example, fundamentalists typically seek to return to an alleged golden age when their own particular type of piety and belief was dominant. The roots of this longing lie deep in both the history of religion and the individual religious experience. Fundamentalists support their position by appealing to the "timeless and unchanging truths of Scripture," seldom taking into account the wide variety of expression in humankind's religious past. At issue is not only tolerance and pluralism, but the historical character of religious insight. Characteristically for most fundamentalists, the idea that their own pattern of interpretation is not unique, and the absolute truth, is "unthinkable."

A European critic protests against the judgment that "no one who does not share fundamentalist conviction can be a true Christian."[4] As he sees it, fundamentalism was first a reaction against the process of modernization in religion and the Enlightenment—not just contemporary "secular humanism" or modernism. This is a premise that will be discussed in greater detail in examining fundamentalism in particular religions.

Christian fundamentalism is identified in the European study as a phenomenon directed

1. against every theological, cultural, and political liberalism;
2. against the historical and critical view of Christian faith documents (Scriptures, etc.; against the infallibility of the pope, the infallibility of the Bible is affirmed);
3. against the theory of evolution as compared with a literal understanding of the biblical creation stories; and
4. against every syncretism as seen in all interreligious dialogue, in ecumenics, and (secularly) in the League of Nations and the United Nations.[5]

It is easy enough for opponents to dismiss "the fundamentalist phenomenon" as a kind of passing fanaticism—but this does not inhibit "true believers" from making converts. More than ever before, the fundamentalist cause seems to be growing as "defenders of God" seek to impose their religious views on the community at large. Fundamentalism has been gaining popular appeal both within Christianity and in other world faiths as well during the last quarter of the twentieth century. As it is now a worldwide phenomenon, its ideological as well as its sociological bases also need to be appraised. An alternative strategy to the critics' dismissal of fundamentalism as short-lived or so vague as to defy any analytic definition is to relate its symbols and doctrines to the much older and more encompassing history of religions. This, of course, requires a cross-cultural view. Lawrence writes: "Comparison alone reveals what is common, and also what is unique, in each fundamentalist cadre."[6]

Fundamentalism stands at the far right of a spectrum of ideologies ranging from secular humanism, liberalism, and modernism, on the left, through traditionalism (and neotraditionalism) and orthodoxy (and neoorthodoxy), to evangelicalism and fundamentalism, on the right. In the United States, right-wing television evangelists of "the electronic church" like Pat Robertson, Jerry Falwell, and Jimmy Swaggart dominate television religious programing. Falwell has described his own kind of dogmatic scripturalism as "reactionary Evangelicalism." Although individual revivalist preachers of this type, now using the "larger tent" of television, may come and go, the populist folk piety to which they appeal continues to be a seedbed for their message.

There is widespread consensus among social scientists and historians of religion researching fundamentalism that it is first and foremost a defensive reaction, a negative response to what is seen as the specter of modernity. In the United States, where the term fundamentalism first was coined by Curtis Lee Laws in 1920, Protestant hegemony began to crumble under growing pressure even before the First World War.[7] Generations-long cultural and religious syntheses were challenged by evolution and higher criticism. There were, however, other factors that brought on the disintegration of the "Evangelical Empire" of the nineteenth century.

Industrialization and urbanization contributed to a growing secular ethos. The arrival of large numbers of non-Protestants—Jews and Roman Catholics—as immigrants from Europe brought about significant sociological shifts in the population at large. Protestants were forced to choose between accommodation and defensiveness, modernism and fundamentalism. Fundamentalism was an attempt to protect their domain. Marsden uses the analogy of immigrants coming to the New World to describe the drastic cultural changes that took place. The uprooting was equally as revolutionary as crossing the ocean. Modernists were somewhat similar to immigrants who welcomed the different way of life in the new country. Fundamentalists were like the groups who resisted assimilation and built their own defensive culture. Indeed, they are not only sheltered "behind an ideological ghetto wall, but the wall itself . . . [is] heavily fortified and regarded as the very wall of Zion."[8]

To explain the continuation of this phenomenon today, we need to identify a number of distinctions. It is important to differentiate between Christian fundamentalism and evangelicalism as well as between secularism and secularity. While the term *secularism* is often used to indicate a confessionally neutral area in community life—for example, the separation of church and state—*secularity* implies total exclusion of religious influence from public life.

IN SEARCH OF A MODEL

In reaction against secularity, fundamentalists have sought to impose their own conviction and its symbols not just on personal and family morals but on entire nations. Falwell's role in the Reagan era is an example par excellence. To be sure, the Moral Majority, which he led, now has been disbanded, and he is receiving less national press coverage than before. In his case, the fundamentalists' program is no longer simply one of sectarian separatism or otherworldly salvation (as in the 1920s). Instead, it offers an inclusive ideology and worldview that have been allied with right-wing political causes. Its advocates even accommodate in limited measure to modern science (tapping the resources of technologies and the communication revolution), certain that they can win over skepticism and unbelief.

In principle, "the new fundamentalism" and its model needs to be distinguished from orthodoxy. Its expectations are more messianic and even apocalyptic as believers anticipate the fulfillment of scriptural prophecies in a number of religions. Their view of creation (so-called scientific creationism) as well as eschatology, "last things," is highly literalistic. The beginning of the world (or the fulfillment of history) all too easily is reduced to being one event among others rather than the unique foundation of existence (or the end of time). Our concern will be to "unpack" such a paradoxically literal interpretation of traditional symbols, locating its parallels in the longer history of religion. Whereas orthodoxies have been more cautious, fundamentalists generally give graphic and detailed descriptions of world beginnings. Can the description of these "border" or "limit" situations, standing as they do at the intersection of time and eternity, really remain so unambiguously factual and without mystery?

As will be explained later in detail, in this study, the terms *myth* and *mythical* will not be employed simply in the everyday derogatory sense of an untrue story, a legend or fairy tale. Historians of religion today define myth broadly as a symbolic model or archetype. *Mythos* will be used here in a very specialized sense to identify a group of related myths (or microparadigms) that make up an inclusive archetypal model (or macroparadigm—in short, a larger, more seminal mythology). The premise is that symbol and narrative are more primordial than their rationalization. That explicit theological interpretation is a later development is something fundamentalists almost entirely ignore.

Actually, fundamentalism is not as radically novel as is often alleged. In the larger context of the history of religion, it soon becomes clear that most of its claims have precursors and parallels in the past. What is intensified, if not entirely new, is the revolt against modernity. Emmanuel Sivan of the

Hebrew University in Jerusalem has researched recent Jewish and Muslim as well as Christian fundamentalisms.[9] He confirms that (as we have already suggested) they project a mythical view from the past—often an earlier golden age—into the future; actually, this has been a widespread phenomenon throughout the history of religion. From such a symbolic model, more powerful than a simply political one, religious revivalists seek the transformation of today's world and the resolution of its malaise in the restoration of an earlier sacred order.

THE EVOLUTION CONTROVERSY

The evolution controversy of the early 1920s highlighted dramatically what was going on in the United States, where the "fundamentalist phenomenon" was first described after the turn of the century. The satirist H. L. Mencken quipped, "Heave an egg out of a Pullman window, and you will hit a Fundamentalist almost anywhere in the United States."[10] Mencken despised what he regarded as inexcusable parochialism and stupidity. Attending the Scopes trial, at which William Jennings Bryan opposed evolution, he attacked the "silver tongued orator" bitterly. When Bryan died a few days after the trial, Mencken wrote that he "had lived too long and had descended too deeply into the mud to be taken seriously by fully literate men, even of the kind who write school books."[11] Fundamentalism, according to Mencken, was not only obscurantist, but a rural outlook. Bryan delighted in "the tune of cocks crowing on the dung hill." Becoming a country saint, he had died appropriately in a "one horse Tennessee village." Mencken speculated that the politician was moved "by hatred of city men who had laughed at him—if not at his baroque theology, then at least at his alapaca pantaloons."[12]

Critics like Mencken have presumed in their polemics that fundamentalists are obscurantist, radical, extremist, and antisecular. Garry Wills puts the issues in better focus, pointing out that Mencken was an adamant follower of Nietzsche. Mencken was an anti-Semite who applied Darwinism uncritically to human ethics. Mencken wrote: "The struggle for existence went on among the lions in the jungle and the protozoa in the sea ooze, and . . . the law of natural selection ruled all of animated nature—mind and matter—alike."[13] Wills comments:

> Thanks to Mencken and to *Inherit the Wind,* a 1950s play that continually re-creates (quite inaccurately) the famous trial on stage and on screen, Bryan is now best known as the fuddled biblicist of Dayton. . . . It was a sad end to a career launched with the "Cross of Gold" speech at

the Democratic convention of 1896. For thirty years after that, Bryan was the most important figure in the reform politics of America. . . . he . . . championed in their embattled earlier stages—women's suffrage, the federal income tax, railroad regulation, currency reform, state initiative and referendum, a Department of Labor, campaign fund disclosure, and opposition to capital punishment.

Wills adds:

> Bryan's career had been a sign of the possible integration of progressive politics and evangelical moralism. That seemed an incongruous union to Darrow and others, who meant to end it by destroying fundamentalism. Science demanded nothing less.[14]

To be sure, Bryan's opposition to evolution was in keeping with his failure to recognize the radical character of the scientific revolution since Galileo. His critics saw more clearly than he that religion could not ignore the change of model brought on by evolution. The creation paradigm of a fixed world order which, it was believed, could be verified empirically by common sense was destroyed in Darwin's discoveries. Bryan supposed that it was still possible to harmonize religion and science in terms of the model that premises a "two book" theory. The two books of nature and Scripture witness harmoniously to divine truth, it is premised. Fundamentalism, which still invokes this model (in scientific creationism), sees harmony where others see only the survival of the fittest.

Confusion has arisen, paradoxically, because the new religious Right has become more sensitive to problems of language and communication than commonly supposed. Its leaders now widely recognize that names have symbolic power, and only a small party of believers welcomes the appellation *fundamentalism*. Hence, in the second post-world-war wave of the movement, Billy Graham and his entourage used the name *Evangelical* to distinguish their outlook from an earlier, less open, and more polemical stance. But Graham's first premises remained premillennial-dispensational.

Fundamentalists, Muslim and Buddhist as well as Christian, perennially call on common sense in support of their outlook. Without any symbolic grid, they are only reading reality directly, they allege. Such claims are widely supported by folk piety. Their religious message and preaching (terms analogous to *mythos*) in this setting often are claimed to be given directly, even propositionally, in revelation. Viewed externally, of course, there is a variety of revelations, each claiming authority.

COMTE'S POSITIVISM AS A SECULAR OPTION—REJECTION OF MYTH OR REDEFINITION?

The popular debate has been not simply about religious models such as modernism and fundamentalism, but between religious and secular models as well, including so-called secular humanism. There can be little doubt that a widely accepted secular futurology stands in contrast to religious eschatologies. From the fundamentalist point of view, human beings claim to have taken charge of history, and God's providence is no longer accepted, they point out. What is at stake can be illustrated by reference to the three-stage scheme proposed by the French sociologist and "father of positivism," Auguste Comte, in the middle of the last century.[15] Comte recognized that initially, at the outset of their life on earth, human beings looked to religious myths for explanation of the world. In a new era, however, such symbolism became gradually rationalized and transcended in philosophical speculation and reflection. In a third period of human history, the answers formerly provided by religious beliefs and symbols as well as by philosophical reflection are being replaced by the factuality of scientific discovery.

On Comte's view, religious myth became outdated. Dismissing what is now called "onto-theological" metaphysics, he claimed to have discovered a framework that could accommodate all of the meanings necessary for human understanding and survival without any recourse to "obscurantist mythology" or the sacred. Fundamentalists, of course, reject Comte's view of religion. But paradoxically, as Langdon Gilkey, who taught theology at the University of Chicago, pointed out, their literalism has affinities with Comte's positivism.[16] Like Comte they leave little or no place for symbolic interpretation.

Comte's chronological scheme has not stood the test of time. It, too, has been used as an alternative inclusive macroparadigm with its own symbols and mythology. A less positivistic, less reductionistic approach to religion's past is needed to explain the fundamentalist phenomenon. As we have already suggested, scholars from a variety of disciplines, literature and philosophy as well as theology, now use the term *myth* in a more positive sense. They speak of a family of related myths making up an encompassing paradigm or worldview, a pattern (macroparadigm) that we are identifying by the term *mythos*.

IN SEARCH OF A MODEL—A TYPOLOGY OR TAXONOMY OF FUNDAMENTALISMS

An alternative strategy to any simplistic description is consideration of fundamentalism's distinctive characteristics in a variety of settings. This may serve to clarify the fundamentalist model more than any single definition. Indeed, it is the widespread strategy employed in trying to interpret the phenomena (of the new religious Right) both sociologically and historically.

Scholars reflecting on fundamentalism are sure not only that it exists across religious boundaries, as I have already emphasized, but also that it is contagious. Typically, they point out, fundamentalism is ideologically reactive with a Manichaean-like sense of good and evil and stresses inerrancy, messianism, and millennialism. The guiding fundamentalist premise, of course, is that truth is religious and that religion exists in sacred texts. Known through revelation, religious truth is interpreted by accepted authority figures. In this setting, reason is subservient to revelation. Researchers identify an enclave dynamics of small, close, and exclusive groups of right-wing believers in a diversity of religions. Personal identity is founded on membership in the group, and the spirit is antipluralistic.

It would, however, be false to view fundamentalism as being simply irrational. On the contrary, advocates see themselves as existing in a well-ordered world that is now challenged by nihilism. Analysts speak of a binary perception of past and future: Both are perceived as having been in principle good before a watershed decline set in. For fundamentalists, the sacred house is on fire. Their goal is not just conversion or reform. They are motivated as well by fear that the tradition that guarantees them religious truth is threatened and dying out.

Robert Frykenberg has researched fundamentalism internationally, in various parts of the world, over three decades.[17] The term *fundamentalist* was first used in the United States in the early twentieth century, following the publication of a series of pamphlets, *The Fundamentals*. It now has become detached from its American, Christian, Protestant, and Evangelical origins, Frykenberg notes. Frykenberg argues that there exists a generic connection between fundamentalisms from different cultural settings, even though they vary in quality and intensity. In support of this thesis, Frykenberg develops what he calls a "taxonomy" or "typology" of fundamentalisms as they have grown up since World War II in particular. He finds that a fundamentalist movement generally consists of a conjunction of at least four kinds of doctrinal elements.

First, the Truth, the central corpus of the ideology or message. Usually its mythos (as we refer to it) is objectified in a body of scripture or a text, sometimes in an oral tradition, as "The Faith once delivered to the Saints." A sacred or transcendent status is given to this nucleus—the Law, the Gospel, the Word, or the ideology. A distinctive worldview and sense of ultimate reality is at the core of this mythos. It serves as a point of division and separation in almost Manichaean terms. Generally accompanying such truth is a broker of truth, a magic personality, a charismatic preacher or prophet who brings a wisdom from on high, generating a mixture of enthusiasm, awe, deference, reverence, and submission.

Second, in keeping with this view of mythos, there is strict delineation of insiders and outsiders, true believers and unbelievers, in the fundamentalist model. Outsiders are pagans, idolaters, gentiles, goyim, or kafirs. The insiders are united by a sense of being a specially chosen or peculiar people, the faithful, a brotherhood or elect nation. Third, the fundamentalist paradigm almost always includes hope of a heaven on earth—a new heaven and a new earth in the near future. In short, there is millennialism and utopianism accompanied by a sense of preordained destiny. Fourth, opposition from a sinister (often mythologically defined) enemy, godless and heathen, is expected.

Frykenberg also identifies what he calls the "functional" or "tactical" features of fundamentalist movements: (a) radical conversion; (b) radical reconversion or revivalism; and (c) militant separatism (in order to preserve purity). He defines conversion as an "altogether total transformation, a complete and drastic change" (whether a single event or a process) from one condition or state of being to another; from one worldview or way of life to another; from one set of beliefs to another. Revivalism, by contrast, is a strategy for bringing back and restoring the vitality of convictions.

A MYTHICAL MODEL, AN AMERICAN CASE STUDY

Fundamentalism is a phenomenon both universal and culture-specific. This will become clearer in the following as we consider a specific American example. Nancy Ammerman, of Emory University, whose sociological research we draw from, has reflected that until recently, modernity has reigned with little challenge. Now this is no longer the case, and it is no longer an unquestioned good. In this setting the society and its culture are ready for something different. Still, to Ammerman it is not at all clear that fundamentalism can lead and provide a way to the future.[18]

Ammerman's case study, *Bible Believers, Fundamentalists in the Modern World*, in many aspects describes a very simple fundamentalist model. She researched and interviewed members of a New England congregation that she gave the pseudonym "Southside Gospel Church" in writing. The congregation advertised itself as being "Independent, Fundamental, Premillennial and Baptist." Members regularly read fundamentalist literature—periodicals and books—published nationwide. Ammerman concluded that Southside Gospel Church exemplified the distinctive paradigm of low-church Protestant fundamentalism: separation from the world, dispensational premillennialism, and biblical literalism. In short, its members were self-consciously fundamentalist and not just evangelical. She distinguishes between the two, remarking:

They also shun the Evangelical's "civil" responses to cultural pluralism in favor of old-fashioned "hell-fire and damnation." Fundamentalists are convinced that their differences from others make them superior
not only because they have something better but because theirs is the
only truth, the only right way to live.[19]

Outside of the congregational church setting, the world is evidently chaotic and without sensitivity to right and wrong, the members believe. Ammerman describes the fundamentalist project as follows: "At the most basic level,
salvation itself is an exchange of right living for blessings in this life and the
one to come."[20] To the Bible believers whom she studied, God's plan of salvation does not appear mysterious (mystery generally is not a fundamentalist
category). God's revealed will provides structure and brings blessings to the
saved. From a sociological point of view, fundamentalists construct a world in
which God is in control, Ammerman observes. Life is no longer a puzzle. "Being saved is the first step in God's plan. It opens all the doors that make understanding of the rest of God's will possible."[21]

In this setting, Christian faith is a practical, not just theoretical, matter.
The shared premise of the Southside Gospel Church is that God shows concern for everyday matters, such as jobs, food, clothes, travel, and repair of au-
tomobiles, and family life, including the choice of a mate. In short, God is not
far away. Moreover, he has an "orderly and absolute plan" for each Christian
life. Ammerman interprets what is going on in terms of Peter Berger's concept
of a sheltering sacred canopy: The orderly world of the fundamentalist is such
a sheltering canopy.

The sacred cosmos, which transcends and includes man in its or-
dering of reality, thus provides man's ultimate shield against the terror of
anomy. To be in a 'right' relationship with the sacred cosmos is to be
protected against the nightmare threats of chaos. To fall out of such a
'right' relationship is to be abandoned on the edge of the abyss of
meaninglessness.[22]

Basic to Christian life in this model is trust in the Bible, and its authority
is claimed unequivocally: Its revealed truth is timeless and as authoritative as
when it was written. Fundamentalists do not deny that much that goes on in the
world contradicts Scripture, but from their point of view they know the Bible's
truth is not just to be argued about but to be lived out. They affirm that it is
not only true literally, but an encyclopedia of all truth: Anything that is true
must somewhere be found within its pages. Of course, the Book is interpreted
authoritatively for the congregation by its pastor; hence the importance of

choosing the right church. With "spiritual eyes" and with the help of fellow believers, God's will is discerned; God is seen to be "opening and closing doors."[23] Liberal churches do not seem to be real churches to members of the Southside congregation. In their intense concern to know and do the will of God, they recognize "signs"—mostly in hindsight. Providence becomes evident, and the claim is made that "God was leading in this way!"

What distinguishes fundamentalists—and makes them sectarian from a sociological point of view—is their eagerness to show and tell others how different they are from the rest of the world. Believers are expected to witness to the world, even as they remain separate from it and upright in life. More than many other Christians, fundamentalists are missionary-minded. Having experienced the new birth, they recount their own experiences of salvation and quote Romans 10:9: "That if thou shalt confess with thy mouth the Lord Jesus, and shalt believe in thine heart that God hath raised him from the dead, thou shalt be saved." Faith is active, and it gives them a clear identity in which salvation is the cornerstone of their lives. Of course, such a Puritan model prohibits vices such as swearing and drunkenness.

Ammerman observes that clear lines exist, as between God's eternal favor, right and wrong doctrine, and correct living, on the one hand, and apostasy, promiscuity, and damnation, on the other. Differences have to do with worship and authority—but most of all with lifestyle. Ammerman quotes a member whom she interviewed: "When you're with someone who's not saved, you can almost sense a total difference. Sense? I think that's the word. Not feelings or vibration, but like a sixth sense."

For fundamentalists, the model is one of a "social world in which their ideas make sense and another in which nothing makes sense." Christians alone are on God's side in their struggle against sin and evil in an evil world. Ammerman sums up:

> For the members of Southside Gospel Church, the outside world can be dangerous and unpleasant. . . . the whole world seems to be wanton, permissive, and selfish. They venture into that outside world only to try to snatch away the few people who seem open to salvation. For most believers, the orderly world inside is so much more attractive than the chaos outside that they choose to leave behind nonbelieving friends, family members, and organizations to devote all their time to the Bible, the church, and Christian friends.[24]

How do the fundamentalists Ammerman studied vote? Of course, the political issues concern not just individual morality but the life of institutions as well. To merit fundamentalist approval, an institution must either be run by saved persons or, if this is not the case, at least follow biblical rules. Not just Christians, but also unbelievers, can adhere to the latter pattern. The congregation Ammerman studied believed strongly that Americans, whom they see as belonging to a Christian nation, can and should honor God. But even when this is not the case, fundamentalists seek autonomy for their own institutions, such as Christian schools. Still as Ammerman observes, the boundaries of God's kingdom can change. Fundamentalists who expect the near end of the world at times do adjust to the needs of the hour without giving up their trust in God's long-term plan. Remaining critical of both doubt and pluralism, they have built their own institutions even if they were not able to dominate society.

Seen from the longer historical perspective, the Southside Gospel Church model is only one Christian model among others, and not necessarily the only true one as its members suppose. Peter Berger, whom Ammerman cites, identifies three options the believer has in facing the challenge of modernity.[25] The first is the cognitive surrender that fundamentalists refuse: simple acceptance of the fact that the majority is right and the adaptation of oneself to that point of view. At the opposite extreme is cognitive retrenchment. For example, the fundamentalist rejects out-of-hand the basic assumptions of the modernist position. Berger states the matter bluntly: "The rest of you go climb a tree; we believe this, we know this, and we are going to stick to it. And if this is irrelevant to the rest of you, well, that is just too bad." A middle stance, what Berger calls "cognitive bargaining," recognizes that there are two conflicting views of the world and begins to negotiate. An attempt is made to arrive at a nonfundamentalist cognitive compromise. Berger's triad, of course, also applies to fundamentalism in other cultures outside America.

FUNDAMENTALISM "FROM THE INSIDE OUT"

Lawrence emphasizes that the fundamentalist restorationist model does not necessarily imply blind reaction against all features of contemporary life.[26] Fundamentalists do have a point, he argues, as they offer a critique of modernism. Social scientists researching fundamentalism often attribute its growth and power to the disintegration of self-contained societies. Communities like the Southside Gospel Church seek to revive a sense of identity and meaning in their own setting. Researchers point out that the governing myths, the accepted paradigms by which thought and life have been organized, often seemed to have lost their power in the late twentieth century.

Two powerful "thrusts" can be identified in fundamentalist movements. On the one hand, there is an individualistic thrust that is separatist and sectarian. On the other hand, the social thrust of fundamentalism has been described by sociologists as "revolutionary traditionalism." Its political spokes-persons appeal to what they claim are the beliefs of the "moral majority." New charismatic leaders engender mass followings, condemn moral laxity, and seek a remedy in personal religious experience. Their appeal is widely heard in the American setting, as ethical norms (in all but the most secularized parts of so-ciety) are still reinforced by religious models, and it is to them that believers turn. Opposing an apostate worldliness that refuses traditionally accepted re-ligions and family standards, conservative churches have experienced new waves of growth while more liberal denominations have lost membership.

Ian S. Lustick, extending the discussion of fundamentalism beyond Christianity to Judaism, sees it as (1) basing its activities on uncompromisable injunctions and (2) considering the activities of its devotees to be "guided by direct contact with the source of transcendental authority."[27] To secularly minded critics, these traits seem to be a liability. On the other hand, it may be said positively that fundamentalism has much deeper existential implications for the everyday life of the believer than any rational presentation of its tenets can suggest.

Backing words with deeds, fundamentalists have developed effective po-litical strategies. This is true in the United States, but even more so in other parts of the world: Modernity and "the West" are often attacked together. Ad-vocates of the new religious Right are outspoken not only about the atheism of a "secular humanism" that "leaves God out"; they also attack "situational mo-rality" and with it the "nihilism" of the so-called counterculture.

Paradoxically, the new Right has engendered a very unsymbolic argu-ment about religious symbolism. Resisting the contextual as well as modernist premise of historical growth and development in religious truth, fundamen-talists are generally convinced that the fundamentals of their religion (one might say "symbols" or "myths") cannot be given up or compromised with modernism or its ally, secular humanism. These include not only their own distinctive models of deity and the moral law, but particular confessional or kerygmatic tenets—for example, the verbal inspiration of Scripture, literalist belief in creation, or the immanent end of the world as similarly untouched by historical criticism. In principle, doctrine is timeless.[28]

A WORLDWIDE PHENOMENON

Social scientists commonly note that fundamentalist movements are so-cially divisive of society and often lead to violence.[29] Such movements, indeed, reflect the failure of secular elites to come to grips with deteriorating economic conditions. Their leadership is replaced by new charismatic figures who have more direct contact with followers. Fundamentalists claim that the older religious establishment has not succeeded or preserved purity. The growth of their movement is accelerated when there is no other platform for protest but religion. Nationalism at times is accepted and used, at other times opposed.

Enlightenment doctrines of human rights often are a target of the new religious Right, as T. N. Madan of the University of Delhi in India argues. Fundamentalism, often sectarian, can be totalitarian as well.[30] Another Indian scholar, Harjob S. Oberoi, focuses his critique on Hegel's theses about the Enlightenment as well as their contemporary defense by the living German philosopher Jürgen Habermas.[31] According to Hegel, the Enlightenment had established (1) effective individual freedom, (2) the right to criticize established authorities, (3) autonomy of action, and (4) acceptance that one can know oneself independently of religion. These claims are disregarded and denied in most fundamentalisms, Oberoi emphasizes.

Fundamentalist militancy has become increasingly widespread since World War II, and in particular since the growing Arab-Israeli and Muslim-Hindu confrontations. Lawrence identifies Islamic fundamentalism as "a major new departure" in Islamic history, one whose advocates seek to confront, challenge, and in the end defeat modernity and the secular West.[32] The worldwide attraction of the religious Right, like that of the political Right, coincides most conspicuously with the collapse of liberalism. It grew especially in the era of the war in Vietnam and the Arab defeat in Palestine. A phenomenon that at first seemed to be local soon had major consequences for international politics.

There are, no doubt, significant outstanding differences as well as parallels between fundamentalisms in different world faiths, for example, Christianity and Islam. To say the least, fundamentalist ideology varies even within particular religions, as, for example, between Southern Baptists and Pentecostals in low-church Protestantism. The pattern is not the same among the majority Muslim party, the Sunnis, and Khomeini's Shi'ite followers. It is clear that the causes championed are not always the same. In spite of all differences, our conclusion will be that fundamentalists all over the world share a common revivalist paradigm whose "built in" dilemmas are intrinsic to their ideology, and that these cannot be resolved apart from a comprehensive revision of their symbolic models—which need to be not only demythologized but historicized.[33]

Of course, when developments are analyzed sociologically and psychologically, the modern phenomenon of nationalism must be taken into account. Fundamentalists have drawn strength from it, but at times also opposed it, as in Egypt, where fundamentalists reacted against Nasser's union of socialism and nationalism. Moreover, fundamentalism in Asia—among, for example, the Sikhs in India, Hindus, and Muslims—needs to be seen against the background of communalism. In the end, however, the reaction against secularity in the growth of fundamentalism cannot be ignored and calls for careful analysis of its religious roots.

THE CONTEMPORARY SETTING—IN THE WAKE OF TWO WORLD WARS

To a significant extent, fundamentalism's appeal grew out of the pessimism resulting from the tragedy of two world wars. For better or worse, an earlier "Christian"-European dominance (and colonialism) had come to an end. The accompanying synoptic vision of Christianity as the highest religion, confirmed by the progress of Western civilization (so Hegel believed), was radically challenged.[34] Revivalists and nationalists in other major faiths have rejected this vision most emphatically.

The question remains why historical developments often led to fundamentalism instead of pluralism and a renewed realism. (The term *fundamentalism* is a twentieth-century one; the roots of the phenomenon, of course, are much older.) One answer is that the optimistic rationalism that had grown up in Europe since the Renaissance and in particular the Enlightenment, was under siege. Christendom as it was imposed on other parts of the world (in the later colonial era) found itself in crisis. The relation between religion and culture was a much more important issue than fundamentalists realized. More than they have understood and at times even unwittingly, they have raised again the question of how much the norms of civilized life are based on religious symbolism. As we noted, fundamentalists have not given up their belief in a millennium (brought by God), in spite of all the evils of the time. Today, they also are more than ever convinced that the present world cannot be surrendered to antireligious forces.

Chapter 2

American Fundamentalism

REVIVALISM

The American fundamentalist movement had retreated to the background during the era between the two world wars, following the scandal of the Scopes trial. It reappeared in the larger world of culture and politics with fresh zeal after the Second World War. With religious modernism quickly going out of style even before the war, the fundamentalist movement gained strength as it nurtured its own enclaves and networks—schools, publishing houses, and missionary boards—while working against the modernists who seemed to dominate major denominations. The new religious Right found an easily identifiable target in the Supreme Court's postwar rulings against prayer in public school classrooms as well as the Court's rulings on abortion.

It was the fundamentalists, most of all, who identified a widespread sense of impotence and meaninglessness and advocated personal conversion as the answer. The mythical symbolism of the American revivalistic cultus is reinforced by an intense emotional state that accompanies "twice born" conversion—a sense of the need for radical change of life and belief. Lowell D. Streiker, in his book *The Gospel Time Bomb, Ultrafundamentalism and the Future of America*, describes fundamentalism as a movement, a creed, and a mentality.[1] Streiker delineates the conversionist paradigm of low-church fundamentalism:

> acceptance of the authority of the preacher, church, evangelist . . . sect or cult as the mediator of the presence of God and the authoritarian interpreter of the Bible; . . . a pessimistic view of one's own nature and human nature in general; . . . renunciation of control over one's life and the acceptance of divine control as mediated by intense feelings, the Bible, the church or sect, religious leaders, and so forth.[2]

The symbolism of the new birth is basic to low-church Protestant fundamentalism. The Lutheran church historian Eric W. Gritsch emphasizes that the "Nicodemus factor" is at the center of Christian fundamentalist evangelism. Gritsch refers to Jesus' conversation with Nicodemus, described in the third chapter of the Gospel of John, in which he tells this Pharisee and respected political leader, "You must be born again." Gritsch points out that there were numerous versions of the myth of the redemption of the world through the disclosure of "secret knowledge" (gnosis). The author of the Fourth Gospel used one of them to emphasize "that Christ is the only path from the darkness of sin into the light of redemption," one accomplished "by way of an existential encounter with the man Jesus rather than through any sophisticated philosophical procedure."[3]

Of course, the theme of the new birth, present in the New Testament, is a long-standing one in the history of religions. Faced with the problems of finitude and guilt, humans have for millennia sought a rebirth into eternal life. An earlier unbroken relation with deity and the sacred is to be restored. Christianity, unlike Judaism and Islam, is a faith of the "twice born." In all of these Western theisms the orientation is not a temporally cyclical one, as in Greek or Hindu thought; on the contrary, redemption is historical. The limitation of fundamentalist eschatology (and apocalyptic) from the critical point of view is that it is often accompanied by a reaffirmation of a mythical, symbolic worldview that remains unrecognized and unexamined.

Gritsch observes: "Fundamentalist interpreters of the Bible are not so much concerned about the historical accuracy . . . as they are . . . about . . . theological inerrancy. They argue that something 'inspired,' be it Scripture or prophetic utterance based on scripture, can never be false. Their hermeneutical (interpretative) key to Scripture is not the modern historical-critical method, but the rational harmonization of inspired inerrant truth."[4] The dilemma that follows from such a premise is that fundamentalists often refuse to "listen" to the biblical text.[5] Rather than reading it with an open mind, they apply their own grid to it, arbitrarily harmonizing passages from diverse historical eras. From a historical point of view, the division, as in the *Scofield Reference Bible,* a widely circulated publication, of the human past into seven dispensations—innocence (Adam), conscience (after the fall), promise (Abraham), law (Moses), grace (Jesus Christ), seven years of great tribulation, and the millennial rule of Christ on earth—suggests an implicit recognition of a variety of levels in understanding the Scriptures.

Such an interpretation (including myths of world beginnings and world ends) does have practical consequences. It is not just individual congregations that have adopted the fundamentalist model. In fact, it is being accepted by entire denominations. The claim for biblical inerrancy has become a tool in a new power struggle in which moderates are being challenged and overthrown as denominational leaders.

THE "GENESIS CONTROVERSY"

An example of this new power struggle is that the largest American Protestant denomination, the Southern Baptist, has been marked by more than a decade of sharp warfare and division. In this traditionally conservative church, fundamentalist claims have been voiced uncritically in the outspoken biblicism of a former president of the Southern Baptist Convention, W. A. Criswell, long pastor of the First Baptist Church of Dallas, Texas. His congregation helped sponsor a new seminary under the direction of Paige Patterson, a key combatant in the fundamentalist struggle for power. Criswell argued the fundamentalist case for biblicism as follows:

> The divine origin of the Scriptures is now disputed in the name of scholarship, science and religion. This is being done by those who profess to be friends and champions of the Word of God. Much of the learning and theological activity of the present hour is dedicated to the attempt to discredit and destroy the authenticity and authority of God's Word. The result of this crisis is that thousands of nominal Christians are plunged into seas of doubt.[6]

Controversy has centered on the first eleven chapters of the Book of Genesis. Were Adam and Eve, Cain and Abel, and Noah really historical persons? Before, the fundamentalists had objected to a commentary volume authorized by the Sunday School Board's Broadman Press. Ralph H. Elliott, the author, taught at the denomination's Midwestern Baptist Seminary in Kansas City. Elliott had identified the early stories of Genesis as being nonhistorical: "These stories are what Alan Richardson called parables—'parables of nature and man in order to convey deep historical insight.'"[7] K. Owen White, at that time pastor of the First Baptist Church in Houston and later professor at Southwestern Baptist Seminary, objected. He described the book's content: "death in the pot . . . liberalism, pure and simple, . . . a sort of rationalistic criticism [that] can lead [us] only to . . . disintegration as a great New Testament denomination."[8] Broadman, the Southern Baptist publishing house, eventually withdrew the book, and when Elliott allowed another firm to publish it, he was dismissed from Midwestern Seminary and became the pastor of a Northern Baptist Church.

Elliott was expressing a widespread nonliteralistic view that understands the Genesis narratives in terms of the history of salvation. A believing Christian, he still was prepared to take seriously the history of human life on this planet. His opponents—invoking a long-standing Baptist position—claimed the Bible as their only authority. But in a change of polity as fundamentalists, they now added the test of biblical literalism. Of course, they oversimplify the matter by equating revelation with Scripture. In fact, no one reads a sacred text without presuppositions—acknowledged or not. As we have already suggested, Protestant fundamentalists typically view biblical material through their own literalistic "grid."[9]

Today, the so-called scientific creationists (among the fundamentalists) still debate stories of divine origin as if they were recounting empirical facts. Mythical descriptions of the end of time (as well as of its beginning) are interpreted literally in the premillennial-dispensational scheme. Television evangelists like Robertson and Falwell as well as Billy Graham forecast that European, Iranian, Arab, African, and/or Chinese armies will invade Palestine. Millions of Israelis will perish, but a remnant will continue to live and in time will accept Jesus as the Christ. Believing Christians will already have been physically raptured from the earth to meet him in the air. He will return to earth and lead an army of saints in the battle of Armageddon in which the Antichrist will be vanquished.[10]

It is their anticipation of the immanence of the end of the age that distinguishes fundamentalists most from other conservative Protestants, the evangelicals. The fundamentalists are the most right-wing, and their focus on the immanent fulfillment of a mythical "plan of the ages" often consumes and displaces other theological interests. Millions of copies of premillennial books on this topic are sold annually. Hal Lindsay's *The Late Great Planet Earth* is reported to have had total sales of over fifteen million.[11]

The fact is that something novel has been added to evangelical Protestantism in the fundamentalist paradigm, namely, a new premillennialist futurology. Its advocates believe that they have rediscovered long-forgotten truths about the meaning of history in biblical prophecies soon to be fulfilled. Their "dispensational mythology" entered the American evangelical setting—only in the latter part of the last century—through the influence of an Englishman, John Darby (1800–1882). Darby was a member of the Plymouth Brethren denomination, which had broken away from a "worldly Anglicanism."[12] Premillennialism premises that the world will grow increasingly evil, and Christ will come again and rapture true believers, taking them away from the earth into heaven. There will then be seven years of great tribulation with the reign of the Antichrist. Jesus will return bodily and rule the earth for a thousand years. This theory does not belong to traditional orthodoxy, but became influential in the United States as it was espoused by the late-nineteenth-century preacher-evangelist Dwight L. Moody. In the last century, in the United States, the majority of Protestants were more evangelicals than premillennial dispensationalists, giving priority to conversion and belief in scripture.

So-called postmillennialists expected continued progress and growth in human goodness. By contrast, premillennial belief that Christ will return as wickedness covers the earth marks a turn toward pessimism. Theologically, it represents an attempt to make the end of history part of its sequence, calculating in literalistic fashion what will happen, how, and when. Eschatological symbolism and myth are given a spatiotemporal locus. Such a position, identified at times as "chiliasm," has been out of bounds for orthodoxy throughout most of Christian history. Already in the later first century, it became evident that the world was not going to end in the immanent future. Even St. Paul had had to admonish his converts to return to work![13]

Actually, eschatology and the more vivid apocalyptic description of the end of time are major themes of both the Christian New Testament and the Muslim Qur'an. In the Jewish and Christian biblical paradigm as well as the Muslim model, the universe is not understood as self-sufficient or eternal; it has its beginning and end in God's providence and remains dependent upon deity for its continuing life. Characteristically, modernists downplayed these themes in biblical exegesis and theology as they affirmed the growth of human goodness and progress.

Among Christians, Albert Schweitzer, who was not only a missionary doctor and organist but also a New Testament scholar, pointed in his *The Quest for the Historical Jesus* to the eschatological themes in the New Testament.[14] Indeed, he argued that they are central in the teachings of Jesus and cannot be excised. Jesus' sense of his "freedom from the Law" was based upon his strong sense of the immanent coming of the Kingdom of God. However, Jesus, recognizing the mystery of "last things," envisaged no "timetable" or cosmic plan comparable with modern dispensationalism.

Something more specific is being said in the genre that employs the symbolism of the Books of Ezekiel and Daniel, Matthew 24–25, and the Book of Revelation to predict terrible events soon to come. Everything that is to happen is seen as beyond human control; no human initiative can arrest the darkening apocalyptic panorama of history. Shi'ite Muslims such as the Ayatollah Khomeini look not for the Second Coming return of Jesus but instead for the return of a twelfth and hidden Imam—once represented by Khomeini, who reigned in his stead.

PARADIGM THEORY

Fundamentalism has often been described historically and sociologically, but less often appraised from a philosophical or theological perspective. Can we identify an underlying religious pattern, as distinguished from a psychological or sociological one, in evaluating the fundamentalist turn to the right? My argument will be that a defensive literalist model can be recognized in a variety of settings, irrespective of all cultural differences. If, as we have already suggested, disputes about doctrines often have deeper roots than words in conflicting archetypal symbolism, fundamentalism needs to be understood in terms of its own distinctive paradigm.

In identifying its basic model, we can begin from a very common experience: Two individuals—even of the same religious background—debate doctrinal issues without any mutual understanding.[15] One is allegedly the more open and liberal, the other follows a defensive restorationist model. In spite of being members of the same community or denomination and having the same religious allegiance, such individuals lack empathy for each other's convictions. At issue is not sincerity. They simply do not communicate, as they view religious truth from divergent frames of reference. Very different mentalities determine their understanding.

The divergence can be explained significantly by the fact that they work from conflicting patterns or archetypes, contradictory presuppositions and perspectives that often are not clearly identified. These are indeed psychological, but also theological. Sometimes, but not always, more implicitly than explicitly, the divergence between moderates and fundamentalists is both conscious and unconscious. In terms of religious understanding, there is what may be described as a different "existential" and (not just rational reflective) paradigm. Moreover, such models, contrary to what fundamentalists claim, are not timeless but contextual.

JAMES BARR'S CLASSIC STUDY OF FUNDAMENTALISM

Critical research on the fundamentalist model began in Protestantism. The English scholar James Barr wrote a seminal book on this subject. Titled *Fundamentalism*, it was published in 1977.[16] The models and categories that he introduced in his analysis have been expanded by other researchers in attempts to understand fundamentalist ideology in non-Western societies and religions.[17]

Barr identifies four distinctive characteristics of the Christian fundamentalist pattern and psychology: First, claims for the inerrancy of Scripture protect the fundamentalist system against criticism by a web of secondary elaboration. Inerrancy becomes a test of faith, guaranteeing access to the divine. Second, the Christian fundamentalist model is characteristically salvationist in orientation, dominated by soteriological and eschatological beliefs. Moreover, salvation conceived as personal and individual is not necessarily associated with membership in any social group or church.

Third, the model typically compartmentalizes religion; individuals are seen as acting primarily alone as they witness to their belief. A historical sense of Christendom or of any inclusive larger corporate body of believers is lacking. Protestant fundamentalists tend to be conservative and to support the economic and social establishment in the community with little or no sense of tension between belief and their everyday activities. Fourth, historical sources of tradition are concealed. It is as if beliefs and dogmas had appeared ex nihilo.

PERIODIZATION

The fundamentalist model needs to be seen in relation to other models. Hans Küng develops a theory of religious paradigm or model changes that he borrows from Thomas Kuhn's analysis of scientific revolutions.[18] Can it be applied to fundamentalism as well? Küng uses periodization of theological models together with a limited historicism to criticize the growing conservativism of his own religious community, the Roman Catholic Church. We will apply it to the fundamentalist outlook.

Our use of model theory in a similar way, will serve as a means of developing a historical typology. Thomas Kuhn's book on scientific revolutions has been widely read and debated, and Kuhn himself has qualified his initial paradigm analysis. Kuhn, a historian and philosopher of science, made it his thesis that a given paradigm reigns in the scientific community during a particular era until it is challenged by changed cultural circumstances, new data and ideas. Eventually, one model is supplanted by another: for example, the Ptolemaic by the Copernican worldview, Newton's physics by that of Einstein, or Paley's fixed teleological model by the evolutionary outlook of Darwin. Scientists already familiar with the tradition of a particular model commonly resist change, Kuhn observes. It was biologists, not just theologians, who initially opposed the Darwinian revolution. Kuhn's point is that scientific models are not as self-evidently empirical or as timeless as has been commonly supposed. He emphasizes that paradigm changes often result in radical discontinuity.

How would such a periodization help to clarify the phenomenon of fundamentalism, with its one-dimensional and at times positivistic dogmatic view of such themes as creation and eschatology? The history of its recent growth and development from earlier evangelical roots in revivalism and millennialism makes clear that fundamentalists, too, have their paradigm, one that is conditioned by the ethos of the time. Basically theirs is a reaction against modernity, theories of evolution, and the historical-critical study of Scriptures, the so-called higher criticism. In their intransigence, fundamentalists allow only a single paradigm.

Common to fundamentalists is an intolerant absolutist and atemporal model that ignores the history of religion and consequently allows no dialogue within religions or between them. Of course, there are long-standing precedents for such a stance. Religious tolerance developed in the West only at the time of the Enlightenment. More than modernism, fundamentalism seems to honor the major symbols of tradition (creation, eschatology, Christology, Buddhology, or Muhammad's role as Prophet). At the same time, such recognition is undermined by its atemporal dogmatism. Rejecting any sense of development, not to mention evolution, its advocates continue to think ahistorically as if their beliefs and doctrines have been handed down ex nihilo. Falwell describes the position clearly:

> To Fundamentalists, the authority of Scripture is ultimately linked to the legitimacy and authority of the Bible. They view the Bible as being God-breathed and thus possessing the quality of being free from error in all of its statements and affirmations.[19]

Falwell is explicit in saying that the Bible is absolutely infallible with respect to matters pertaining to geography, science, and history. He protests that the social order is disintegrating because men and women disobey the clear instructions God gave in his Word. The same outlook is evident among fundamentalists in other religions with respect to the Torah, the Qur'an, and the Hindu, Sikh, and Buddhist Scriptures.

In contrast to fundamentalists' exclusive appeal to one single model, Hans Küng's claim is that there have been paradigm changes in the history of religions—somewhat comparable to those in the sciences. On his interpretation, a model is not simply intellectual; it is rather both psychological and historical-cultural—a life stance, a grid, through which the self and the world as well as deity are interpreted.

Of course, periodization challenges any view of religion that premises a timeless absolutism—as in the case of fundamentalism. Truth is not denied by such a reference, but any exhaustive description or formulation is. Through historicization, paradigm theory makes clear the indirect and symbolic character of knowledge in both science and religion. When a cultural synthesis of the past is defended aggressively—as in fundamentalism—the timebound character of religious knowledge becomes doubly evident, Küng argues. The absolutization of a particular historical model from the past in the end only masks old problems and creates new difficulties.

Thomas Kuhn acknowledged, when Küng discussed the issue with him, that his kind of paradigm theory could be applied to theology. Model shifts, of course, imply both discontinuity and continuity. Hans Küng's thesis is that in Christianity there was an early apocalyptic-eschatological model, a Patristic model strongly influenced by Greek philosophy, medieval, scholastic, Reformation, and Counter-Reformation models, as well as Enlightenment and post-Enlightenment models. Küng periodicizes not only Christian history but also the history of other faiths, such as Islam and Buddhism. (This periodization was welcomed by the distinguished Japanese Buddhist historian H. Nakamura at the Buddhist-Christian dialogue conference held at the University of Hawaii in 1984).[20] Most recently, Küng has extended this type of analysis to Judaism and Chinese religions.[21]

Seen in this perspective, the fundamentalist model is not limited to one single culture or one single religion. Reacting against modernism and secularization, fundamentalism endorses a pre-Enlightenment paradigm in what Küng refers to as a "post-Enlightenment era." In spite of all the differences existing between fundamentalists of the major faiths, they share a common premise: that religious truth is essentially timeless and unchanging. Historical considerations such as the identification of diverse epochs and their respective paradigms are not to be allowed in interpreting revelation. The literal meaning of the text is to be honored (although typology and allegory are seen as being necessary). Nevertheless, the fundamentalist "monomodel" is still a theological paradigm, and the continuing question is whether it can be made all-inclusive in view of the variety of material in written Scriptures themselves.

LATIN AMERICAN FUNDAMENTALISM

An interesting perspective is provided on North American fundamentalism if one considers its partial reduplication in South America. According to

Pablo A. Deiros of Argentina, Protestantism on the continent has had a hard, oppositional edge against modernism and foreign liberalism.[22] Pentecostalism, the most powerful movement, has strong mythical and even shamanistic dimensions. Penny Lernous reports that "every hour 400 Latin Americans convert to Pentecostals or other fundamentalist or evangelical churches."[23] Out of a population of 481 million, 60 million persons are said to be Protestants.

"Stage figures like Jimmy Swaggart, jumping with the electricity of the Holy Spirit, dramatize converts' attempts to defend themselves against a world which has spun out of control, by struggling for mastery over themselves. Empowered by collective religious enthusiasm, converts ritualize their refusal to allow the 'world'—especially traditions like drunkenness—to exercise its sway."[24] Glossolalia, speaking in tongues, is one of the strongest accompanying manifestations. In a number of countries it has been explained as being the only way to protest in an otherwise oppressive political situation.

The primitivist model is evident. More-traditional mainline Protestant groups, theologically oriented, long only played a marginal role. The recent spectacular growth has given rise to as many as 650 independent groups and 120 separate Protestant denominations. Deiros reports that North American right-wing agencies have initiated mass evangelism techniques. Campus Crusade's young people have gone door to door as "shock troops" of the battle against Communism. Institutionally, Jimmy Swaggart's organization has contributed millions of dollars to the building of new and attractive Pentecostal churches in Latin American cities. Following the pattern of Billy Graham, Luis Paulau, a former waiter who grew up in the Plymouth Brethren tradition, conducts mass campaigns. His effectiveness has shown that Latin American fundamentalism has become indigenous. Evangelists receive good press and television coverage, often cooperating with right-wing regimes.

Protestant growth takes place in a new sociological and cultural setting, mostly in urban areas. Most Protestant congregations are voluntary associations in the free-church tradition. Not all are charismatic. The encompassing mythos is Puritan-pietistic. Present growth contrasts sharply with the lack of conversions to Protestantism in earlier eras. Roman Catholicism was dominant throughout the entire colonial period. Evangelical missionaries found an opening only during the first third of the nineteenth century with the coming of national independence and the establishment of republican governments. The overwhelming majority of missionaries are now from conservative or independent church groups.

The fundamentalist model is one that seeks to change individuals, not culture or government, and results have followed. Deiros cites David Stoll, who states that Christians are addressing the most intimate aspects of life in innovative ways that may have a long-term effect, throughout decades to come, on traditional paternalism in Latin American culture. Fundamentalists have shown themselves capable of responding to the immediate concerns of lower-class masses.[25]

The English sociologist David Martin points out similarities with the earlier Methodist movement in Great Britain and the United States.[26] As an earlier sacred canopy has been broken, pluralism and tolerance have paved the way for evangelicalism. Earlier catholic cultures are being challenged; in the eighteenth century it was the Anglican, and now in Latin America, the Roman Catholic. Fundamentalism is essentially a lower-class movement. Popular piety lives, "seeping up powerfully through the cracks," and is directed against the establishment. Practically, social quietism is at the same time socially revolutionary. Moreover, Martin finds that secularism is not so much on the rise in Latin America as was supposed. Indeed, the culture draws from a larger legacy of the sacred. Pentecostalism is a particularly powerful entrance to it in the new milieu—still preserving part of the Catholic past. Its symbolism is literalistic, but the mythos is immensely vital and alive.

Deiros correctly points out that the sacred and the secular were not as divorced as in modern secularity.[27] Indeed, Romans 13:1 at times is invoked: "Let every soul be subject unto the higher powers. . . . the powers that be are ordained of God." The fundamentalist evangelical model cuts across denominational lines and replaces other forms of Christianity in a changing situation. Of course, it is true that the Bible is often a "germinative factor," but the acceptance of its truth does not necessarily result in political activism.[28] Diverse parties join together to proclaim the Gospel before Christ returns again at the end age.

Pentecostalism has made the difference in success. There is group participation in prayer and even liturgical dancing. At the same time, fundamentalism often has been joined to an anticommunist crusade in which Christianity has been represented as the last chance for freedom. On the premise that its truth is complete, absolute, and unqualified, its polemic is directed against modernism, liberalism, biblical criticism, Marxism, liberation theologies, ecumenism, humanism, and any other "corruptions." In spite of all the interest in the fulfillment of biblical prophecy, there has been little concern for empirical history. The course of events, it is believed, will be beyond human control as the premillennial-style drama unfolds.

H. RICHARD NIEBUHR'S TYPOLOGY

We have emphasized that fundamentalism embodies a single model. H. Richard Niebuhr in his *Christ and Culture* proposed a typology—sociological and theological—that gives a more inclusive range of options.[29] In so doing, it provides a basis for criticism of fundamentalism in both Christianity and other religions. For its relevance to be understood, it needs to be described in some detail. Niebuhr's scheme parallels, in part, Berger's triad that was cited above. If it were applied in another context, the term *Christ* might be replaced by *Torah* in Judaism or *Buddha* in Buddhism.

The Christ-against-culture model embraced by the fundamentalists Ammerman studied as well as their Latin American counterparts is one of Niebuhr's models. Niebuhr's typology is fivefold, explaining the different ways in which the Christ figure has been related to society and civilization: (1) Christ against culture (fundamentalism), (2) the Christ of culture (modernism), (3) Christ above culture (Catholic-Thomistic), (4) Christ in polar tension with culture (Lutheran), and (5) Christ the Converter of Culture (Augustinian-Calvinist).

According to Niebuhr, the Christ-against-culture paradigm not only has appeared in contemporary sectarian fundamentalism, but also was embodied in the initial Christian mythos during the Roman Empire when the religion first was being persecuted. In this model, the kingdom of God has nothing to do with the kingdom of Caesar; the latter soon will be destroyed. Christians indeed live in a sinful world, but they do not belong to it. Civil government was not their concern. Very soon God's sovereignty and righteousness were to do away with wickedness, and Christ would return in power and glory, they believed. But the world did not end, and even in the New Testament this was not the only model. Paul's view of civilization in Romans 13 was more positively affirmative.

The opposite pole is what Niebuhr designates the "Christ of culture" paradigm: The modernist, culturally accommodating Jesus is equated with the highest and best of civilization and its meanings. This outlook came to the fore in the nineteenth- and early-twentieth-century attempts to show that Christianity is compatible with all that is good in human progress, in particular with modern science. The pattern was evident already in Gnosticism in the early period of Christianity, Niebuhr believes. Gnostics claimed to have a worldly wisdom that explained Christian truth much better than the faith of simple believers. Actually, it was an eclectic synthesis of oriental and Greco-Roman notions and challenged the Hebrew-Christian doctrine of creation.

What is lacking in both the Christ-against-culture and the Christ-of-culture pattern, from Niebuhr's point of view, is recognition of the tension between church and world; in Berger's terms, there is no cognitive bargaining. The polarity between church and world necessary to a religion premised on special revelation and a linear view of history affirming eschatology, is absent. Niebuhr identifies three other "middle positions" that in his judgment identify the tension between faith and culture in which Christians live.

The Christ-above-culture paradigm envisages two realms, nature and grace. One, as it were, stands above the other as in the Thomistic medieval synthesis. The model integrates a long-standing acceptance of earlier Greek wisdom and philosophy, expressed, in particular, in terms of natural law. Christ judges and redeems culture and expects his followers to be a part of it even as he directs them to a goal beyond it. The predominance of this model in Roman Catholicism explains why Catholicism can be traditional without being simply fundamentalist or sectarian.

Two other (nonfundamentalist) middle positions also are envisaged by Niebuhr in his typology. The first is Christ in polar tension with culture, as expressed in Luther's doctrine of two kingdoms: Christians live in the kingdom of this world and the kingdom of God and have to account to both. They ought not to evade their obligations to civic order, to justice, and at times even to the use of power and force. At the same time, they have an obligation to the kingdom of God to further brotherhood, love, and eternal life. The two kingdoms are in polar tension; one is not simply higher in terms of supernature as in the Catholic synthesis.

The other paradigm that attempts to relate religion and culture positively is that of Christ the converter of culture, espoused by Augustine and Calvin. Niebuhr's book favors this model, although he does not advocate it exclusively. Both Augustine and Calvin accepted that conversion is never complete in time and history. The eschatological dimension remains in tension with that of the present world, pending final fulfillment. But conversion in this setting is not just personal or individual; it extends to the whole of life with continuing social concerns. As we have already suggested, Niebuhr's typology might be applied, in part, to any religion that does not understand the history of salvation and the history of humankind as fully converging in the present.

PRIMITIVISM

It is important to observe that there is a strong element of primitivism in fundamentalist revivalism. This designation, *primitivism*, identifies more than folk piety, namely, a restorationist theological model. As noted above, revivalism perennially views the paradigm of the first decades or century of a religion as normative. Specifically, a primitive pattern of so-called New Testament Christianity is enshrined in mythological terms. A similar theme is emphasized in some statements of Islamic fundamentalism: that is, the words and deeds of the Prophet at Medina are to be emulated. In addition, other themes long at work in the history of religion supplement primitivism—separatism and sectarianism. Both obviously are the antitheses of a more inclusive historical view that appraises change and development in religions more broadly in relation to diverse cultures and eras of civilization. But necessarily, their developed forms invoke a more complex range of relationships than primitivism, notably in the interface between religion and civilization. Seen from this perspective, the primitivist revivalist hope for a return to a simple innocent era or its model, religiously or politically, does not take into account this essential aspect of the dynamic of religion.

Fundamentalists do live in the world and are conditioned by the political order in which their lives are set, whether they acknowledge the fact or not; they often are caught up in a dilemma between activism and quietism. Our conclusion is that the Southside Gospel Church model (devoid of any sense of Christendom) is less common in Christian history than fundamentalists suppose.

THE ENLIGHTENMENT VERSUS FOLK PIETY

Niebuhr's models are limited largely to traditional Christian history. They reflect the impact of modernity against which fundamentalism has developed at best only in a secondary way. It is this revolutionary impact that needs to be addressed. "Whatever the outcome of the fundamentalist challenge," Lawrence argues, "its origins are inseparable from the specter of its declared enemy: the Enlightenment. To study fundamentalism is to assess the Enlightenment as at once the precursor and the foil of all fundamentalist thought."[30] Earlier we cited a similar opinion, held by the German political scientist Thomas Meyer. Of course, as an intellectual revolution, the Enlightenment has had both positive and negative consequences for religion. Its claim for equality and universal reason—all persons are created free and equal—was often invoked against earlier sacred hierarchies. Humankind's longer religious past (in Christendom, for example) was regarded as a source more of intolerance than of guidance by a number of the statesmen who founded the United States. Religious tolerance was enacted into law in the constitution on Enlightenment premises.

Fundamentalism is now widely recognized as a world phenomenon, evident in Africa and Asia as well as the Americas. It is contagious. In spite of all differences, there are patterns and manifestations of fundamentalism in the United States that can be found in other cultures. Significant for the contemporary situation is the fact that the Enlightenment never extended to Islam or Hinduism. Fundamentalists in these religions are more overtly anti-Enlightenment (as well as anti-Western) than fundamentalists in the United States. This coincides with a decline in the West of Enlightenment belief in universal reason.

The growth of fundamentalism reflects the crisis of the transition between earlier and later eras and their worldviews. Very soon it becomes evident that some other chronological scheme is called for besides the (allegedly biblical) division of history into seven distinct world eras with a special divine intention (or dispensation) for each. Human beings fail in each age as they are put to the test. Today, in many areas of the earth, earlier sacrosanct worldviews are only beginning to be challenged by Enlightenment cultural pluralism and science. The situations remain premodern, and traditional piety can flourish.

"THE GREAT WESTERN TRANSMUTATION"

The Enlightenment often is seen as primarily an intellectual movement, and its ideas by no means encompass the full pattern of change. Westernization frequently seems to result in nihilistic destruction of cultural traditions. Marshall Berman describes this process aptly in his *All That Is Solid Melts Into Air: The Experience of Modernity*. Berman writes: "To be modern is to experience personal and social life as a maelstrom, to find one's world and oneself in perpetual disintegration and renewal, trouble and anguish, ambiguity and contradiction."[31] Marshall Hodgson, a historian of Islam gives priority to what Hodgson labeled "The Great Western Transmutation".[32] The term seems particularly appropriate in the case of Islam, the religion that was Hodgson's specialty.

As conceived by Hodgson, the Great Western Transmutation had no allegiance to any specific place, race, or religion. It was tangential to the moral plane, and the rate of change was ad hoc and sporadic.[33] It has to be understood against the background of the recognition that in many respects the Enlightenment and modernism were a disappointment. Now their outlook is challenged by a growing fundamentalist sense of the sacred. Today, rationalists and empiricists alike are surprised by rising folk piety. Küng argues that the changes in the wake of two world wars have resulted in a new and very different situation in an emerging global civilization. Here is Küng's version of the Great Transmutation, less Western oriented than that of Hodgson: (1) European political power (Christian and/or secular) no longer sets the course of history for the larger world, as it seemed to be doing in the colonial era.[34] (2) Western "Christian civilization" has lost prestige as warfare has taken on new and terrible dimensions with the advent of atomic and hydrogen weapons. (3) Finally, the non-Christian religions, often supported by nationalism, have shown new and renewed vitality. It is in this postwar, postmodern setting (in Küng's sense) that fundamentalism has now been identified as a worldwide phenomenon that often revives mythology in an uncritical folk piety. Christianity can no longer be defended simplistically as the "highest and best." In the new dynamic, other faiths, too, have developed their fundamentalisms that have become sources of intolerance, conflict, and fanaticism.

Chapter 3

Mythos in the History of Religion

THE NEW STATUS OF THE FIELD

Fundamentalism leaves no place for the history of religion. How is such a manysided phenomenon to be understood? The historian of religion, Mircea Eliade, once commented to a group of colleagues that now—in the latter part of the twentieth century—for the first time it has become possible to write a complete history of the religious past.[1] At this point, scholars now can say (as they could not before) what it has been in virtually every era and place on the globe. To be sure, there are esoteric meanings—of stories as well as rituals— that remain closed for lack of written records. Yet thanks in particular to modern anthropological and archaeological research, there is greatly expanded knowledge in the late twentieth century. It is this new knowledge that significantly illumines the phenomenon of fundamentalism in the twentieth century.

Eliade's analysis provides an especially valuable point of reference in relation to fundamentalism, because of his emphasis on the so-called primitive tribal and archaic periods. (The national religions of ancient Egypt,

India, and China, for example, are classified as "archaic.") It illumines "proto-history"—simplistically put, what happened in the period "from Adam to Abraham to Moses." Traditional religions have equated their own views of sacred history with world history. Thus it is said that all human beings were Muslims until they were corrupted by persons from other faiths. Hinduism is supposed to be able to include all other religions. And the sacred history recorded in the Hebrew Bible, for Christians the Old Testament, was supposed to explain the origins of nations. Today, such inclusive use of traditional outlooks has been challenged by a vast accumulation of new data from fields as diverse as anthropology and psychology as well as archaeology and philology.[2]

More recently, the discovery of the Dead Sea Scrolls has illumined the scriptural background of the Hebrew and Christian traditions.[3] New knowledge of preliterate tribal peoples and their oral traditions provided by anthropology has yielded parallels with earlier religious history.[4] Late in the nineteenth century, scholarly translations of Eastern scriptures, Hindu, Buddhist, and Chinese, became available for the first time.[5] With the host of discoveries (including the discovery of evolution) that made the nineteenth century a singularly creative era for the history of religion, a number of older stereotypes were destroyed. It became increasingly necessary to recognize myth as myth and not as science.

A much clearer line could be drawn between myth and the data of "empirical history." For example, it became evident not only that there are two different creation stories in Genesis, but also that there were a host of different creation stories circulating in the ancient world long before they were set down in writing. The Hebrews evidently borrowed in part from the mythological frameworks of other cultures in telling their own stories.[6] Obviously, the earth is much older than biblical literalists suppose. At the same time, new data gathered by researchers in the history of religions confirmed that such mythical themes as creation were worldwide; they were by no means limited to Western theisms and had a much longer past. Except for fundamentalists, scholars became interested in them not as science but as mythology, in short, as archetypal symbolism.

Paradoxically, many of the pioneering nineteenth-century researchers dismissed both myth and any continuing relevance of the sacred. Their research often was grounded on the reductionistic premise that religion could be not only understood but explained on terms other than its own. Sir James Frazer, author of the many-volume *Golden Bough*, can be cited as example.[7] Frazer collected a vast amount of new and interesting materials from the history of religions. He himself was convinced, however, that the key to life's mysteries lay ultimately not in religion but in modern science.

Eliade's interpretation was the opposite of the widely accepted developmental evolutionary theory Frazer held. Eliade refused, for example, to distinguish a definitively primitive mentality from later, more logical ones and emphasized by contrast early humans' rich, deep-rooted religious sensitivity and imagination as expressed in myth and symbol. In choosing this model, Eliade made an anthropological, a philosophical, and even a religious judgment. He was well aware of alternative views that interpreted the history of religion in terms of progress leading either to Christianity or to modern naturalism. He was sure that the religious consciousness of the sacred had been very rich and creative "from the outset." He knew, from his own experience of yoga and the study of shamanism, that this consciousness was not simply deluded. At the same time, he rejected popular supernaturalism and scholastic dogmatic theism.

In this chapter, I will use some of Eliade's ideas as a point of entrance into the field of the history of religion. Other research projects will be related to his outlook. In short, Eliade's outlook will serve as a reference for analyzing fundamentalism. He would be in agreement with fundamentalists that humans have been religious from the outset. To be sure, early phenomena were not all-inclusive in terms of subsequent possibilities or at the time moralized in our later sense. Eliade, for his part, pointed out the religious basis of cannibalism (a theme fundamentalists would derogate). The power and "raw vitality" of myth lives on even to the present (for example, in fundamentalism). The early insight about the sacred, expressed in myths, was singularly rich and creative, Eliade believed. A community sense of solidarity was very strong; modern individualism had not yet developed. To the present, Eliade found humankind's mythical heritage still reflected in literature. It can be suppressed but not destroyed, as it is archetypal. Political and social myths persist in modern times as well, he noted. Indeed, Eliade was sure that modernity's lack of a sense of the holy is a singular loss that has precipitated a spiritual crisis.

Eliade's interpretation of mythos is particularly relevant, because fundamentalists in a variety of faiths, as we have seen, often (but not always) leave this dimension of belief and practice unrecognized. In the West most of them dismiss mythology as "pagan" and treat the history of religion apologetically, only from their own literalistic outlook. In their premodern model in a postmodern era, there is no dialogue of world faiths, because of disagreement over belief and practice. One religious (dogmatic) paradigm is fully true, and all others fully false.

Primarily a historian of religion and not a theologian, Eliade wrote books on yoga and shamanism that are classics in the field.[8] His lasting concern, throughout his lifetime, was to relate archaic and Eastern forms of religions life to Western ones, a meeting that he believed would be singularly seminal and creative. Early in his career, he had left Europe to study in India. After the Second World War, he taught as distinguished professor at the University of Chicago. A number of his most distinctive insights about the history of religion were synoptic and intuitive rather than analytical, and his generalizations continue to be criticized by some social scientists for their wide-ranging cross-cultural character. Even if he did not focus directly on fundamentalism, his ideas remain significant for theories about it.

SACRED TIME AND SPACE

In *The Sacred and the Profane* Eliade emphasizes how much sacred space and time have been particular loci of the holy.[9] The roles of both sacred places and sacred days and seasons are virtually universal. Devotion has come to center about them, as with respect to Jerusalem and Mecca, for example. Earlier, temple cities were believed to be located at the center of the universe, where tradition said the world had been created. Holy times (the Sabbath, for example) held cosmic importance, serving, like holy places, as special manifestations of religious power. The mythology of holy places and times long preceded critical rational reflection. As centers of power, they not only gave order and meaning; experience was organized around them. They are patterned from cosmic archetypes and mirror a higher order that is not just temporal but comes from the realm of the divine.

It was in the preliterate stage, when cultural traditions were conveyed in oral form, that vital archetypal myths and symbols first appeared. To the present, major religions have had a limited number of symbolic models by which they understand reality. This premise is basic to our critique of fundamentalism. It works against what has been called "the big-bang theory" of religious origins. All religions have a history and employ (or convert) existing symbolic models as well as develop new ones. For example, as we have noted, new birth and passage into another life were symbolized in stories long before the advent of Christianity. Christian theology, most nonfundamentalist theologians now recognize, has never been exhaustive in conceptual terms; mystery remains and has been set forth in a variety of symbols and narratives with respect to deity, creation, the fall, salvation, and eschatology.

So-called primitive tribal groups and archaic national religions (of Egypt, Babylon, and China, for example) laid the basis for the later religions with founders (who indeed modified them radically). Eliade reflected:

"Sacred history"—mythology—is exemplary, paradigmatic: not only does it relate how things came to be; it also lays the foundations for all human behavior and all social and cultural institutions. . . . Basically, man is what he is because, at the dawn of Time, certain things happened to him, the things narrated by myths.[10]

Against fundamentalist naiveté, this reveals continuities, in particular the dependence of later religious symbolism on earlier myth and ritual. Indeed, these continuities are evident to the present even in fundamentalism. It was taken for granted that in the time of beginnings, when heaven and earth were open to each other, heavenly beings communicated with human beings (the premise was largely unquestioned.) The "events" of this time are looked to for understanding of patterns of family life, vocations, and the organization of nations. Such mythical archetypes reflect a wholeness from above, not just one of the temporal order. The evidence is that when early human beings tried to understand themselves and their world, it was in terms of stories and not abstract ideas. It would be a modern reductionistic view to see these stories as simply untrue.

MYTH, RITUAL, AND THE SACRED

Historically, myth and ritual have been central in human beings' concern with the sacred. Eliade described them as being worldwide, citing a wide range of examples that he correlated phenomenologically rather than historically. Critics charge that it is not always fully clear as where the history of religion left off and philosophy began in his attempt to relate humankind's earlier religious past to the present.[11] Intellectually, he appropriated the phenomenological method of the German philosopher Edmund Husserl—that is, *epoché*, the bracketing of value judgments.[12] Eliade's interpretation of the history of religion was neither confessional nor "secular naturalistic." It relates in particular to fundamentalism because his exposition of myth and the sacred was not intended as an abstract philosophy of religion or a systematic theology. Moreover, in Eliade's description the shaman almost appears as an existential seer!

Eliade finds the religious consciousness to have been highly creative virtually from the emergence of human life on earth. When the distinctively human and religious first appeared on our planet cannot be dated exactly, he concluded. But as soon as *Homo sapiens* was capable of speech, the evidence is that it showed a profoundly religious understanding of "limit situations," death, suffering, and the possibility of rebirth.

Eliade emphasized that before later rationalizations and orthodoxies, religious life centered on the narration of sacred stories and their ritual reenactment. To the present, religions recount their archetypal symbols in powerful narratives. More than either fable or legend, the mythical models they use are not just factually true data, but serve to establish paradigms for understanding. As archetypal models they phenomenologically embody a symbolic meaning that antedates rational analysis. In short, major myths, most of all creation myths, are primordial. As we have already suggested, every major religion has an indispensable symbolic (macro) model embodied in these models that cannot be reduced to an idea alone. Its myths and rituals express and embody this pattern. For persons of a given tradition, it remains archetypal and exclusive. As a modern phenomenon, fundamentalism recaptures some of this primordial power. C. Colpe, a Danish scholar who has taught the history of religion in West Berlin, gets to the point in arguing that, in a similar way, ever since the Enlightenment, the notion of the sacred—and its expression in myth—was minimized, when not outright rejected, in the Western European intellectual tradition.[13]

Eliade challenged this stance directly by trying to show that attempts such as Frazer's ended in a blind alley. The long history of humankind's sense of the sacred, expressed symbolically in myths and ritual, cannot be dismissed as simplistically as before, Eliade argued. Accounts that regard mythos as simply untrue narrative miss the point. Historically, it has been creative as it has attempted to understand reality.

Today, a significant number of scholars—anthropologists, literary scholars, and philosophers as well as historians of religion and theologians—share Eliade's interpretation of mythos as being not historical fact but paradigm and symbol (in a variety of traditions). The late Joseph Campbell's books and television appearances directed attention to the role of mythos even more than did the writings of Eliade. His fascinating description of human beings' early "primitive and archaic" religious life interested a wide readership and later many viewers as well. However, Campbell was not as methodologically probing, and did not range through the history of religion as systematically, as Eliade.[14]

OTHER SCHOLARS IN THE FIELD

Eliade's scholarship in the history of religion takes cognizance of a variety of research. In Germany, the neo-Kantian philosopher Ernst Cassirer, in particular, in the second volume of his *Philosophy of Symbolic Forms*, called attention to the importance of mythic thought as a kind of knowledge.[15] Major myths have their own intrinsic patterns and cannot be reduced simply to nonsense—to be outgrown as humankind allegedly becomes more rational and secular. Cassirer came to view myth as a form of a priori understanding very different from, and yet somehow similar to, the forms of understanding that Kant identified. Moreover, he concluded that in organizing life and the world, as a priori structure of meaning, mythos was a first step toward the later logos of rational understanding.

A different but related contribution was made to the history of religion by the French anthropologist C. Levi-Strauss, a leader in the structuralist school of language analysis, in his four-volume work *Mythologiques*. Levi-Strauss attempted to decode the structure of myths, emphasizing that this form of expression can have highly complex and sophisticated meaning.[16] Armed with wide anthropological and philological knowledge, he advanced the premise, similar to Cassirer's, that myths ought no longer to be regarded as simply primitive or irrational phenomena but as having a structure of their own that remains to be discovered as their meaning is decoded. He confirmed, in interpretation of different settings, the deep roots and persistence of larger mythical frameworks of meaning. In short, it is the function of myths to provide models; they are paradigmatic.

The psychoanalytic discovery of the subconscious by Freud and Jung was significant in giving myth a new status in the modern world.[17] Eliade was certainly indebted to both Freud and Jung but does not follow them uncritically. Their research made it clear that myth continues to figure in the lives of contemporary persons—at some times creatively and at others destructively. They did not agree on its meaning in relation to the sacred. Freud found little, if any, positive value in religious mythology. Jung believed that he had discovered archetypal religious symbols deep in the unconscious, present though often suppressed. Even in apparently very secular persons they became evident under psychoanalysis. Indeed, the forms they assumed seemed to repeat earlier myths from the past, and Jung came to believe that he was dealing with universal archetypes of the collective unconscious. Although myth played a more positive, creative role in his analysis than in that of Freud, its truth value remained ambiguous, as Jung limited himself primarily to psychological description.

Indebted to Freud and more particularly to Jung, Eliade initially took his cue from the pioneering study by the German historian of religion Rudolf Otto, *The Idea of the Holy*.[18] Otto argued that if we wish to understand the dynamic of religion—past and present—we ought not to turn first to dogmatic theologies or the history of ideas but to the awe, wonder, and fear we feel before the holy. Eliade saw this outlook as a confirmation of his own nonreductive phenomenological approach—bracketing prejudgments and attempting to understand the phenomena not in modern categories but in terms of their own rituals, myths, and symbols. Otto, of course, and Eliade after him, was no longer willing to accept the limitations of Enlightenment rationalism (or scholastic philosophy and theology). Anthropological research, in particular, has confirmed on its own, more empirical grounds that mythos exists in its own right.

THE CENTRALITY OF MYTHOS

Part of the strength of Eliade's scholarship is not only that he recognized the many-sided richness of myths, but that he called attention to meanings often overlooked in the religious past. So-called moderns only reflect their own subjectivist bias in presuming that the sacred is simply invented rather than encountered and discovered. Implicitly in agreement with fundamentalists on this point, Eliade premised an archaic ontology and argued that humans perennially seek salvation in a quest for being in the face of finitude and death. For him, there was no simply primitive ignorance to be overcome progressively (no difference in principle as between earlier and later psychology).

Human beings simply cannot live without mythos, Eliade affirmed. Mythos projects order and structure, giving a positive orientation toward existence. Eliade, confident from his own research as a historian of religion that archetypal myths have been diffused universally throughout most of the human past, interpreted them as the key to the phenomenon of the holy. Identifying myth as "a sacred history," he described it as

> relating an event that took place in primordial time, a fabled time of the 'beginnings.' In other words, myth explains how, through the deeds of supernatural Beings, a reality came into existence, be it the whole of reality, the cosmos, or only a fragment of reality—an island, a species of plant, a particular kind of human behavior, an institution. Myth, then, is always an account of a 'creation'; it relates how something was produced, began to be.[19]

The primordial myth of creation is seen as a pattern for other new beginnings later in human time: Abraham migrating to a new life in obedience to Yahweh; Moses leading the Israelites to a new land; the return of the Jewish remnant from exile; Easter morning; the new revelation of the Qur'an (Sura 96); or Mohammed's flight from Mecca to Medina, the *Hijra*. Of course, Eliade's almost exclusive focus of the mythological consciousness on cosmogony, world beginnings, has often been criticized, but he continued to defend it.

Encounter with the sacred can be illustrated by the biblical story of Moses and the burning bush. When Moses is confronted by the numinous and holy, the bush burns but is not destroyed. Theophanies are not simply imagined, in Eliade's view. Such manifestations of sacred power, hierophany, extend throughout the whole universe. The sky—heaven above, for example—is one of the oldest and strongest symbols of transcendence. Earth, rivers, mountains, people holy by vocation—shamans, priests, and prophets—all exhibit sacred power.[20] The holy as the most real and powerful cannot be ignored. In Eliade's judgment, it is equivalent with what has been defined more speculatively and philosophically as "being"—the most real. Eliade writes:

> Religious man thirsts for being. His terror of the chaos that sur-
> rounds his inhabited world corresponds to his terror of nothingness. The
> unknown space that extends beyond his world . . . this profane space rep-
> resents absolute nonbeing. If by some evil chance, he strays into it, he
> feels emptied of his ontic substance, as if he were dissolving in Chaos,
> and he finally dies.[21]

Symbols of the sacred are not empty but full of "reality." Eliade's conclusion was that the vitality of a particular religious tradition turns not so much on its rational theology as on the vitality of its symbolism—its mythos.

The question that fundamentalists do not ask is what symbolic model (mythos) is present. In fact, they implicitly eschew it by reaffirming an earlier exclusivistic paradigm. In the history of religions, archetypal models are diverse. One can identify both macro- and micromodels, and at crucial times these passed from one religion to another. In fact, the religious past—in particular, its major symbols—is not the property of any single faith. No doubt, earlier symbol systems were expanded and converted in terms of later faith traditions and conviction. But in this process, the symbols were not created ex nihilo or revealed simply "from above." Eliade's claim, that most, if not all, major religious symbols antedate the religions with founders, radically challenges fundamentalist presuppositions.

THE PHILOSOPHICAL ANALYSIS OF PAUL RICOEUR

The way in which Eliade's research can be used as a background for philosophical and theological reflection is evident in Ricoeur's important study *Symbolism of Evil.*[22] Ricoeur accepts and uses Eliade's phenomenological perspective, modifying and expanding it philosophically. Van Leeuwen points out in his analysis that Ricoeur interprets myths as "heuristic stories." Van Leeuwen writes: "They must be demythologized as far as they suggest historical, geographical, or biological knowledge. Precisely then they can be recognized as interpretative models which explore or reveal possible ways of experiencing the world. To interpret the myth is to discover 'the field of experience *opened up* by the myth.'"[23]

Ricoeur develops a philosophical description of the symbols of evil that were set down in writing in the mythology of Babylonian religion, Gnostic and classical Greek myths, and what he calls the "Adamic" myth. He formulates his analysis at three levels: The first level is that of primary symbols and the metaphors they invoke. The second level is one of narrative, specifically myths; and the third level, one of speculative symbols. On the second level, myth "processes" first-order symbols.

Ricoeur's premise is that symbolism is not just a purely linguistic phenomenon. Evil, real enough existentially, cannot be understood simply empirically. Like philosophy it has prereflective bases in experience, existence—fear and dread, for example. Ricoeur's summary phrase is *Symbol gives rise to thought*.

Why is it necessary to focus on the mythological dimension? Ricoeur answers: (1) Myths recapitulate the totality of humankind in one exemplary primordial person. This person exemplifies "a concrete universality" that can be applied to the existence of everyone. (2) As myths reenact the beginning and end of human experience, they take on a dimension of time, a sense of evil and perdition as well as its defeat in salvation. (3) Myths tell about how human beings became alienated and the actual situation became one of guilt. A mythical account performs its symbolic function by means of narration of a situation that is already dramatic. The leap from innocence to guilt is imagined in dramatic narrative. Thus mythical reference to the totality of humankind and history is necessarily symbolic.

FUNDAMENTALISM AND PROTOHISTORY

We have already suggested that Eliade's research bears directly on protohistory—in biblical terms, what took place during the period "from Adam to Abraham." The history of humankind is not limited to sacred history as fundamentalists believe. Initially, human beings probably lived on berries and simple plants in a food-gathering stage. This kind of existence antedated the hunting culture that has continued in some areas virtually to the present but is now about to come to an end. The agricultural revolution took place in different areas at different times and began at most eight thousand years ago, replacing hunting cultures. It came earlier in some areas and later in others. Religion had different symbol systems in these diverse settings.

The claim of historians of religions like Eliade, that existing evidence shows that a sense of the sacred expressed in story and ritual antedated any abstract interpretation, is crucial. In short, mythos, and not rational logos, was "in the beginning." It is not that primitive tribal and archaic paradigms exhaust or even control the whole later history of religion. But they continue to have power, showing themselves where they are not expected and leaving a vacuum when they are not present; especially the sense of the sacred that attends them is perennial, and now it has surfaced again with power in a resurgent fundamentalism.

The new religious Right expresses, often in its own dogmatic way, a return to an earlier mode of mythos. To be specific, television evangelists—especially in the Pentecostal tradition (Oral Roberts and, in lesser measure, Pat Robertson and Jimmy Swaggart)—at times seem to have an archaic shamanlike quality. The theme of shamanism is explored in one of Eliade's major books.[24] He views the shaman as a pivotal figure in the history of religion, whose esoteric qualities loomed large in primitive and archaic religion. Could one then not say that there is a counterpart in modern television evangelists' emphasis on faith healing, ecstasy, and glossolalia? Of course, primitive and archaic eras did not make our abstract distinctions between natural and supernatural, immanence and transcendence. Dominant in their world (as in the folk piety of many fundamentalists) was the manifestation of sacred power, *kratophany.*

In the total history of ideas, diverse religions as "living symbol systems" have been accessible only in a limited sense to outsiders. As Rudolf Otto explained, the phenomenon of the sacred is sui generis, unique and distinct, and cannot be reduced to another dimension—philosophical, psychological, or sociological—but must be understood in terms of its own reality. The researcher should not dismiss strange and unfamiliar myths and rituals. This is a danger of both modernist secularism and fundamentalist dogmatism. Instead, one must attempt to understand what is going on in terms of the history of the sacred.

EXTENSION OF MYTH TO THE LATER RELIGIOUS HERITAGE

Biallas shows how Eliade's view illumines later developed religions:

> For example, for the Jews, Jahweh is liberating his people now (not just at Passover); for the Christians, Jesus is risen today (not just at the first Easter). Because myths (and rituals) are not mere commemorations but true experiences of sacred beginnings, Eliade asserts that they are the most precious human possession. They are sacred, exemplary, and significant.[25]

In conclusion, it must be said that in a number of respects, Eliade is more helpful in explaining earlier, rather than later, periods of religious history. The Swiss-German philosopher Karl Jaspers has identified a religiously axial period from 800 to 500 B.C.E.[26] At that time, religion was moralized and internalized in a revolutionary way. This was the era of Confucius and Lao-tze in China. It was also the time of Gautama Buddha in India, the Hebrew prophets in Israel, and the Greek philosophers. It may have been the time of Zoroaster in Persia, although of all the leading founders of religions he is among the hardest to date. In the axial period, most of the inclusive symbol systems that differentiate religious worldviews to the present were established.

The continuing power of mythos, reflected in the appearance of new paradigms, makes it clear how different mythos is from magic. As exemplary and paradigmatic, it needs to be distinguished from magical attempts to bring the world into harmony with an objectively real world that cannot be otherwise controlled. The mythical worldview organizes and shapes the environment. Myths are not just attempts to gain control over the environment as in magic, although magic and the sacred have not been as fully distinguished as has often been supposed.

Myth has lasting significance, because it addresses the whole person, putting him or her in touch with the entire cosmos in a very existential sense, not just intellectually. Issues such as goodness versus evil, life versus death, unity versus diversity are highlighted. Biallas writes: "They speak to the similarity of existential situations in which humans find themselves: similarities of social relationships (of male and female, of parent and child), of physical environment (storms, sunshine, drought), and of individual experience (of birth, growth, maturity, old age, death)."[27]

And Eliade concludes:

> It matters little if the formulas and images through which the primitive expresses "reality" seem childish and even absurd to us. It is the profound meaning of primitive behavior that is revelatory; this behavior is governed by belief in an absolute reality opposed to the profane world of "unrealities"; in the last analysis, the latter does not constitute a "world," properly speaking; it is the "unreal" par excellence, the uncreated, the nonexistent: the void.[28]

The question is how this bears on the problem of fundamentalism. It does so directly in the recognition that the history of religion includes much more than the appearance and history of the biblical monotheism of the Hebrew and Christian religions or Islam. The history of these religions needs to be understood in terms of the larger religious history of humankind, and not the latter simply in terms of their myths. Historians of religion need not limit themselves to just one outlook alone, East or West, but can seek to understand the diverse models that have appeared throughout the past. A number of the pioneering scholars who first became aware of the new diversity of data in the history of religion supposed (mistakenly) that humankind first had been without religion and in the course of time had invented its rites and symbols. Or religion was believed to have grown out of magic, or developed from dreams or sex-related wish fulfillment. But preliterate mythology itself was often highly complex and sophisticated, and mythological consciousness is alive, not dead, up to the present.

Chapter 4

The American Paradigm

PREMISES OF ANALYSIS

Fundamentalism has its background in the setting of low-church evangelical piety in the United States. This chapter will focus on this heritage as it divided between left and right, fundamentalist and modernist, early in the twentieth century. Revivalism already was predominant throughout the nineteenth century. I will interpret the American experience in terms of the two foci we have already identified: archetypal symbolism and its periodization. Paradigms reflect external history—geography and wars, for example—and their internalization. American history is made up of not simply events, but symbolic narratives about them (in terms of the exodus from the Old World, for example). Each of the periods we will identify has had its own set of governing beliefs, in short, mythos.

In terms of the mythos or paradigms of religious life in the United States, one may speak of prerevolutionary evangelical America, the Enlightenment pattern at the time of the revolutionary war and the writing of the Constitution, the pre–Civil War and post–Civil War nineteenth-century periods, the era of the First World War, the depression, and then the Second World War, and the paradigms of a diverse nation now approaching the twenty-first century.

We will be concerned especially with the way in which the once-inclusive religious pattern of the country was challenged by secularity—claiming science as an ally—in the late nineteenth and twentieth centuries. In contrast to this paradigm, attempts now are being made to reassert the early convictions in the name of fundamentalism. The sense of the sacred, reaffirmed by the new Right, has deep roots in the past. Revivalists seek forcefully to preserve and extend its sphere of influence. One needs to distinguish different periods in the American experience and to relate them to dominant archetypes, past and present. Life has been set more and more in worldwide context since the first and second world wars; isolationism has been abandoned. When the American experience is contrasted with other cultural traditions, its presuppositions stand out more clearly.

THE PRESIDENCY

European observers—religious and secular alike—continue to be dismayed by fundamentalist manifestations in American political life. Of course, they know that religion often is joined with nationalism. Still they were puzzled by the evident piety of presidents Woodrow Wilson and Jimmy Carter, one a covenant-minded Presbyterian modernist and the other a Southern Baptist Sunday school teacher.[1] Even less understandable with respect to a nation where religion is disestablished by the Constitution was Ronald Reagan's open alliance with fundamentalist television evangelists during both of his election campaigns. Reagan had his own distinctive religious rhetoric, and it was significant in his election to the presidency.

Addressing a prayer breakfast in the Convention Center at Dallas, Texas, on 23 August 1984, the day of his renomination for a second term in office, Reagan affirmed:

> The truth of politics and morality are inseparable. As morality's foundation is religion, religion and politics are necessarily related. We need religion as our guide. We need it because we are imperfect. And our government needs the church because only those humble enough to admit they're sinners can bring to democracy the tolerance it requires in order to survive.[2]

In his attempt to attract votes, Reagan, the "Great Communicator," employed the highly symbolic, often mythical speech on which revivalism thrives.[3] His mother had been a very pious woman, his father a drunkard, and their son's early life had been nurtured by middle western folk piety. In 1980, four years before the Dallas prayer breakfast speech, candidate Reagan had gone to the same city, against the counsel of advisers, to appear on the platform with the nation's leading television evangelists. Reagan, who had toyed with premillennialism, exclaimed: "I do not ask you to endorse me, but I endorse you." They did support him against Carter, who faithfully emphasized and practiced the long-standing Baptist doctrine of the separation of church and state.

There has been no major anticlerical party in the United States to oppose Reagan's appeal. But in Europe, a traditionalist who subscribed to the union of throne and altar would not have needed to say any more to evoke strong protest. The orientation of the new religious Right was stated succinctly by Francis Schaeffer, one of its most competent and theologically sophisticated spokespersons. He argued that "the world view which produced the founding of the United States in the first place is increasingly now not allowed to exert its influence." Another outlook, premised on "material energy" and chance, has supplanted the natural-law consensus that originally supported freedom. It is now producing its own widespread negative results, Schaeffer claimed.[4]

Schaeffer's forthright claim was that when the nation was first established, the Founding Fathers virtually unanimously believed in God. The outlook was not anticlerical, as in the case of the French Revolution. They intended freedom for, but not necessarily freedom from, religion. Schaeffer's argument was not without historical bases. But the paradigm of the common faith was not fundamentalist but Enlightenment rationalist. Both are now being challenged by a new secular mythos that Schaeffer complains is defended by the Supreme Court in the name of the First Amendment of the Constitution. Actually, what is being proposed politically is the replacement of one kind of model, liberal and individualistic (exemplified in the statements of Walter Mondale, Reagan's opponent in the presidential race), by another, more right-wing conservative. How do these relate to American history?

THE EVANGELICAL EMPIRE

At the time of the founding of the United States, popular religion was at low ebb. A sense of the sacred seemed to have receded, even though many of the clergy declared the Revolution to be a holy cause. Revivalism was significantly a frontier phenomenon that renewed folk piety, and was not an elitist movement. As the frontier moved westward, so did the evangelical low-church model. The national symbolism, affirmed even by the practical-minded Benjamin Franklin, came from the Bible: one of exodus, a new beginning in a new land.

Many of the early immigrants who came to North America fled from religious persecution in Europe. Freedom of conscience and the separation of church and state, championed by Jefferson and Madison at the time of the nation's founding, were protected by the Bill of Rights of the Constitution. Actually, the country was overwhelmingly Protestant and low-church throughout the nineteenth century. Deism, belief in a creator God not immanently present in the world, was receding even before the turn of the century. Throughout the nineteenth century, Enlightenment and Christianity merged to form a new and positive paradigm in the United States. It was different from the one dominant in Europe, where church and state often remained linked to each other in the union of throne and altar. The North American paradigm has been described historically as one of the "Evangelical Empire." It was the dominant nineteenth-century pattern in the United States, and fundamentalism arose as it began to disintegrate.

Martin Marty, in the forward to a book by the American historian Donald G. Mathews, comments on the continuing importance of the evangelical mythos: "A hundred and more years later, revivalism, evangelism and the religion of personal experience of Jesus Christ are a part of the lives of Presidents, legislators, athletes, entertainers, millionaires, and poor Appalachians alike. No one is likely to comprehend their scope or depth unless he knows his way around the South in the crucial period of Evangelical development."[5] Mathews, writing in his *Religion in the Old South*, shows how the evangelical pattern spread across the United States in the nineteenth century. It had its roots in earlier frontier revivalist awakenings in both the North and the South.

The major paradigm shared the outstanding features of low-church Protestantism elsewhere and, in particular, emphasized "personal turning" and "community identity." Today, it is from the South more than the North that this paradigm has renewed its influence. Television evangelists like Graham, Robertson, Falwell, and Swaggart are all from the region of the Confederacy. The South, having lost the Civil War, turned in on itself and became more intensely religious.

By contrast with the conservative white denominations (such as the Southern Baptist), black congregations have remained evangelical but have not become fundamentalist premillennial.[6] Martin Luther King's concern for the future suggests a more open-ended model that takes cognizance of positive opportunities in the present and tries to reform social conditions.

Evangelicalism is the chief expression of what Mathews identifies as a "general, widely dispersed trend toward intense religious commitment in Atlantic Protestant civilization." Such Evangelicalism is the background of modern fundamentalism in the United States. In spite of the struggle over slavery in the last century, a common Protestant piety was shared throughout the land, with both sides reading the same Bible, as Lincoln emphasized. Evangelical sentiment stood in contrast to the rationalistic intellectualism and ecclesiastical aristocracy of cultural elites that later gave priority to the impersonal aspects of the cosmos. Instead, the new birth was primary.

It is this paradigm, which (paradoxically) drew part of its individualism from the Enlightenment, that needs to be understood, because it continues into the present. Thousands of persons, in a movement extending geographically from Germany to England to New England, rejected a simply rationalistic or credal reference and turned instead to a different model, one of personal experience. Already as early as the time of Jonathan Edwards and the awakenings, Calvinists had begun to look more to religious experience than they had in the Reformation period. On the frontier, ritual acts and scholastic theology could not satisfy the needs of religion any more than could reason and nature. Populism laid claim to knowledge of God from the most vital source, religious experience. The psychological basis of contemporary fundamentalism can be found in its subjectivist internalized conversionist paradigm.

In short, a new orientation—coming from the second wave of the Reformation (seventeenth-century Anabaptist and free church)—bred its own new mode of social organization in North America more than in continental Europe. There were only remnants of the religious establishment to struggle against. Jefferson sought and received Baptist support against the Calvinist clergy in Virginia. But long before his time, widespread dissatisfaction was present against existing authority structures. Traditional ways of assigning prestige and respect were given up for existential, and not just intellectual, reasons; a new way to affirm one's own significance and that of one's children had become available in religious community.

In the nineteenth century, all levels of American society—education, government, social and private ethics—were shaped by Protestant Evangelicalism. For the individual, it premised self-discipline as a way to personal holiness. Conversion, the experience of the new birth, provided new bonds of community. It was a renewed sense of the sacred that flared in frontier revivalism. Preachers—often noted more for their enthusiasm than their theological training—called on their hearers to come out of the world. At the same time, new social distinctions were being created. All of humanity stood before the judgment of God, the preachers emphasized. Nations as well as individuals were condemned. As in the contemporary fundamentalist paradigm, the Gospel message brought clear distinctions between saved and unsaved, God and the world.

Socially, the disorder of the world was to give way to the order of Christian society. The premise was optimistic, millennial, but not apocalyptic. It was an expression of hope for a new day in a new land. In an evangelical ethos in which proclamation, more than celebration, had high priority, the Bible was the locus of the sacred, indeed a holy object reverenced in preaching. Mathews describes the preacher's role:

> [The preacher had a] "gift," as Evangelicals called it, to make the life-death-resurrection of Christ a contemporaneous event, and he did so with such vivid and evocative imagery that many who heard him experienced the meaning of the Christian religion through a familiar, reassuring ritual: the conviction of pervasive sin, the nausea of just condemnation, the joy of Christ's salvation. . . . no high mass ever more effectively presented the "risen Lord," nor priest more dramatically reconstituted the community through a symbolic reenactment of the myths of the Christian faith.[7]

THE GREAT REVERSAL

Even an omnibus periodicization of the United States' religious history cannot ignore the change of paradigm (from certainty to probabilism) that the American historian, James Turner, has identified as "The Great Reversal."[8] Fundamentalist "revolutionary traditionalism" clearly has its basis in this change. The designation identifies the end of the nineteenth-century Protestant Evangelical Empire (with its reform optimism) and a shift toward a more pluralistic secular society. The fundamentalist movement emerged when low-church Protestantism "divided" between the modernist Left and the more conservative Right. The unique synthesis of the Reformation and the Enlightenment that had grown up in the country (in contrast to Europe) fell into disarray. One cannot really understand the new religious Right and its folk piety if one does not take into account this watershed.

Although the Protestant revivalist and reform mythos of the Evangelical Empire lived on after the Civil War into the later so-called Gilded Age, it was already in decay. Stephen Toulmin, who teaches philosophy at the University of Chicago, has formulated a parable about the growth of scientific specialization as opposed to the more comprehensive understanding of nature that interested the Founding Fathers. The parable can be applied more widely to the change of paradigm, the Great Reversal, that evoked fundamentalism.

> You go away on vacation, leaving behind a flourishing and active department with clearly defined terms of reference, an established staff, a suite of offices, even perhaps—as the carpet advertisements put it—"a Bigelow on the floor." Having come back from the Bahamas two weeks

later—the nightmare goes—you faced strangers. Your job, your department, and your office no longer exist. . . . You cannot even say, trium-
phantly, "Look! this is the *room* I used to work in," for there is *no* longer
such a room to be recognized. (It is a film theme worthy of the Italian
director Bertolucci.)[9]

Toulmin's story expresses well what Turner in his *Without God, without
Creed, the Origins of Unbelief in America* identifies as a drastic and revolutionary
change of paradigm, in short, the Great Reversal. "Since the end of classical
antiquity, God has provided the axiom from which followed all comprehension
of man, nature and cosmos," Turner writes. Nineteenth-century North American civilization shared this conviction. "Then His existence itself became de-
batable, and the center fell out of Western intellectual life," Turner adds.[10]

Theistic belief in God was no longer the shared basis of thought and
experience. The new cultural mythos was one in which human beings could
live without deity and without belief in one. American and Europeans both had
believed—every one within the orbit of European culture—that a superhuman
power had caused the universe and set the purpose of life. The consensus now
dissolved. What Turner calls "a simple, universal axiom" of tremendous importance became optional. Fundamentalists simply do not accept this reversal,
and they seek to alter the situation in a revolutionary way not only in the
United States but worldwide. Instead, they emphasize the certainty of scriptural revelation. Their strategy is one of both personal conversion and political action.

Questions about the relation of religion to public life have been raised
anew by the fundamentalist Right, intentionally and dramatically. Our argument is that the interface between politics and religion was distinctive in
the New World of the North American republic. Free from any established
church, there was not the tension between the old religious order and a new
secularism that existed throughout most of Europe. Protestant and Enlightenment conviction shared a unique myth of personal liberty. Individualism,
including individual religious experience, was reinforced by life on the frontier.
While Europeans continued to struggle against establishment and clerical-
ism throughout most of the nineteenth century, revivalism flourished in the
New World.

Not only was there numerical growth of Protestantism; the Catholic past
was largely forgotten or derogated. A range of sacred values, unchallenged
and at times unrecognized, was expressed in a long series of crusades, including
the antislavery crusade, and extended into the twentieth century in, for example, crusades against the use of alcohol and for women's suffrage. In the view
of many Europeans, Christianity appeared to have been abandoned in the

United States when the government lost control of religion under disestablishment. The centuries-long union of throne and altar was excluded. Actually the question of the relation between church and state is not the same as that between religion and society. As Father Richard P. McBrien of the political science department at Notre Dame University, observes, society is a more inclusive term.[11]

SEPARATION OF CHURCH AND STATE

Historically, in the Evangelical Empire in the United States, church and state were separated, but not religion and culture. (For Lincoln, for example, as for the society at large, it was not as simply a private matter as Jefferson supposed.) The ambiguity of the cultural situation in the United States lay (perhaps paradoxically) in the fact that although atheism was not intended from the outset, no religious belief was allowed to be prescribed. God was not dead, nor the sacred excluded, in Nietzsche's sense. The arrangement was not a priori but a posteriori, arising from particular experiences and circumstances—most notably, of course, the American Revolution against the throne.

Sociologist Robert Bellah has researched these historical issues in detail. They were not as simple as the modernist-fundamentalist controversy suggests. Belief in God was accepted in what Bellah has called "civil religion." The Founding Fathers "had a rather complex view of the relation between religion and politics," different from the current liberal theory: Commonly accepted ideas about the ends of life are necessary for a free society. They believed that religion contributes to them.[12]

Bellah, illustrating his own position, cites Alexis de Tocqueville, who visited the new North American republic early in the nineteenth century and observed:

In France, I had almost always seen the spirit of freedom (and religion) pursuing courses diametrically opposed to each other, but in America I found they were intimately united, and that they reigned in common cause over the same country.[13]

I do not know whether all Americans have a sincere faith in their religion, for who can search the human heart? But I am certain that they hold it to be indispensable to the maintenance of republican institutions.[14]

The generally accepted model presupposed a common universal reason. Nature's God was also the nation's God. Of course, a different polity would have

been favored in a Middle Eastern or Asian cultural setting where European Enlightenment influence had not been felt. In the United States, individual human
rights were primary. Religion was not to determine legal precedents as in traditional Islamic or Christian societies.

ENLIGHTENMENT INFLUENCE

A critical and illuminating interpretation of the Enlightenment paradigm
is made by American historian Carl Becker in his book *The Heavenly City of Eighteenth Century Philosophers.*[15] Becker argues that the Enlightenment had a deep
indebtedness to the earlier Christian medieval vision (including the theme of
natural law). Hans Küng writes about the more sustained controversy between
science and religion that took place in Europe, where the diverse models of
both fields became identified and confused:

> the challenge was not in principle to biblical religion but to an ancient
> science. . . .
> According to the ideas of the natural scientists of the sixteenth and
> seventeenth centuries, Christian theology and the Church should have
> become allies of the new science; but, because of their failure to do so . . .
> they contributed substantially to the establishment of both scientific and
> political atheism.[16]

The situation in the New World was more positive. The statesmen who
founded the United States of America clearly intended to do so on modern
Enlightenment premises and honored both science and religion. By and large,
earlier painful controversies about science and religion (as well as reason and
faith) were avoided. The harmony of science and religion was a basic American
Enlightenment premise. Both were welcomed gladly, and their patterns of
meaning seemed to converge. As men of the Enlightenment, both Franklin and
Jefferson, for example, had strong interests in natural science. At the same time,
they accepted religion as socially necessary for good government.

Religious sectarianism, fundamentalist-style, was disavowed. The God of
the Founding Fathers was not simply "the God and Father of our Lord Jesus
Christ." The national God was more related to order, law, and right than to
salvation and love. Still he was not just an absentee world-maker. Rather, in
nondeistic fashion he was believed to be active in history, with special concern
for America.

The American Enlightenment synthesis of science and religion, based
in particular on the idea of timeless reason, was challenged by the theory

of biological evolution. (The impact of evolutionary thought was delayed somewhat by the Civil War.) Evolution introduced a kind of wild card, as it were. A new mythical picture emerged. Loren Eiseley, in his carefully researched study *Darwin's Century*, describes the dramatic change in model that came about with Darwin's discovery of biological evolution. Eiseley likens time—in the new evolutionary paradigm—to "a vast chaotic Amazon pouring through unimaginable wildernesses" its burden of "houses and bones and gardens, cooks and clocks." Above the earth, "stars and men and worlds emerged out of the interstellar vapor, flared briefly, and passed again into darkness. If the eternal stars transformed themselves, why should one quibble over the powers contained in a meadow mouse, or an ape who forgot to go back to his tree." Man became "the child of change" along with all other forms of life, and the majestic natural law governing the universe, honored by eighteenth-century deists, was replaced by a war of nature."[17] The point is that it was a war in time and not eternity; a new sense of history was emerging, one that soon enough extended to the biblical sources. Actually, evolution was not the only issue. Debate about the nature of history and religious authority was implicit.

Two of the questions we have already raised, that of historical development, so much highlighted by evolution, and the demythologizing of biblical cosmology, are especially related to the new scientific paradigm. The Baconian empirical model had helped to pave the way for fundamentalist literalism and positivism. The historian of fundamentalism George Marsden observes that by the beginning of the nineteenth century Evangelicals had come to read the Bible with a flat-footed literalness unparalleled in Christian history. Even as scientific developments made "Biblical facts" increasingly questionable, Protestant leaders in a continued appeal to a Common Sense Baconian paradigm continued to understand its truth as depending on them.[18]

The dialogue with Darwinism hardly could have been carried out on less satisfactory premises. On the one hand, nonsymbolic literalist doctrines of creation and eschatology were defended fundamentalist-style. On the other hand, accommodation by modernists gave up long-held beliefs in an often reductionistic view of the origins and future of humankind. The left wing accepted, and the right wing rejected, the historical-critical study of scripture imported from Europe. A new and stringent biblicism developed among the latter. Liberals expected this-worldly social evolution and progress; fundamentalists looked for the second coming of Jesus. Science and religion—and their respective models and symbolism—were confused, to say the least. Divided between fundamentalists and modernists, even to the present (as Garry Wills points out) the overwhelming majority of the United States' population continues to profess belief in God.[19]

Virtually until the Civil War "believers could rest secure in the conviction that the evidence for God was as certain as science itself," Turner observes. It was only in the second half of the nineteenth century that agnosticism grew and became a major option. He designates the decades immediately before and after the Civil War as the time of transition in the United States. It was the era in which the American people were probably their most religious. At the same time, there was a growing agnostic naturalism and secularity. In sociological terms, the nation became more urbanized, less rural. As industrial work moved indoors, there was greater freedom from nature's cycles. Socioeconomic change distanced people from the natural environment.[20] To quote Turner: "God remained central to thinking about important scientific questions. . . . Yet, by the end of the 1860s, science had little use for God. . . . After Darwin's *Origin of Species* appeared in 1859, God rapidly became redundant in the whole business."[21]

Modernist Protestantism in its new archetype attempted to reconcile evolution and providence in a doctrine of progress. William A. Hutchison reports that the modernist impulse in American Protestantism found greater diffusion in the North than in the South from the 1870s to the 1930s. In his judgment, "Modernism generally meant three things: first and most visibly, it meant the conscious, intended adaptation of religious ideas to modern culture."[22] Hutchison identifies two "further and deeper notions": The immanence of God as revealed in human cultural development and the belief that human society is progressing toward the kingdom of God. Turner is highly critical of the decisions of theologians and ministers in the late nineteenth century whose choices, in his judgment, boiled down to a decision to defuse modern threats to the traditional bases by bringing God into line with modernity.

Fundamentalism grew up as a reaction. All did not turn on evolution, which, although often in the forefront, was not the only issue. Turner points out that the notion of a unitary conception of language had begun to break down in the nineteenth century as scientific language grew more exact. It was not atheism but agnosticism, a permanent suspension of belief in God—the distinctively modern unbelief—that twenty years after the Civil War emerged as what Turner designates "a self-sustaining phenomenon" in the United States.[23] By the 1880s, unbelief was a widespread available option in North America. In spite of the dramatic growth in church attendance between 1860 and 1910, there was an overpowering change of mythos. Belief in God became, and in Turner's judgment remains, subcultural. Earlier it had functioned as a unifying and defining element of the entire culture. In the later part of the nineteenth century, the common heritage it provided, underlying diverse worldviews, was dissolving. Turner concludes that if anyone were to be arraigned for deicide, it should be "the godly Beecher family" or perhaps the Anglican Bishop

Samuel Wilberforce (who debated Huxley), not Charles Darwin or the American skeptic Robert Ingersoll.

LINGERING ISSUES

The historical judgment must be that in the collapse of the dominant religious mythos at the end of the Victorian era, there was loss as well as gain. The perennial philosophical questions had not all been answered as much as Herbert Spencer, Darwin's favorite philosopher, liked to think. The issues addressed again today in fundamentalist eschatological and apocalyptic speculation—even in their singularly undemythologized form—concern the nature and meaning of time and history. Fundamentalists had sensed something very important; however, their literalism has precluded their accepting a modern (or postmodern) outlook.

Over the long run, interpretation of the meaning of history in a symbolic worldview or mythos is probably inevitable. Perennially a new destiny has been expected in the New World. In the early period, the New England Puritans had a religiously inspired vision of a city set on a hill. They sought freedom of worship for themselves, but not tolerance for others. Later, the myth of manifest destiny inspired the growth of the nation across the continent, most of the time in secularized form. During the Civil War, it was sung about in the "Battle Hymn of the Republic": "Mine eyes have seen the glory of the coming of the Lord." Today, fundamentalists in their own literalistic fashion are again raising primary issues about the meaning of history and national destiny. Unintentionally they have once again introduced the question of mythical model.

Chapter 5

The Case for Mythos

MYTHOLOGY DEBATED

Characteristically, both sides in the fundamentalist-modernist controversy have disregarded religious symbolism. Throughout their arguments, both fundamentalists and modernists have often given priority to "the facts" with no reference to symbolism. The thesis of this chapter will be that consideration of the theme of mythos shows a way out of the dilemmas posed by fundamentalism. What Tillich called "the religious situation" can be clarified by reference to his definition of myth as "historical symbol."[1] It is important to identify not only myth's place in the religious past, but also, in particular, its paradigmatic character. Dutch Protestant theologian Hendrikus Berkhof emphasizes that each world faith has its own distinctive model and mythos. It is interesting to note that in clarifying his position he speaks of myth, message, and/or preaching—together.[2]

Swiss-German philosopher Karl Jaspers remarked:

How wretched, how lacking in expressiveness our life would be, if the language of myth were no longer valid! To fill myth with banal content is to commit an unpardonable error. The splendor and wonder of the mythical vision is to be purified, but must not be abolished. . . . Does the splendor of the sunrise cease to be a tangible, ever new and inspiring reality, a mythical presence, just because we know that the earth is revolving around the sun, so that properly speaking there is no sunrise?[3]

Kurt Hübner, a German philosopher of science, follows Jaspers in endorsing mythos. Even though his own special field is the philosophy of science, he enthusiastically describes contemporary historical research on the role of myth in humankind's past as "a not yet recognized revolution in knowledge."[4] Hübner seeks to show that mythos has a foundational character and embraces a primordial unity in an inclusive view. Far from being illusion, it can embody a kind of aesthetic seeing into reality. Hübner's philosophical claim is that the separation between subject and object is not as uncompromising as it has seemed (unnecessarily, in his view) in much of Western European thought ever since Descartes's emphasis on mathematical method. For his own part, Hübner is prepared to adhere strongly to the claim that mythology can be "a presentational form of knowledge."[5] Myths deal with the concrete and not just the abstract, with both the whole and the part.

Hübner is convinced that both myth and science can be sources of insight and knowledge and that their modes of knowledge are not fully antithetical if one accepts myth's archetypal character. Hübner cites as an example of aesthetic "seeing into reality" the German poet Hölderlin's contemplation of the unity of a landscape in its entire natural setting.[6] Another dimension than conceptual abstraction or mathematical analysis is present. In an aesthetic and even religious way, myth has a presentational unity, disclosing the sacred. This unity is evident as well in the music of Richard Wagner. It is the reduction of myth to irrationality that Hübner protests against, as he is convinced that it is a way of understanding the most real and sacred.

In the remarks cited above, Jaspers was responding to the German New Testament scholar Rudolf Bultmann's "demythologizing." Bultmann's clear and informed rejection of biblical mythology in his so-called demythologizing initiated an important debate more than half a century ago.[7] He long has been a target of fundamentalists. Bultmann's original concern was a seminal one. Myths, fantastic and contradictory, have been judged to be meaningless, especially since the Enlightenment, and in most respects Bultmann shared this conviction. What he proposed was forthright: simply to give them up. It is important to note that he did not evaluate demythologizing comprehensively from the perspective of the history of religion. The issue is crucial—not just in Christianity alone.

Jaspers claimed that mythical stories and symbols are older than rational reflection in human consciousness and are related to a first order of knowing.[8] In terms of his own philosophy, they "point" existentially to what he identified as "the Encompassing," the most real. There is a watershed at this point, which I described initially in terms of Comte's positivism. It was necessary and good that humankind relinquished mythos, Comte argued.[9] A contradictory claim made by its defenders like Jaspers is that this mode of understanding has been productive and creative. Indeed, it has been indispensable in providing a rich seedbed of metaphor, symbolism, and ideas out of which later reflection and analysis have developed. In short, it is not as much irrationality and madness as its critics often have supposed.

Historically, it might be said that the major religious traditions have sought to tame the mystical consciousness of the sacred in powerful mythical symbols. Taken seriously as more than legend or fable, myths explain sacred history using models from a world "beyond" that transcends ordinary experience. In such an appraisal they are to be understood as symbolic, often archetypal, and not simply factual as in fundamentalist literalist style. Understanding and interpretation are not timeless, but proceed along a horizon from previous understanding. The so-called hermeneutical question (Hermes was the messenger of the gods) is what, if anything, an earlier message, taken out of its initial setting, can mean today.

THE MEANING OF DEMYTHOLOGIZING

The debate initiated in Europe by the New Testament scholar Bultmann more than half a century ago was limited in focus, addressing primarily the nature and role of myth in a Christian biblical exegesis.[10] At the outset, Bultmann premised an unbridgeable antithesis between mythical thinking and the modern scientific outlook. In short, he raised the question most fundamentalists avoid. His claim was that demythologizing, the replacement of obscurantist outmoded religious symbolism, was imperative before there could be any relevant Christian religious statement. This much can be said positively at the very least: Bultmann had identified the hermeneutical problem of translation, which characteristically is ignored by fundamentalist apologists.

Bultmann protested that Christianity still remains impregnated with mythological conceptions that contradict modern common sense. For example, the New Testament cosmology is one of a three-sphere, mythical world made up of heaven above, the earth, and hell below. Not only is a higher world affirmed; its reality is seen as intervening in, and bursting into, human life. Strange, uncanny, and disquieting powers of a variety of types are alleged to appear and even dominate the scene. Bultmann was sure that modern science—conforming to the law of empirical causality—can allow no such supernatural forces. Critically, such outdated thinking must be given up—demythologized.

In his historical research, Bultmann showed that the New Testament writers draw on mythical images of Jewish apocalypse and the Gnostic symbolism of redemption as well as on the mystery religions. The mythical New Testament model envisages the present era as dominated by Satan. In the apocalyptic language, which is used especially in Ezekiel, Daniel, and Revelation, as well as Matthew 24, immanent catastrophe is predicted. Such was the preunderstanding, the symbolic horizon presupposed in interpretation. According to the apocalyptic mode, it was predicted that the present age soon will end and be replaced by another, and the Messiah will come. Gnosticism described the descent of the Son of God, clothed in the body of a man, from the world of light, a theme widely used in Christological speculation.

Early Christianity appropriated both apocalyptic and Gnostic symbolism in its historical archetype. Bultmann's conclusion was that the proclamation of salvation—the saving event in Jesus Christ—no longer finds understanding or is relevant when expressed in a literalist model. All of this symbolism needs to be given up. Of course, Bultmann's ideas have dismayed fundamentalists. One particular reason was that, having initiated the demythologizing controversy, he did not wish to replace the core meaning of Christianity by humanist cultural symbols of moral evolution and progress. His hermeneutical concern was not simply another phase in the modernist-fundamentalist debate. On the contrary, he was attempting to understand Christianity in what he judged to be its existential meaning.

The nineteenth-century philosopher W. F. Schelling, whose ideas continue to have influence in the present, in particular through the theology of Paul Tillich, wrote from a different point of view:

It [revealed religion] does not create the matter in which it develops; it finds it independently present. The formal achievement of revealed religion is to surpass mere natural, unfree religion; but for this very reason it has the natural religion in itself, for the surpasser contains the surpassed. . . . For the kinship between the two [mythology and revelation] has been shown in their common outward destiny.[11]

FUNDAMENTALISM VERSUS DEMYTHOLOGIZING

Bultmann's demythologizing did not stop with cosmology but proposed a program for Christian theology in general. The issue is relevant to other religious traditions as well. Bultmann argued specifically that major scriptural themes are no longer negotiable, unless they are existentially reinterpreted. Fundamentalists also interpret these themes existentially but do not demythologize them.

In the literalist model, the tension between Christianity and a sinful world is expected to be resolved by the return of Jesus to the earth. Of course, it must be said that, in practical terms, the perpetuation of a living faith of the type Bultmann affirmed is often more effective in a revivalist setting than in either theological modernism or neoorthodoxy. It is commonplace that revivalist evangelists who expect the second coming of Christ continue to make converts when demythologizers do not. The mythical narrative they invoke is not symbolically abstract but describes the destiny of the world, human persons, and angels and demons in compellingly powerful, concrete terms.

When men and women first described themselves and the world, they told stories; historically, abstract analytic concepts came later. Jaspers in his book on the interpretation of history concludes that initially all human thinking and language had a mythical reference.[12] His concern in the passage quoted at the beginning of this chapter is not the truth or falsehood of a particular symbolic narrative, but its distinctive mode of meaning—in short, the nature and meaning of myth. It was the development of mythos (and not, initially, logos) that distinguished human beings from other animals and provided their first "rationale," as it were.

For nonfundamentalists living in the contemporary world, the question is not whether demythologizing is necessary; indeed, it is inevitable. A further issue is whether remythologizing can be avoided. In short, can religion be converted into fully nonmythical terms?

Schelling concluded, in antithesis to demythologizing, that

> mythology is inevitable; it is an inherent necessity of language, if we recognize language as the outward form of thought; it is . . . the dark shadow which language casts on thought and which will never vanish as long as speech and thought do not fully coincide, and this can never happen. Mythology in the highest sense of the word is the power which language exerts on thought in every possible sphere of cultural activity.[13]

Northrop Frye, a classics scholar who taught at the University of Toronto, explains further:

> Man lives, not directly or nakedly in nature like the animals, but from within a mythological universe, a body of assumptions and beliefs developed from his existential concerns.... One of the practical functions of criticism ... is, I think, to make us more aware of our mythological conditioning.[14]

EARLIER CRITIQUES OF MYTHOLOGY

Actually the downgrading and rejection of myth did not begin in modern times.[15] In their apologetics, the early fathers of the Christian church dismissed mythology as pagan nonsense. They believed that their own Christian narratives were true stories and that the non-Christian tales of the gods were untrue and to be rejected. Humankind had moved out of the darkness of myth into the clear light of Christian revelation. The modern rationalist or empiricist rejection of myth has very different bases. Myth is viewed generally as the antithesis of scientific discovery.

The problem with both the Christian and the secular rejections of myth is that, as I have already argued, it is perennial and keeps reappearing today. Mythos (archetypal myths) has come to the fore again because of psychotherapy, the discoveries of Freud and Jung.[16] Modern sociologists and psychologists identify it as a powerful factor to be taken seriously in politics and community life. In popular religion, myths proliferate both outside of as well as within the Western monotheisms. Thus one may speak of the myths (archetypal patterns, the first premises and presuppositions) of Europe, the United States, or Islamic civilization and history.

Early Christian polemic against myth drew on the attack of the pre-Christian Greek dramatists and philosophers dating back to two and a half millennia ago. They rejected polytheistic stories, viewing them as untrue and, more often than not, immoral. Yet Plato himself, from whom Christian apologists drew heavily, left a place for limited recourse to myth.[17] He granted that it could be employed to identify a kind of insight about reality that empirical description and rational explanation do not express fully. It might even be said that it remains at the border of understanding as a kind of reference without which one does not attain a maximum of insight. Of course, the myths that the Greek playwrights and philosophers rejected are only a part of a larger legacy. In the form in which their critics came to know them, mythical narratives had already been rationalized and stereotyped. Myth was not just told and retold, but written and rewritten as the oral form of transmission was abandoned. Moreover what was preserved (in Homer, specifically) was not the model of the common people, but a literary genre. (The poems of Homer were the unifying scripture of the Greek city-states.)[18]

Even when the initial frame of reference is demythologized, the mythical symbolism remains, psychologically and culturally, in the background and is only partially transcended.[19] German philosopher Hans Blumenberg, the main representative of "metaphorology," from his own premises recently has argued that human beings perennially create myths to avoid what he calls "the absoluteness of reality."[20] Myths, in being archetypal, are synoptically inclusive, not just confused history or primitive explanation of nature. They give human beings at least limited control as over against a predetermined universe that otherwise has them completely at its mercy.

J. J. Bachofen ranks among the most important researchers of mythology in the last century. His statement is classic:

> The symbol [i.e. mythological symbolism] awakens intuition where the language of abstraction can only offer rational explanation. . . . The one is directed inwards, the other outwards. Only the symbol can combine a wide variety of notions into a single total impression; the language of abstraction, on the other hand, arranges them in succession and presents them to the mind piecemeal, whereas they ought to be presented to the soul at a single glance. Words reduce the infinite to finitude, symbols lead the spirit beyond.[21]

THIELICKE'S THEOLOGICAL CRITIQUE OF BULTMANN'S DEMYTHOLOGIZING

Such reflection leads to the question whether the rational patterns identified as logos are always the full antithesis of mythos. Challenging Bultmann's demythologizing as a fellow German Lutheran theologian, Helmut Thielicke, appealed for a "restatement of the New Testament mythology" that includes reference to both logos and mythos.[22] Arguing that "myth is a permanent element in human thought, and therefore an indispensable vehicle for the expression of Biblical revelation," he holds that myth can express true but not exhaustive knowledge, derived from illumination or revelation. Thielicke's criticism of Bultmann's radical existentialism is that it "really leaves no room for a historical revelation in time."[23] For his own part, Thielicke concludes that mythology in itself is timeless. Still, the symbolism and imagery used is conditioned by the worldview current at the time.[24] The paradox of

Bultmann's position is that he rejects myth cosmologically but accepts it as true personally and existentially.[25]

Dutch scholar Theodoor Marius van Leeuwen states the issue clearly in his reinterpretation of demythologizing; he uses the term in a sense different from Bultmann's:

> *Demythologizing* is an urgent necessity of modern thought, but *demythizing* would cause a deplorable impoverishment. In fact modern man has been the first to discover the proper *symbolic dimension of myth*. Our modernity is born out of the distinction of history and myth, and out of the desac-ralization of nature. It is after this 'crisis' that man recognizes myth as myth. . . . Mythical language does not explain reality in a scientific sense. The events told in myth can not be co-ordinated with the time-scale of history; its places are not found in geography.[26]

From this, van Leeuwen draws the following conclusion:

> Myth as *explanation* must be dissolved. Its logos, its pretension to be an account of history or an explanation of nature, is pseudo-logos. But the demythologization of myth is the condition for a rediscovery of myth as symbolic narration. The 'greatness of myth' . . . is that it has more meaning than a history which is, objectively, true. This meaning is not etiological but *explorative*. Myth explores the possibilities of man and his place within being. It is 'an opening up and a disclosure' . . . of a field of human experience.[27]

FRYE'S LITERARY ANALYSIS OF BIBLICAL MYTH

In what sense does an understanding of New Testament religion require remythologizing? The alternative to comprehensive demythologizing, as well as fundamentalist literalism, is clarified in Northrop Frye's *The Great Code*. The author addresses the problem of mythos.[28] In Frye's terms the Bible is mythic in the sense that it tells a story, organizing the story around certain values and symbolic insights. He illustrates what he means by "mythos" by referring to Gibbon's *The History of the Decline and Fall of the Roman Empire*. Gibbon, he argues, gave more than simply a factual report. The historian used his information with a narrative principle to select and arrange his material. Without such a mythos, his book could not have taken shape. Of course, the biblical stories are sacred because they are believed to be revealed; the distinction between natural and revealed is something that Frye claims is not to be found in primitive societies. As a literary critic Frye observes that the biblical accounts are both historical and symbolic. He writes:

If we read the Bible sequentially, the Bible becomes a myth, first by tautology, in the sense in which all myths are *mythoi* or narratives, and second in the more specific sense of being a narrative with specially significant material that we find in all mythologies: stories of creation, of legendary history, lists of laws and rituals with narratives explaining their origin, and so on.[29]

Frye, who bases his claims on a rich knowledge of the history of religion, affirms that myth is inseparable from things to be done or specified actions. Thus ritual actions that accompany the rehearsing of the myth point in the direction of its original context. He emphatically states that this type of analysis does not reduce the biblical stories to fiction. His judgment is that the history of salvation, *Heilsgeschichte*, and world history, *Weltgeschichte*, can never fully coincide. The former by its very nature in a sense falsifies the latter. "Thus the Exodus is a myth of the deliverance of Israel from Egypt which clearly bears only the most oblique relation to the historical events of whatever period it may assume."[30] Frye notes that a consensus of belief about the legitimacy of such mythical stories persisted in the West until the eighteenth century, when rationalism and historical relativism challenged it. He writes:

The linguistic fact [is] that many of the central doctrines of traditional Christianity can be grammatically expressed only in the form of metaphor. Thus: Christ *is* God and man; in the Trinity three persons *are* one, in the Real Presence the body and blood *are* the bread and the wine.[31]

Frye explains that in a secondary sense myths take place in a larger setting of mythology, an interconnected group of myths. (At this point his analysis relates positively to our definition of mythos as an inclusive paradigm.) Folk tales, by contrast, he notes, remain nomadic. To be sure, mythologies often contain a great deal of legendary and traditional history; myths delimit a particular area of culture and mark it off from others. At the same time, they are autonomous, a factum and not a datum of human culture.[32]

Frye's analysis provides a substantial answer to Bultmann by extending the category of myth. Of course, it is important that Bultmann himself believed that Christianity has an indispensable kerygma (message) that cannot be reduced to concept alone. With respect to the history of religion, the same may be said of other major faiths as well. Religions as symbol systems include narratives that are not to be simply equated with either fables or untrue stories. But narratives are not just "factually true data," as many fundamentalists seem to presuppose. Such a claim addresses the issue of truth, which goes beyond the scope of the history or phenomenology of religion.

KOLAKOWSKI'S PHILOSOPHICAL DEFENSE OF MYTH

At this juncture we need to ask how our reference to myth can be justified in terms of the insight and knowledge that it provides. Rather than considering further the role of myth in religion, I will attempt to appraise the field of mythos in nonconfessional terms from the vantage point of philosophy. Among contemporary philosophers, Leszek Kolakowski (existentially oriented and anti-Marxist, but not a professing Christian) significantly clarifies philosophical issues in his book *The Presence of Myth*.[33] Mythos, Kolakowski argues, is an indispensable "transcendental" reference as an archetypal model; it is paradigmatic. Kolakowski describes the mythological dimension as follows:

> I use these terms [*myth* and *mythology*] in their proper meaning with reference to situations which precede empirical reality and empirical time, but which give them a coherent meaning and create a nontemporal paradigm removed from real becoming—a paradigm which is necessary in real becoming *to equal.* . . . (the nature of humanity, the essence of thought, the essence of law, transcendental values, and so on) fall under this heading. In these mythologies, perfection is fulfilled in Being which antedates history, while myth shows us that non-temporal model which we have to emulate.[34]

Kolakowski is not just concerned with religious myth, although this is included when he described it as "a permanently constitutive element of culture." His analysis proceeds from what he calls the "primary recognition" that "myth" is a living reality in a variety of areas—art, history, and politics as well as religion. He is sure that it is not to be explained simply empirically or functionally and insists rather as a philosopher on its epistemological necessity and nonreducibility. In his judgment, mythos not only helps to remove the otherness of the world. It also helps us to understand why this is not fully possible. Mythologies are "principles for understanding things in their preempirical order; reserves of fundamental values which do not prejudice every single situation."[35] They are "instruments of relativization of empirical occurrences."[36] Kolakowski explains:

> Myths. . . . are not translatable into a non-mythical tongue, supposedly apt to convey their genuine content. To believe that we can clar-

ify this content or make it intelligible by this kind of translation is no more credible than to expect that we can hand over to someone the meaning of a musical work by telling them 'what it is about'. Myths would be dispensable if they had metaphysical equivalents. If they both express and conceal an ultimate reality this is because this reality is not expressible in abstracto, not reducible to any theoretical parlance.[37]

An archetypal mythos is a reference that provides the horizon for understanding value, selfhood, and even reason itself in dynamic existential dimensions. As it relates to love and death, in particular, in Kolakowski's view, it enables one to overcome what he calls the "indifference of the world." Only Hume's world is one without myth, Kolakowski argues, and it is not a world in the real sense, but only a succession of experiences. An irreversible paralysis sets in when thought is emancipated from myth. It affects meaning, although not necessarily utility or application.[38]

Kolakowski would agree with Eliade, who argues that the loss of a mythical dimension has resulted in a loss of meaning in the modern world. Though less idealistically oriented than Schelling, Kolakowski probably would agree with him (and Tillich) that history and aesthetics, more than the abstractions of logic, are the key to mythos. At the same time, he has no intention of falling back into a pre-Enlightenment pattern. A simplistic return to mythology could effectively reinstate "a hierocratic despotism over secular life," and Kolakowski finds this unimaginable. On the other hand, a culture totally bereft of mythological elements is equally unthinkable, in his judgment.

What is challenged (successfully) by a philosopher like Kolakowski is the belief (held by Comte, for example) that logos has fully replaced mythos—that the latter belongs primarily to the human race's childhood and now has been outgrown. Kolakowski argues that it is possible to distinguish between the real concentration of insight and a whim. Assuredly, myth can engender fanaticism, but it also is the root of creativity. That there is truth is not self-evident empirically. Without what Kolakowski calls "the myth of truth," no knowledge is possible. In this sense, mythos precedes and undergirds logos.

THE TREATMENT OF MYTHOS IN SUBSEQUENT CHAPTERS:

Fundamentalism has arisen in response to short-term as well as long-term crises of mythos in major religions. Established traditions are being challenged in different settings, and drastic model changes are taking place in religious communities. Problems and issues extend over the confessional barriers dividing them. For example, as noted earlier, Darwin's discovery of biological evolution had a devastating impact on low-church Protestant Christianity. Eventually, other religions have had to confront modern scientific developments. The claim for the verbal inspiration of Scripture and millennialism appeared as defenses against an ever more powerful secular worldview. Today, the problem of adjustment to modern scientific worldviews is not limited to Christianity.

Judaism

In Judaism, fundamentalism has its historical background—the causes that provoked it—in such antithetical developments as the Enlightenment and the Holocaust. Both had a revolutionary impact on traditional quietism. The fundamentalist response has been radical—a renewed messianism and millennialism—with both mythical and utopian bases. Politically, messianism and millennialism have come to be joined with nationalism.

The background of contemporary Jewish fundamentalism is the Six-Day War, through which, in June 1967, large territories were "returned" to Israeli rule. It was followed by a change of government policy and a move away from socialism and secularism. Now, the long-term issue has become the relation of Torah not only to the Enlightenment but also to the post-Enlightenment contemporary world. The short-term issue is one of political order in the Middle East. Judaism's eschatology is being reanimated and is being given new life by fundamentalists in the Gush Emunim movement, and what the lasting changes in mythos may be is not fully clear.

Islam

The fundamentalist crisis in Islam, as in Judaism, is both long-term and short-term. Its historical setting is the collapse of an earlier inclusive culture at the beginning of the modern era, followed by colonialism and now the national independence of Muslim states. Having made Islam into a political program, today fundamentalists seek renewed victory. Of course, they often link religion and government polity simplistically.

To critics, it seems clear that traditional Islamic law, which is to be all-inclusive under fundamentalist revivalist rule, offers few resources for dealing with the complex demands of modern society. How long can the rejection of the separation of civil and religious law endure? How long will Muslim fundamentalists regard Islam as the only "house of peace," with all other communities and religions being regarded as a "house of war"? The short-term political and social crisis is matched by a long-term crisis of mythos. At issue is not only how much Islam will continue to react against the secularism of the West, but how it will relate to modern science and the globalization of world culture.

Hinduism

In Hinduism, in India, a growing fundamentalism is being supported by a union of religion and nationalism. How long can the Republic of India remain secular, even in Mahatma Gandhi's limited sense? Gandhi advocated freedom of conscience and tolerance for other religions, not the full separation of religion from culture and government. A short-term crisis is evident. Amid growing communalism and riots, economic progress has been much slower in India than hoped.

At the same, the questions debated between Gandhi and his opponents (who accepted the use of force on secular and/or religious grounds) continue to be reappraised in a long-term crisis of mythos. For example, issues such as tolerance are being considered exegetically in relation to Scriptures, and fundamentalists seek to restore an earlier worldview in the late twentieth century.

Sikhism

The growth of Hindu fundamentalism in India is feared by Sikhs, and hostility now is directed especially against Hindus as adherents of the majority religion rather than, as earlier, against Muslims. Problems arise partly due to the fact that the Constitution of India both protects individual freedom of conscience and at the same time acknowledges the communal rights of minorities. As these two aspects clash from time to time, how can particular confessional groups relate to the rest of the nation without violence?

The Sikhs, long honored for their military prowess by the British, still continue their own unique lifestyle and dress, with uncut hair and beards. This pattern has shown great power in preserving minority distinctiveness. The short-term crisis obviously is political in relation to the secular republic of India. A long-term ideological debate accompanies it and concerns more than just geography or language. How will the Sikh religious model (which conceives of God as formless) have enough power to survive against a militant Islam and Hinduism?

Buddhism

I will limit the discussion of Buddhist fundamentalism to Thailand and Sri Lanka, and to one party in Japan, Soka Gakkai (a dogmatic form of Nichiren Buddhism). How does fundamentalism fit into the Buddhist setting, if at all? Today, there are both short-term and long-term issues. The short-term issue is how Buddhism is to adjust to modernity and develop a social ethic. Long-term issues are internal to Buddhism itself—paradigm differences such as those between Theravada and Mahayana schools, as well as those among Zen, Pure Land, and Tibetan interpretations, as they embrace modern secular views.

Chapter 6

Jewish Fundamentalism

HISTORY

> After more than eighteen centuries of dormancy, the distinctive [fundamentalist] blend of messianic expectation, militant political action, intense parochialism, devotion to the Land of Israel, and self-sacrifice that characterized the Jewish Zealots of Roman times caught the imagination of tens of thousands of young religious Israeli Jews and disillusioned but idealistic secular Zionists.[1]

This is the report of Ian S. Lustick in *For the Land and for the Lord, Jewish Fundamentalism in Israel.* In Israel, fundamentalism has emerged as a response to both long- and short-term crises. The long-term crisis was occasioned by the threat of modernity, especially as ghetto separation broke down under Enlightenment influence. A more violent attack on Jewish identity took place in the Holocaust initiated by the Nazis. Of course, the impact was particularly strong on the Jewish consciousness, as it should be on the conscience of the entire world.

Today, the short-term crisis arises from the ideological and dogmatic opposition to the State of Israel by the Arab states. In the Six-Day War in 1967, Jewish victory brought major territorial gains to Israel by force of arms. Jewish fundamentalists' attempts to preserve them has brought about a "short-term" change of paradigm under their influence that is debated to the present. Zionism has been given a religious significance that was long denied it by Orthodox leaders.

Can the term *fundamentalism* be used in this context? The question is whether any other term is more appropriate. Scholars researching the background of events often begin by distinguishing the new fundamentalists from quietistic ultra-Orthodox Jews, commonly called the "Haredim" (literally, the "fearful" or "God-fearing" ones), who long have refrained from any political action. Some interpreters argue that the ultra-Orthodox Haredim should also be included under the designation *fundamentalist*, together with the ba'alei teshuvah. The latter are Israeli Jews returning to religious observance, most of them associated with ultra-Orthodox yeshivot. They belong to the circle that has always rejected Zionism in any form, secular or religious, as an anticipation of God's intervention to bring about the end of the exile. The apparent success of the Zionist movement, including the rise of the State of Israel, has not caused them to give up their outlook, and their number continues to grow.

This chapter will be concerned primarily with the Gush Emunim movement, given its confrontation with modernity. The fundamentalist movement began in force when Gush Emunim was formally organized as the Bloc of the Faithful in 1974. Gush Emunim is often said to have had its predecessor in the secretive youth movement (Gahelet) of the 1950s. Suddenly, in 1967, with the defeat of the Arabs, Israel had gained new lands. If these were providentially given, was there also a religious mandate to rule Judea and Samaria? Gush Emunim fundamentalists—sophisticated and determined—argued that there was.

Gush Emunim advocates, no less ultra-Orthodox than the Haredim, share one conviction with them—the belief that salvation can come only from God. But by contrast, calling for political responsibility rather then spurning it, they have been ready to work to speed the fulfillment of biblical prophecies. Gush Emunim drew from a diversity of groups in organizing the opposition to the older secular establishment—demobilized soldiers, intellectuals, and kibbutz members.[2]

Jewish fundamentalism cannot be fully grasped simply by considering sociological, psychological, or political factors alone; it concerns a faith model.

Lawrence focuses on our issue when he asks: "Is it then a choice between myth and reality, or is it a choice between two ideologies each of which is partly myth-making, partly reality-defining?"[3] He describes the current situation as a struggle for the soul of Judaism: "It is a fight to prove that Jews are not merely a special race with a piece of territory but a divine instrument with a universal mission."[4] Lustick emphasizes that "what otherwise might be considered 'mundane' Levantine politics" takes on cosmic significance from the fundamentalist point of view.[5]

As in other religions, Jewish fundamentalism does not simply reassert traditional views. The present era has special meaning for Jewish history as well as world history, because of Israel's uniqueness. At this point, a traditional Jewish conviction is reasserted against Enlightenment secularity and assimilation. What is distinctive is that the new religious Right in Israel not only affirms the modern world (as against traditionalism) but reinterprets it as a distinct stage in the fulfillment of the divine promise of messianic redemption.[6] Earlier, Jewish groups had often legitimated this-worldly activity defensively on the basis of their own needs and interests. Now, such activity is seen as a mechanism through which redemption can come to pass.

"Peoples of the world had learned to mourn for Jews but not to live with them," it was said. On this premise, Gush Emunim's goal has been to build a renewed Jewish presence in the Middle East on the back of a messianic dream. Its revivalist political program is territorial, ethnic, and cultural, Schnall points out.[7] Gush Emunim, invoking mitzvoth (commandment), the sages, and pietist tradition in the movement's activism, has been adamantly religious.[8] It came into public view initially with projects to popularize the strategic importance of Judea and Samaria—candle-lighting ceremonies, marathons, marches, and so on. Membership lists have never been made public officially, and it is not a political party. The inner circle is small. Its leadership's concern for settlement on the West Bank and in other Arab areas has been admired by nationalists who do not share all of its of religious convictions.

What is distinctive (and fundamentalist) about the Gush Emunim model is that religiomystical elements have priority. Commentators note that Hasidism (with similarities to Christian Pietism) and the mystical lore of the Kabbala are drawn upon. Its assessment of state institutions has been described as almost Gnostic-like; they are not absolutized as in Muslim theocracies. Government agencies are employed as a means toward the higher Zionist goal of Jewish settlement and renewal. The state is not to be seen as autonomous and secular (nor is it to be idealized, as in many Islamic views), but with its institutions is subject to halakha ("the way a faithful Jew should walk," scriptural law, especially as interpreted in the Talmud).[9]

Gush Emunim members have defied governments and acted against statutory law, when necessary. Jewish resettlement of Palestine is seen as ultimately justified even when it goes in the face of legal regulations and formalities. Every piece of the land is holy—a present from God.[10] To return any of the land would be a violation of his command. In spite of these radical premises, Gush Emunim advocates seek to portray their movement as being part of the Zionist mainstream.

As against a long-standing earlier Zionist secular model, another paradigm is championed, a religious one that sees the Land of Israel and the process of redemption together. In contrast to the new Right, the early Zionist leaders were little interested in religion. Today, the early Zionist ideology—often it was socialist—along with the communal dining halls and child-rearing experiments it fostered, have waned. Young people who wear the distinctive Gush Emunim knitted skullcaps set up religious study sessions before their tanks at the front line. The Yeshivat Hesder program, approved by the government, allows them to divide their time between a program of study and military service—alternately—over a period of six years.

Fundamentalist reassertion of piety and obedience to religious law has an evident historical background in government support of religious institutions; it is not simply a spontaneous process. When the new State of Israel was founded, Orthodox Judaism was established and given its own educational system with government subsidy. Reform Judaism was excluded from state recognition at the outset. The Gush Emunim constituency comes not from the older generation of secularists but from the nationalist families whose children attended Orthodox religious schools in Israel. The Orthodox schools, which only a minority of the young population attend, have been paid for by the state. There is virtually no middle party such as the groups representing Reform or even Conservative Judaism in the United States.

In Israel today, orthodoxy and radical secularity exist side by side—with a different balance. The impact of the new fundamentalism on national life cannot be ignored, irrespective of the outcome of international negotiations about West Bank settlement. Gush Emunim's advocacy of settlement has had a wider appeal beyond its own distinct fundamentalist constituency, and its settlement initiatives have been implemented with the help of a larger spectrum of citizens. University graduates who want to live near big cities have been able do so in well-built dwellings. These unique and often amply furnished bedroom communities, resembling in some respects American suburbia, appeal to the non-Orthodox as well as the religiously active.

EXAMPLES OF THE NEW RELIGIOUS MILITANCY

A group of some sixty Israeli Jews chose to come to the Arab city of Hebron on the eve of Passover, 4 April 1968.[11] The population of that city was almost exclusively Arab. This visiting party, made up of ten families with their children, arranged to meet at the two story Arab Park Hotel which they had rented for the Passover season. At the hotel, they checked in as tourists from Switzerland. Government military authorities were told that they would stay only two days. Led by activist Rabbi Moshe Levinger, the group first set up a kosher kitchen in the place and then celebrated a Seder in festive spirits. Then they announced that no power on earth could force them to move from this town of the Hebrew patriarchs where Abraham once had lived and from which David for a time ruled.[12] The national government found it much more difficult to respond to the crisis they provoked because the Arab mayor of Hebron had cooperated with the Jewish occupation.

There had been a Hebrew community in Hebron until 1929 when it was destroyed in a massacre by Arabs. At the height of the violence and killing a rabbi had rescued the Torah from its burning synagogue; later he died of burns. After the 1968 return, his grandson felt charged to fulfill his last dying wish, namely, that the Torah scroll be returned to Hebron. Amid heavy nationalist and religious pressure, the ruling Labor Party in Jerusalem decided to compromise. In August 1968 it allowed a yeshiva to be opened in Hebron; enrollment was to be limited to 103 participants. Jews but not Arabs responded positively. On 9 October 1968 a hand grenade was thrown into a Jewish crowd, wounding forty-seven persons. The government still seeking to satisfy Jewish settlers as well as restore peace authorized the building of a new Jewish community at a site overlooking ancient Hebron. Its was to be called by the biblical twin name for Hebron, Kiryat Araba, and in time it grew to have a population of over three thousand Jewish citizens.

In 1978, Likud party rule replaced long-standing Labor dominance. Reversing the older policy, the government in Jerusalem has worked closely with Gush Emunim and its settlement activism. Fundamentalists have often provided the cadres necessary for implementation of settlement policies. To be sure, there is also opposition to Gush Emunim's strategies from parties like the Peace Now movement as well as its other religious groups. But as with fundamentalism elsewhere, more liberal religious beliefs have seemed less compelling compared to emotionally appealing programs, which in Israel have had immediate potential for results in settlement.

In dealing with Gush Emunim, the government has often seen its presence and power in terms of an "iceberg image," presuming that there is more-widespread support beneath the surface than is evident immediately. After all, it is noted, few Jews can accept that it is illegal to reside anywhere they choose in a land with such historic Jewish roots. There has been a radical change of orientation from left to right, secular to religious, as Gush Emunim has moved from the fringe to the mainstream.

In its program, antireligion and secularism are to be overcome by redefining secularism. Gush Emunim drew powerfully from Jewish nationalism in its reappraisal of secular-religious distinctions, Liebman observes, even as it premised that divine redemption was immanent.[13] Expansionism increases the scope of traditional Jewish symbols, he points out. Liebman views the fundamentalist program as a form of domination. Expansionism, initially rejecting modernity, reinterprets it through the prism of the Jewish tradition.[14] Secularism is judged as superficial and lacking in inner content (claims that are echoed in fundamentalism in other religions).

Gush Emunim emphasizes that all Jews—whether practicing or not—share the eternal bond between the Jewish nation and the Land of Israel, on the one hand, and with God and his Torah, on the other. Seen from this perspective, many of the earlier Zionist efforts to return to the Land of Israel were not simply secular even when they seemed to be. An earlier liberalism is transcended. After the State of Israel had been founded, its leader, Ben Gurion, called a conference of intellectuals to chart the future course of the new nation. No religious Jews were included. Now, because of fundamentalism, this type of polity belongs to the past.[15]

> One Jewish fundamentalist has gone so far as to declare there is "no difference between red apostasy and blue apostasy, between apostasy with a cross (converting to Christianity) and apostasy without a cross (becoming a secular Jew)."[16]

Throughout the centuries of exile there had been persecution and endless suffering. Now the passivity that had characterized the past was to be given up. Gush Emunim revivalism explicitly rejects the Diaspora model in a new concern for settlement in the land. The spiritual experience of Diaspora was characterized by closedness, divisiveness, spiritual weakness, and detachment from nature. The Diaspora was an unnatural state, it is argued, and, not surprisingly, so-called secular Jews reacted against its excessive spirituality. Part of its self-segregation stemmed from the necessity to preserve and strengthen the dimension of holiness in the life of the people.

PERIODIZATION

Jewish piety, by and large, has not engaged in speculative theology as much as Catholic Christianity (for example, in Christology). Priority rather has been given to law and ethics—halakha. Lawrence remarks: "One must draw attention to the fact that Judaism is more intensely related to practice, right practice, or orthopraxis, while Christianity stresses the notion of right belief or orthodoxy. If Jews are more prone to ask one another: 'what do you do?' Christians are more likely to demand: 'what do you believe?' "[17] The difference is reflected in Jewish and Christian fundamentalism, respectively.

Lawrence identifies the content of the classical myth as follows: "(1) living by the commandments of the Torah (the *mitzvoth*), (2) obeying the directives of the sages who have been ordained to determine the *halakha*, (3) believing in the truth of everything that the Torah teaches according to the interpretation of scholars whose greatness in *halakha* also invests them with superiority in this area."[18] Of course, there have been outspoken Jewish critics of fundamentalism both in Israel and elsewhere.

One of the most widely read Jewish historians of religion in the United States, Jacob Neusner, invokes periodization in understanding the history of his religion. At the same time, he prefers not to use the term *fundamentalism* with respect to developments in Judaism. Neusner argues that Judaism changed radically in response to Christianity during the early centuries of the common era. He periodicizes the history of the different models in terms of the destruction of the First Temple by the Babylonians in 586 B.C.E., the destruction of the Second Temple by the Romans in 70 C.E., the Muslim conquest dating from about 640 C.E., and finally the coming of modernity in 1787 and 1789 with the United States Constitution and the French Revolution. Neusner speaks of an early age of diversity in which there were many different paradigms or Judaisms. This claim itself excludes any simple fundamentalist appeal to the past. Neusner writes:

> Archaic Judaism constituted a rich, mythic structure, realized in every sort of experience. The issue of modern Judaism is not whether Jews still believe in the old myths, but rather how the old myths have been transformed.[19]

Beginning with the destruction of the Second Temple in 70 C.E., a single Judaism emerged. It was based upon the premise of a dual Torah—the written and the oral. The latter included the writings of the sages, the Mishnah and commentaries on it, as well as the Talmud. One version of the latter was produced in Israel about 400 C.E., and another in Babylonia about 600 C.E.

THEOLOGICAL CONTROVERSY

Clearly, in the contemporary discussion in Judaism, there is a theological watershed with respect to halakha, observance of Torah. Of course, orthodoxy needs to be distinguished from fundamentalism. The issues in the present paradigm debate are identified clearly in Rabbi Robert Gordis's essay "A Dynamic Halakhah: Principles and Procedures of Jewish Law."[20] Gordis seeks to refute the view that "halakhah is . . . locked in mortal combat with the contemporary age, the demands of which are, therefore, to be resisted with every means at its disposal." He argues that in fact Jewish law has not been "monolithic and unchanged in the past," and he finds "no grounds for decreeing that it must be motionless in the present and immovable in the future." Gordis is convinced that a "healthy tradition" is "sensitive to the age and responds to it." Indeed, it is the secret of Judaism's capacity to survive.

Gordis calls on the "past two centuries of brilliant and dedicated research in Jewish law, literature, and life." Optimistically, he finds a dialectic of continuity and change at every point. Halakha is comprised of two elements, in his judgment: "continuity with the past and growth induced by the present." Its driving force is, first, the necessity to respond to new external conditions and, second, the need to give recognition to new ethical insights.

Rabbi Louis Jacobs counters that "traditional halakhah is based on fundamentalism, if not of the Bible certainly of the Talmud." He argues that "resistance to change is not only due to the need for legal stability, but is also based on a most powerful religious dogma, the Word of God is unchanging and His Law immutable, this Word and this Law being mediated through the Talmudic Sages and through no others."[21] The central contested question is one of change and subjectivity. Rabbi David Singer, himself Reformed, describes the Reform movement as having cut the Gordian knot by declaring traditional procedures of Jewish law to be inoperative. Rabbi J. David Bleich, author of the book *Contemporary Halakhic Problems*, opposes all such "cognitive retrenchment," speaking of "Halakhah as an Absolute."[22] Jewish law simply does not change, in his judgment. Contesting Gordis's interpretation as much as Rabbi Jacobs's, Rabbi Bleich writes: "The Judaism which he describes is not my Judaism; the halakhah to which he subscribes is not my halakhah. Most fundamentally, I suspect that the Deity he recognizes is not the God who revealed himself at Sinai." Rabbi Bleich's claim is that "all of halakhah is inherent in the original revelation at Mt. Sinai." He concludes: "The application of normative, unchanging legal canons to multifarious situations, is not at all a process of change."

HISTORY OF RELIGION AND THE JEWISH TRADITION

The debate, of course, is much wider and larger than fundamentalist controversy in Israel. In considering contemporary Jewish history-of-religions scholarship, I will refer to Neusner's *The Way of Torah, an Introduction to Judaism*.[23] Periodicizing, as does Küng, Neusner speaks of not one but many Judaisms: "We must remind ourselves that the contents of the Torah have varied from one Judaism to the next."[24] He understands the reasons for using the term *myth* in the history of religions and also works with paradigm theory. Viewing Judaism as a whole, Neusner attempts to describe its paradigms in terms of three elements: a worldview, a way of life, and a social group that, in the here and now, embodies the whole.

Before proceeding, we had best clarify the meaning of *mythic structure*. By *myth*, historians of religion do *not* mean something that is not true. They mean, in Streng's words, "that the essential structure of reality manifests itself in particular moments that are remembered and repeated from generation to generation." These moments are preserved in myths. This meaning is wholly congruent to the Judaic data we shall now consider.[25]

Neusner argues that myth, when present, "must infuse all details of the faith . . . ; it must be somehow hidden in every ceremony and rite, every liturgy, every sacred gesture and taboo."[26] In short, Neusner knows that the question of the status of myth and symbol in the Jewish religious heritage cannot be avoided. He premises what he calls an "ecology of religions," the interrelationship between a religious way of viewing the world and living life and the historical and social circumstances of its followers.[27] The dualism between worldview and history—identified by him—is generally overlooked or denied by fundamentalists in their exclusive focus on absolutes.

In the case of Judaism, the archetypal paradigm is one of monotheism. The Jewish biblical paradigm centers on history as opposed to a nature mythology. God is "above" history and yet active in it providentially. The Hebrews borrowed cosmological symbols and myths from other countries and cultures, in particular, Mesopotamia, Syria, Palestine, and Egypt. Even these were in part historicized. Nature was no longer regarded as divine, but understood as existing separately from God even though related to him. Demythologizing belonged to the strategy, but it was not carried to the point of the rejection of all symbols or myths. The Hebrews modified and converted; they did not accept uncritically the symbols and structures that they borrowed. Stories of world beginnings in creation, and world ends, were transformed from polytheism to monotheism, historicized and moralized. New meanings were substituted for older ones in reevaluation, and a whole pantheon of gods was dismantled.

The Hebrew biblical mythos and its structures can be identified in terms of the symbols of creation, revelation, and redemption.[28] Creation, revelation, and redemption, in this view, are not just events in the past, Neusner emphasizes. They take on mythical significance and are affirmed to have perennial relevance as they are reenacted ritually in the cultus. The Torah scroll in the ark in the synagogue visibly symbolizes the Law of God. Liturgically it is proclaimed: "This is the Torah that Moses set forth before the People, Israel, at the instruction of the Lord."[29] Writing as a historian of religion, Neusner does not attribute the writing of the Torah literally to Moses, but dates it later. Although oral traditions were collected in the period of the monarchy, the larger written Torah dates primarily from the period after the Exile, he accepts. According to Neusner, Torah symbolism expresses what the New Testament scholar E. P. Sanders has called covenantal monism, "meaning the keeping of the religious requirements of the Torah as an expression of loyalty to the covenant between God and Israel."[30]

Commonly, Orthodox scholarship ascribes the writing of Scriptures to earlier personages. Thus Moses was credited with the authorship of the Pentateuch, David with Psalms (at least some of which come from the period of the Second Temple after the return from exile), and King Solomon with Proverbs (a collection of sayings). But on critical historical reading, Leviticus, the third book of the Pentateuch, probably is a priestly manual from the Second Temple period. In any case the Pentateuchal material is diverse, and critical historians judge it to be a compilation. The written Torah shows internal evidence of being edited and reedited even after the Captivity. Of course, it is important to note that the division between Reformed and Orthodox Jews turns in part on biblical higher criticism, as in the case of the Christian modernist-fundamentalist antithesis.

Neusner believes that it was with the exile to Babylonia in 586 B.C.E. that Judaism proper was born as a religion. He is explicit that "Judaism is not the religion of the 'Old Testament'; rather, it is a development out of the ancient Hebrew Scriptures as much as Christianity is."[31] The conviction of "a faithful remnant" that survived the Exile and Captivity preserved faith in the God of Abraham, Isaac, and Jacob. After the return of part of the nation under the Persians and the building of the Second Temple, a priestly theocracy and exclusivist ethos were reinforced. "The classical myth," one in which meaning is found primarily in the correspondence between heaven and earth, became dominant, Neusner explains.[32] But this worldview is not accepted literally by any but the Orthodox and fundamentalists today. Neusner is as sure as Bultmann that religious truth does not depend on an earlier worldview—but he uses myth much more inclusively.

Neusner describes the present era as one of "reversionism," saying that it marks the conclusion of the age of modernization.[33] At this point, his historical analysis joins the questions raised by fundamentalism, a controversy that he

does not invoke at length, although he notes that Jews are again asking press-
ing questions about Torah, not as source of historical facts, but as God's
Word: "Why do I live, what do I do to serve God, what should I do with my
life?" The issues have shifted from human questions framed by humanity in
God's image and in God's likeness to an altogether different set of urgent
concerns that include matters of politics and economics. The impact of the
Holocaust and the founding of the State of Israel are foremost in this setting.
Liebman writes:

> The Holocaust, the central myth of Israeli society, conveys the
> message that without a state Jews are victims of non-Jews who are per-
> petually hostile to then. The tradition, in turn, legitimates Jewish rights
> to the Land of Israel, the only territory upon which a Jewish state can be
> built and the only land where Jews can realize their national destiny and
> assure their security.[34]

THE IDEOLOGY OF CONTEMPORARY JEWISH FUNDAMENTALISM

Christian premillennialism envisages the literal fulfillment of all of the
prophecies made with respect to the land and people of Israel. To be sure, it
qualifies them in relation to the new Christian dispensation and the role of the
Christian Church. Today, not only Christian, but Jewish fundamentalism sets
forth its expectations in a temporal scheme. The latter expects redemption
through a series of events that will lead to the building of the Third Temple in
Jerusalem and, if God's chosen people are faithful, eventually to the coming of
the messiah. For the Jewish outlook, redemption is primarily communal, not
individual, and the pattern of expectation is worked out accordingly in terms
of recent events.

Gush Emunim ideology specifies three stages in which messianic redemption is to occur. First there will be a repentance out of fear with the
return from Diaspora to the promised land of Israel. Secondly, national reconstruction will be heralded in a symbiosis of the People and the Land. Finally,
in a third stage, a repentance out of love will begin, one that will ultimately usher in the messianic era. If they wish, the Jewish people can attract the
messiah, accelerating the redemptive timetable by an "increasing level of religious observance."[35]

Historically, the fundamentalist paradigm goes back at least to the
early period of Jewish resettlement in Palestine.[36] Following the First World
War, the British under their mandate in 1921 appointed Rabbi Abraham Isaac,
known as Rav Kook the Elder (1869–1935), to serve as the Ashkenazic chief

rabbi. Unlike its secular proponents, Rav Kook the Elder understood Zionism as a return from a spiritually purgative exile as Jews reassumed their "Divine vocation" and began to achieve "the splendor of redemption."[37] Although ineffective politically as a leader, the chief rabbi nonetheless laid the religious basis for the present fundamentalist movement and its advocacy of "the whole land for Israel as commanded by the Torah." By contrast, the vast majority of rabbis in Europe at the time opposed the Zionist cause—looking for religious fulfillment in God's own good time rather than political salvation by human effort.

The senior Kook's intention (he was known as "Harav" to his students) was to resolve theological problems raised by Zionist secularism in particular. He saw that sparks of holiness that stem from a divine source are being hidden throughout all creation. All human beings are partners in religious efforts, but the primary responsibility to expand the influence of the sacred in all areas of life rests upon the Jewish nation. Rabbi Rav Kook's philosophy of an "all-encompassing unity" assumed that everything good comes from Judaism and Torah, even if no direct relation is evident at first sight.[38] Liebman finds that such a naively optimistic expansionism does not stand the test of contemporary Jewish experience. He attacks, in particular, its assumptions about the benign nature of secularism. The first Kook lived before the Holocaust, Liebman notes. By contrast, his son, Tzvi Yehuda Kook, 1891–1982, endorsed a more defensive nationalism. Both premised that "the Jewish nation [people] possessed absolute sanctity unconditioned by their behavior—a result of their natural and unchanging qualities."[39]

Tzvi Yehuda (the younger Kook) in particular emphasized the undivided integrity of the land and the importance of Jewish settlements: "The State of Israel was created and established by the Council of Nations by order of the Sovereign Lord of the Universe so that the clear commandment in the Torah 'that they shall inherit and settle the Land' would be fulfilled." "It is these mitzvot [full control and resettlement] that, by means of our rule, can accomplish the act of Redemption."[40] The Rabbis Kook were a "bridge" between the secular and religious parties. As in the case of fundamentalism in other places, its outreach has gone far beyond the inner core group of advocates, which is estimated as having anywhere from two thousand to twenty thousand members.

It seemed a sign of the times when the long-reigning Labor party lost in a national election and Menachem Begin became prime minister in 1977. As a symbolic gesture, he personally visited Tzvi Yehuda, the younger Kook, at Markaz HaRav (the Rabbi's Center), the yeshiva that the elder Kook had established in Jerusalem. An amazed student who was present described the occasion as follows:

He came as if to Canossa, as if this man, Tzvi Yehuda, was God's representative. Suddenly the Prime Minister kneels and bows before Tzvi Yehuda. . . . What greater empirical proof could there be that his fantasies and imagings were indeed reality? You could see for yourself that instead of treating him as if he were crazy, people looked upon him as something holy. And everything he said or did became something holy as well.[41]

Tzvi Yehuda taught that redemption was the crucial challenge of the time and enjoined practical political action to help bring it about. Lustick explains:

As his father had, Rav Tzvi Yehuda communicated to his followers a mystical, romantic interpretation of Zionism, redolent with the language of messianism and redemption. But he went substantially beyond Rav Kook the Elder by specifying the political and spiritual stages that the redemption process would entail and the concrete steps that had advanced it and would advance it toward its glorious conclusion.[42]

Whereas initially Israeli state leadership refused Gush Emunim's resettlement plans and efforts, today its parliamentary representatives and their friends have been given charge of large sums of state money, which are dispensed to settlers. A key to the movement's success has been its leaders' permissive attitude (dating from the time of Rav Kook the Elder), reflected, for instance, in the lenient observance of halakhah by the majority of citizens in Israel. The senior Kook enjoined patience:

To reject these children who have strayed from the ways of the Torah and religious faith, having been carried away by the raging currents of the times—I say unhesitatingly that this is not the way God wants . . . The inner essence of Jewish holiness remains hidden in their hearts.[43]

Of course, with respect to principle, Gush Emunim adherents refuse compromise and believe that ultimately religious norms have to be imposed on all groups of Jews in Israel, including those of secular and atheistic conviction. The long-term goal is religious rule, and it was the Kooks who supplied the paradigm and ideology to support it. Lustick insists that the break with centuries old traditions is greater than their followers acknowledged.[44] Jewish fundamentalism is far from simply ultra-Orthodoxy; like Christian fundamentalism it appropriates millennial traditions urgently in a new way.

This (Jewish) fundamentalism is based on the belief that the oral Torah is the necessary extension of the written Torah, and this is justified in both practical as well as theoretical terms. The boundaries of Eretz Yisrael are imprecise in the written Torah, and they are made explicit in the oral Torah. It is in the latter that southern Lebanon is given by divine decree to the tribe of Asher. The Gush Emunim belief is that other nations will benefit, both physically and spiritually from the redemption accomplished in Israel. Indeed, even the Arabs will benefit, in spite of defeat. Arab opposition to Israel is only the latest and most crucial episode in an eternal battle to overcome the forces of evil.

As I mentioned at the outset, some of the roots of the new fundamentalist paradigm are to be found in Hasidic pietism of the late pre-Enlightenment period as well as the Jewish mystical lore assembled in the Kabbala. The elder Kook, in the essay "The Road to Renewal," defended Hasidism on the grounds that it rescued Judaism from the grotesque forms it had assumed in Sabbatianism.[45] The Hasidim were the precursors, indeed "true Zionists," he argued. It is through reexpression in living holy men (like himself), charismatic leaders of the present era, that the religion responds to particular events like secularization that embody challenges to its core values.

As Lawrence points out, Judaism experienced the Enlightenment piecemeal. Even conversion of individuals to Christianity would have been less threatening to the community than defection to Enlightenment rationalism. The loss of internal purity could give rise to disaster, a view echoed by Gush Emunim. "Ritual slippage lessened the spiritual worth of the Jewish collectivity. Worse yet, it delayed the coming of the Messiah and the day of redemption."[46] The counterstrategy, adopted by Gush Emunim, is the scrupulous observance of the mitzvoth, on which the salvation of the world is believed to depend.

The question is inevitable—as well in the case of its Christian counterpart—as to what happens when this millennial scheme is not fulfilled or if "land is traded for peace." Whereas other parties have left a greater space between political goals and effective means for their realization, fundamentalists are absolutistic and uncompromising. The fundamentalist conviction is that true religion cannot be marginal but should dominate the whole life of the community, indeed of all humanity. The question of principle is what happens when the separation of the secular and the holy is repudiated on the pattern of Gush Emunim.

Newman asks, Is Gush Emunim conservative or radical, or really even fundamentalist? What will be its lasting influence? Its premise is similar to that of Christian fundamentalism: Human peace is possible only when it is divinely ordained. "True peace becomes a metaphysical concept involving a millennial recognition of the absolute monotheism of the Lord who is One, and a recognition by non-Jews of Jewish Jerusalem as their 'spiritual capital.' "[47] Part of Gush Emunim's uniqueness lies in its strategy of welcoming the secular into its fold, Newman points out. Politically it has become institutionalized, Newman concludes, but he adds that at the same time the presence of charismatic spiritual personalities has kept it radical. In his judgment, Gush Emunim raises ideological issues that can be solved only theologically.

Critics charge tha [|]the religious right wing is scarcely distinguishable from the secular right wing in Israel. Indeed, its members have cooperated with any secular Zionist party or group that was willing to form an alliance with it. Actually, advocacy of the Greater Land of Israel did not begin with the recent fundamentalist movement. Even as a Labor leader, Ben Gurion was in favor of the Greater Land of Israel. To be sure, he dropped it in 1947 when he accepted partition; this was regarded as a tactical move after the 1967 victory. Moreover, the first Gush Emunim settlements were established during the Labor party government of Yitzhak Rabin under the patronage of then defense minister Shimon Peres, who defended them against Rabin. Today, Gush Emunim is not greatly involved in Haredim attempts to impose greater halakhic observance in Israel through Knesset legislation.

Before the present fundamentalism, Liebman points out, a system of symbols, a set of myths, ceremonials, sacred places, and values, legitimated the social order and integrated the population. But religious and nonreligious Jews lived in separate states, as it were, in a segmented pluralism. Now they have been "pushed together." The common mythos expressed in the life of the state, so-called civil religion, is being transformed and transvalued. It is expanded and utilized by Gush Emunim for its own purposes. For example, Gush Emunim borrowed and adapted Zionist-socialist terms such as *halutziut*, sacrifice or redemption of the Land. Critics point out that less concern is shown for social justice or equality of property.

> At the heart of these conceptions, whether of the religious Zionists or of the civil religion, lie the seeds of an ethnocentric and chauvinistic view of Judaism and the Jewish people. Neither the founders of Israel nor the early religious Zionists shared this view. But Israeli leaders inculcated this view through the mass media, school curricula, army educational programs and elitist rhetoric.[48]

The tension between the sacred and the secular continues, as a major part of the population of the country remains secular rather than religious. Symbolically, Dizengoff Street in Tel Aviv and Kiryat Arba overlooking Hebron are contrasted. One is worldly and the other religious. Secularists and fundamentalists live side by side. This is possible because Gush Emunim demands are outside of the main interest of other Israelis.[49]

MODERATION—THE DECLINE OF FUNDAMENTALIST INFLUENCE

> For about a decade, the movement represented either the promise of a breath of life for both Judaism and Zionism, or a demon haunting them. Either way, GE has recently ceased fulfilling either of these parallel functions in Israel.[50]

So writes Gideon Aran, who teaches sociology and anthropology at Hebrew University in Jerusalem. He observes that the movement, probably at its peak during the mid 1970s, was perceived as a serious threat to existing Jewish and Zionist entities.[51] But the rise of the Palestinian Intifada has changed the play of forces, opening new perspectives toward Gush Emunim. Torah-centered settlers have been attacked by masked Palestinian stone throwers, and there has not been the popular and government support that Gush Emunim adherents had expected. They are disappointed that so few Soviet immigrants have gone to the West Bank. Aran concludes that the movement is still very powerful but no longer as influential as it once was; the high watermark of its influence has passed.

The majority of the population has not been converted. Secular Jews have been put off by Gush Emunim's traditional halakhic foundation, religious Jews by its messianic-mystical basis.[52] Aran concludes: "If there is any Judaization of Israelis, it is not of the revolutionary type which GE proposed but rather a quasi-classical Judaization involving a certain detachment from Zionism."[53] Old problems have not been resolved by millennial hopes: How is halakhic law to be institutionalized in the sacred realms that have fallen under Israel's control?[54] Aran argues that "the existing rabbinic codex, as it is, makes it impossible to maintain a sovereign national entity which fulfills all contemporary social and political functions."[55]

How faithful Jews are to live in the modern world—in which tolerance and pluralism as well as the separation of religion from the state are dominant—remains a problem.[56] Issues such as as relations with the non-Jewish world community as well as the human rights of non-Jews in Israel are still being debated. The religious world and the modern secular one remain compartmentalized, Aran points out, and the tension between them will not be resolved simply by maintaining the unity of the Land of Israel or even rebuilding the Temple. Today, more than ever before, Orthodox parties (as distinguished from fundamentalist), though small in comparison to others, exercise great influence. They are politically influential out of proportion to their numbers, and they often hold the balance between religious and nonreligious Israelis. During what Aran calls the "heyday" of Israeli fundamentalism, "the intoxicated sphere of true redemption" had wide appeal.[57] Now, as Gush Emunim's original goal has remained unfulfilled, it is not surprising that the movement is becoming more introverted.

Chapter 7

Muslim Fundamentalism

THE PHENOMENA

"The growth of Islamic fundamentalism is an earthquake." In this way the former prime minister of Lebanon, Saeb Salam, described the course of events as Shi'ites in his country took up the Islamic Revolution of the Ayatollah Khomeini.[1] Khomeini's ascent to power in 1979 attracted the attention of the media to his fundamentalist movement. "It signaled the possibility of a restoration of Islamic values to the center stage of the world events."[2] Lawrence adds:

> The religious dimension of what has happened in Iran is better encapsulated in the term "fundamentalism" than any other -ism.[3]

Howard LaFranchi comments on Muslim fundamentalism in France: "The growth of a population that publicly proclaims its religious faith is a deep source of worry for many French."[4] His comment comes in response to a demonstration by Muslim school girls and their mothers in a Paris suburb who were defending their right to wear the veil in French public schools. They chanted, "My chador is my protection." As a powerful symbol of the fundamentalist Muslim model, the chador is directed against not just immodesty but also the non-Muslim secular ethos.

Does Islam fit the pattern of having had diverse paradigms throughout its history as well as an inclusive mythos or macroparadigm? A short-term paradigm crisis is evident in Islam as fundamentalists seek access to political power. They have achieved this goal primarily among the Shi'ites in Iran. Among the Sunnis, the other major party of the religion, fundamentalists have become influential but have not been so successful in gaining dominance, even though Saudi Arabia long has been a fundamentalist theocracy using its great wealth to support Sunni institutions and causes internationally.

A long-term crisis of mythos is evident in the difficulties that the followers of the religion have had in entering into the contemporary world. Structural weaknesses have become evident in the Muslim fundamentalist paradigm. The relations among government, religion, and civilization remain a key point of tension today as Islam confronts modernity and postmodernity. Most of its major apologists are not overly optimistic or hopeful about the future, even though the religion is not on the decline in terms of influence.

Fundamentalists champion Islam as a "holistic ideology" adequate "to address every activity of life and every sphere of human society."[5] A leading theorist, Sayyid Qutb, martyred by Nasser's government in 1966, stated the case clearly, arguing that the religion revealed to the Prophet Muhammad embodies a unique ideal beyond history, time, and place. He envisaged it as towering above humanity and events and defined it as being both a doctrine and a method—an organic unity of theory and practice.[6] It is this totalitarian, nonhistorical paradigm that is dominant in contemporary fundamentalism. Islam has become an ideological system—political, social, and economic, as well as theological—that in its own exclusive way provides a defense against the West and modernity.

Even when it does not achieve complete political power, fundamentalism remains a force to be reckoned with in the Muslim world. A key issue in the Islamic paradigm, of course, is religious law. Islamic fundamentalism is based not just on the Qur'an, as an inspired book, but on the Hadith, the sayings of the Prophet, and the whole body of legal traditions, the Shari'a and its authoritarian code of conduct. All are included in the classical model. Such a reference makes possible a much more detailed and inclusive social program than that of most Christian fundamentalisms. Right action has priority over right belief, and inclusive community-wide religious practice is expected.

How is it that a religion of the historical richness and strength of Islam has now come to be associated with a one-dimensional reactionary integralism? Earlier in this century there was a liberal stage led primarily by Westernized elites. Then after the Second World War, in the Nasser era, came an effort to link religion to socialist and nationalist patterns. Sayyid Qutb and others of the Muslim Brotherhood in Egypt paid with their lives for their attempt to reassert the Muslim paradigm in its initial purity. He believed that Muslim regimes had reverted to an earlier pagan state that existed before the preaching of the Prophet. They had to be overthrown by force.

Qutb ranks among the most profound of the fundamentalist champions who seek to impose their own religious norms through Islamic law, the Shari'a, on the entire social community. In principle, no separation of church and state is allowed. Characteristically, the political and religious communities have been unified in Islam. The model has been one in which all that is outside of its own house of peace exists in a house of war. Other peoples of the Book, Jews and Christians, as monotheists were not put to death after conquest but were allowed to live within the Islamic realm as second-class citizens.

Historically, this stance has been challenged by the Enlightenment along with democratic theory. Actually, for a long time there was no traditional religion that championed unrestricted freedom and pluralism before the Enlightenment and the rise of modern democracy. Still, even in this setting the Muslims do not have the worst record with respect to tolerance, in spite of the evident militancy of *jihad* (holy war) in the name of Allah. Persecuted Jews fled to Istanbul and the Ottoman Turkish Empire when they were expelled from "Christian Spain" at the end of the fifteenth century.

Essentially, Muslim fundamentalists (with their "bloc view") envisage an either/or between a secularist and a religious model. In Iran, the clergy have had a major role in revolution and the subsequent control of the country. The recent leader of Shi'ite revivalism in that country, the Ayatollah Khomeini, even as a fundamentalist modified a number of traditional doctrines to support his revolution. Still, as a fundamentalist he was careful to avoid all contact with unbelievers—including adherents of other religions—and warned that those who did not surrender to Islam would be "put to the sword and dispatched to hell, where they shall roast forever."[7] Near the end of his life, he gave international license for the execution of Salman Rushdie because of the author's allegedly blasphemous *Satanic Verses*.

BELLAH'S SOCIOLOGICAL ANALYSIS

Among the populace, fundamentalism is encouraged by the failure of ruling elites to solve economic as well as social problems. (Had Nasser been able to solve those problems, the outlook might have been different in Egypt today.) Social scientist Robert Bellah, in his essay "Islamic Tradition and the Problems of Modernization," attempts to appraise, in sociological terms, the crisis of model evident in fundamentalism.[8] Bellah's conclusion is that the ever-present alternatives in the Islamic world today remain precarious—between a more open, improving society and a decaying one. Religious law, the Shari'a, often blocks any change or compromise.

In Bellah's judgment, a black-and-white Muslim exclusivism—in the traditional paradigm I referred to, which regards Islamic states as the house of peace and all others as the house of war—has become practically non-negotiable amid the pluralism of the modern world. Having said this much, he is not prepared to regard the contemporary Muslim "scripturalism," generally designated as "fundamentalist," as simply mistaken, and he refuses to condemn it as entirely unproductive or meaningless. Paradoxically, "The reassertion of the basic message of the *Qur'an* in the face of the overgrown garden of magic of late medieval Islam has had a profoundly modernizing consequence," he has concluded.[9] To their credit, many fundamentalists advocate *ijtihad*, independent reasoning, and condemn *taqlid*, blind imitation, Bellah notes.

Bellah believes that, as in the case of Judaism, the Islamic genius lies in the claim that revelation breaks with the natural continuum of cosmos, society and self which defined earlier tribal primitive and archaic national religions.[10] The initial early Islamic political model, Bellah argues, was democratic and not totalitarian. He regrets that today fundamentalism works against "the development of a secular political consciousness that may derive moral guidance from Islam but faces political problems in political terms." Bellah cites Soedjatmoka's charge that too much reliance is placed on "visual images," that is, "rhetorical devices as a substitute for any serious and thorough program of political reform."[11] Of course, the majority of the Muslim world has never passed through a stage comparable to the Renaissance or Enlightenment or, in sum, what Marshall Hodgson, the distinguished historian of Islam, called "the Great Western Transmutation." Demythologizing is neither necessary nor possible, in the fundamentalist view.

What makes the situation complex is that Muslim fundamentalism has a longer and more comprehensive tradition, and in many respects has been developed with greater subtlety (scholastically), than its modern Christian counterparts. Muslim fundamentalists appeal to a succession of teachers: Ibn Hanbal (d. 865), Ibn Taymiyya (d. 1328), and Ibn Abd-al Wahab (d. 1792), to mention only a few. We may ask, How does this model from the past translate into fundamentalism today? The paradigm identified by analysts is very specific. Essentially it means (1) renewal by a return to Islamic roots; (2) militancy and *jihad*, holy war, in defense of Islam; (3) a combination of ideology

with political activism in personal life; and (4) a readiness to challenge traditional religious and political authority and willingness to sacrifice for the sake
of Islam.[12]

Bellah observes that the pattern has been one in which there has been
little political development outside of or apart from religion, in the Muslim
world. He describes the situation that arose in later Islamic history as a de facto
differentiation between the two largest parties in the religion—one of Sunni
secularism (and pragmatic adaptation), on the one hand, and one of Shi'ite utopianism, on the other.[13] This complex of factors has long contributed to conflict, representing an antithesis up to the present day. In fact, a concept of
secular citizenship is still largely absent in Islam. Earlier patterns and developments are absolutized as in Christian fundamentalism.

The difficulties that the traditional Islamic model presents in the modern
world can be identified very simply: Sociologically, because the religion does
not distinguish between church and state, all issues become religious issues,
and generally they are dealt with from an unreconstructed mythological
worldview. The result is both a short-term and long-term crisis. Bellah notes
that as "Max Weber pointed out, in many societies that continue to live in a
'garden of magic,' a fictive web of symbols exists that half convince—until the
next famine, civil war, or plague—that all is as it should be, or if not, that some
local holy man can quickly put it right."[14] Today, in what Bellah has called
"dreaming innocence," charismatic revivalists propose simplistic answers for
complex cultural questions.[15] Of course, the extreme opposite of fundamentalist exclusivism and restorationism is the secular city—in which everything is
regarded as a simply human construction—a paradigm that fundamentalists reject. However, as a sociologist, Bellah is convinced that an intransigent literalism cannot cope with the profound problems about the meaning of life raised
by the contemporary experience.

As in other faiths, the spread of fundamentalism in Islam has been facil-
itated by new technology—radio, television, tape recorders, as well as computers—and income from oil. This was clearly evident in the return of
Khomeini to Iran. Powerful emotional symbols inspire mass movements among
the followers of the religion, as in the revolt against the Shah. More often than
not, the feelings associated with them have little to contribute to the solution
of complex economic and social problems in the postmodern era.

LITERALISM AND SYMBOLISM

To the present day, Muslim religious leaders, mullahs and imams, resist
any critical, literary analysis of the Qur'an, the holy book of their religion.

Scripture is interpreted with a "factual" literalistic hermeneutic: It simply tells what happened, and its message is to be accepted or rejected on these terms. In illustration of the fundamentalist model, the following example may be cited. The dominant view of scriptural inerrancy remains the same as when Muhammad Ahmad Khalaf Allah presented his doctoral thesis at Cairo University shortly after the Second World War. His topic of study had been the narratives of the Qur'an, and he attempted to judge them by modern historical and literary standards. His research project was "to cull out the truths of the Qur'an in the context in which they were revealed." In this he was judged to be academically successful, and his thesis was passed by his advisor, Dr. Amin al-Khawli.[16]

In his writing, the doctoral candidate was careful not to deduce anything not specifically intended by the Qur'anic text. However, in his study, Khalaf Allah divided the narratives into three categories: history, parable, and allegory. Such distinctions, of course, are the beginning of a critical-historical reading of the Qur'an. Moreover, familiar with modern critical historiography, Khalaf argued that "the intent of the Qur'an in the narratives was nothing but admonition (*'ibra*) and exhortation (*'iza*) and never was instruction in history or its truth."[17]

The fundamentalist response to this position was vehement. Historical evaluation of the text was opposed as much by Muslim literalists as by Christian inerrantists in their own tradition:

> It is not sufficient for the author to burn it with his own hands or someone else's hands in view of and within hearing distance of teachers and students; it is necessary for him to announce his return to Islam and to renew his marriage vows if he is married. . . .
>
> Burning the thesis is insufficient; first you must burn the *shaytan* who has filled your soul with his drivel and dictated it to you. If you burn the devil, retire from the College of Arts and its doctorate and go to the seclusion of your own room where you can weep about Satan's deceit until God may accept your penitence.[18]

How might one respond to the claim of fundamentalist Muslims that their religion embraces neither myths nor legends? All religions work from archetypal models that are not given factually as is often supposed. In these terms, Islam has a unique and creative mythos of its own (as Bellah indicates), specifically that of monotheism. The Qur'an both criticizes and converts for its own purposes symbols that were already present and developed in earlier religious traditions: creation, the last judgment, a monotheistic rather than a polytheistic model of deity. Its mode of expression is basically verbal and not pictorial, to be sure. Still, the Qur'an abounds with concrete metaphor and image more than abstraction: creation of human beings from a drop of blood, the last judgment, paradise cool with running water as compared with the fires of hell.

Focusing on the vitality of mythos points to the dilemmas of fundamentalism but does not fully identify the fundamentalist dilemma. Muslim fundamentalists, like others of this genre in different religions, continue to affirm a "big-bang theory" of the origins of their faith patterns. Of course, periodization (and identification of diverse microparadigms) works against this. In the Muslim world, divergent paradigms continue to live side by side up to the present day. In Khomeini's attempt at ecumenism, a common front, distinctively Shi'ite, was to be accepted by the rest of the Islamic world. What the various fundamentalist movements in different countries and regions have in common is the rejection of relativism, historicism, and secularity—all three of which are equated with infidelity.

EVALUATION

Today, medieval, modern, and even postmodern paradigms all are present together in societies that never accommodated, indeed have never experienced, the liberalism of the Enlightenment. In the recent period, Jewish, Christian, and Muslim forms of fundamentalism have had different but overlapping timetables. Fundamentalist radicalism grew substantially in both Judaism and Sunni Islam as a consequence of the 1967 war between the Israel and the Arab nations. In the Shi'ite realm, the 1979 Iranian Revolution seemed a providential defeat of Western secularism.

Change is not limited to intellectual developments. The Muslim world, from Dakar on the tip of Africa to Jakarta in Indonesia, is being propelled, as it were, into a technological and pluralistic setting. In a variety of countries, persons who only recently have been taught to read, or may still be illiterate, learn about computers, airplanes, and hydrogen warfare by watching television. The Enlightenment model of tolerance and freedom of conscience, as well as the historical-critical reading of Scriptures, may be dismissed as innovations and outside of the Islamic house of peace; but that house is divided. In a world armed with atomic weapons, fundamentalist revivalism is not providing the resources necessary to the survival of humanity.

Lawrence emphasizes that the pattern of revolutionary change—the paradigm crisis—developed almost accidentally and unplanned in what Hodgson called the "Great Western Transmutation"—in short, the Enlightenment, science, and technology.[19] In this setting, secularity no doubt posed a real and living threat for the dominant religious mythos. While the popular American television serial "Dallas" was still being shown in Egypt, for example, the press reported that nearly a million persons were waiting to see who shot J.R. The eventual banning of the program makes it clear how much traditional family patterns and relations between the sexes are called into question by the communications revolution. If change were simply technological or political, the resolution of issues would be less difficult. In fundamentalists' protest, social, ideological, and religious models are implicated together and overlap. The emphasis on authority and certainty arises significantly from the desire for a clear moral and ethical framework, and those who challenge it are to be restricted by government as they were in Medina at the time of the Prophet.

PERIODIZATION

It was a group of imams belonging to the Shi'ite school of Islam that led the revolt in Iran. Inspired by Khomeini, their achievement in overthrowing a militarily strong-armed regime ought not to be minimized. The Shi'a-Sunni paradigm alternative dates from the early centuries of the religion, and turns in particular on the question of succession to the Prophet Muhammad. Khomeini never claimed to be the hidden imam whose return is expected in Shi'ite mythology, but did claim to rule as his regent. Shi'ite mythology also centers on al-Husayn, the grandson of the Prophet and son of Ali, whose martyrdom is commemorated annually in the Shi'ite celebration of Ashura, which includes even ritual bloodletting. Shi'a has had a greater sense of suffering in its mythos, more than other schools of this very world-affirming religion. Shi'ites characteristically have developed a more revolutionary mentality than the Sunni. This has now been carried into the modern world, reinforced by new oil riches.

In justification of the claim that Islam cannot be regarded as a timeless phenomenon, one can cite great differences, between, for example, African, Asian, Middle Eastern, Indian, and Indonesian forms of the religion. The distinction between micro- and macroparadigm is helpful in dealing with Islam's diverse expressions in different areas. Early in its history, the religion developed a vast empire, extended from Africa to India, and governed first by the Umayyad and then the Abassid caliphs. The model under these dynasties was that of Middle Eastern monarchy rather than one of equality as among Muslims at the outset. As conquests grew, the worldwide Muslim empire stretched from Africa to India. Indeed, it ranks among the greatest empires in history.

The fall and plundering of Baghdad, its capital, in 1258, symbolized a dramatic turning point in Islamic civilization. Still, there were continuing waves of expansion, all of them not simply military; the religion was taken to Indonesia, for example, by trader missionaries, strengthened in particular by Sufi mystical conviction. Scholars working in this area have attempted to critically analyze what brought on the spiritual decline that was clearly evident by the time of the discovery of the Americas. A stagnating Muslim world eventually came under European economic and political domination.[20]

Colonialism was a culture shock—the paradigm crisis par excellence. While a large part of the Islamic world became European colonies, only the three so-called gunpowder empires remained independent: Turkey, Iran, and Mogul India. Eventually, Turkey, in the area where Byzantium had been conquered, came to be known as "the sick man of Europe." Of course, an expanded geography (with the discovery of the Americas) rendered the Muslim heartland, located between Europe and Asia, less important in trade and transportation, and this may be one explanation for the reversal of fortunes between Europe and Islamdom. Or was decline caused by Turkish rule and the organized militarism its model embodied? In a number of respects it was less culturally wide-ranging than earlier Arab Islam. Or was it the rise of an intolerance that was not as evident in earlier periods? Members of other religions were treated with less respect than before.

We have argued that fundamentalism today, as a defensive reaction, has its roots in a long-term crisis of mythos, not just in short-term developments. One might have expected a greater sense of self-confidence and cultural independence with the end of colonialism. In fact, those who inherit oil often interpret their new riches as being sent by God. For the most part, they have not succeeded in solving even short-term social crises throughout the Muslim world, and more commonly than not have produced unfulfilled expectations that have fueled fundamentalist sentiments.

Historical paradigms need to be identified specifically, in order to appraise contemporary parallels and differences. An early period dominated by persons who had known the Prophet in their historical lifetimes was followed by one in which careful attention was given to collecting and confirming traditions about him (that were not part of the Qur'an), the Hadith. As the religion grew and embraced larger numbers of believers, a party of rigorists, the Kharijites, resisted all compromise with political expediency. In the end, they proved too inflexible to set the dominant model; a number of their beliefs are echoed by contemporary fundamentalists.

A party that seemed to give priority to reason more than faith and the revelation of the Qur'an, the Mutazalites, was put down under the leadership of Ashari (d.c. 922), and the archetypal symbolism of the religion was structured in terms of anthropomorphic personal language. In reply to the rationalism of the Mutazalites, Ashari argued that Allah, God, thinks, speaks, and acts, but not as men do. The paradigm is one in which the mode of divine speech, thought, and action is not to be specified more abstractly. In the occasionalist model, God's action is understood as fresh and renewed every moment. He is the lord of destiny and predestines and acts in his own way. Continuity is in his deed rather than in terms of any more-abstract philosophical principles such as have been emphasized in Western European rationalism.

When the rapidly growing mystical movement of the Sufis threatened to radically internalize the external social structures of the religion, it was the theologian al-Ghazali who (from his own religious experience) helped to reincorporate them into the mainline Islamic mythos.[21] His writings continue to be read by Muslims today and are second only to the Qur'an in popularity. Basically his model was fideism (faith alone) as opposed to the confusion of the philosophers. Islamic thinkers intentionally did not appropriate Greek categories on the pattern of Christian theology.

"What distinguishes fundamentalists from traditional Muslims is the force with which they take certain ideas and apply them as a challenge in particular instances," Lawrence explains.[22] Thus it is the thought of Ibn Taymiyya (1268–1328), who opposed the Mongols even after they had converted to Islam, that is cited as pattern by the fundamentalists. But the plurality of models in the tradition becomes more clear among the legal thinkers, who have directed it in practice. Without any priesthood, the body of authoritative lawyer teachers, the ulama, have decided what norms and symbols are to dominate in its mythos. In their decisions, they have relied in differing degrees (liberal to conservative) on the Qur'an, the Hadith, reason, consensus, and analogy. But the fact is that the Qur'an is not primarily a law book. Of its 6,666 verses, only five hundred—some commentators say as few as two hundred verses—deal with legal issues.[23]

My point is that the novelty of Islamic fundamentalism lies in the fact that the religion has been made into a revolutionary social program, in a form very different from that of traditional interpretations. To the fundamentalist consciousness, the Prophet's model for society (which is often compromised by Muslim caliphs) appears to be threatened by forces from outside—Jewish, Christian, and secular. To what extent are the basic metaphors and symbols that form the interpretative basis of the religion to be modified? Do not themes such as creation, last judgment, resurrection, and paradise require mythical reference (in the history-of-religion sense), as does description of deity, if as in the case of Islam final knowledge is reserved to Allah? Fundamentalists allow no modernist modification, defending instead their own dogmatic positivistic paradigm. In short, demythologizing is not accepted, and mythos continues to dominate in a decisive way. Before the revolution in Iran, for example, Jalal Ali-i Ahmad criticized Western influence as being "occidentotic":

The occidentotic is a man totally without belief or conviction, to such an extent that he not only believes in nothing, but also does not actively disbelieve in anything—you might call him a syncretist. He is a timeserver. Once he gets across the bridge, he doesn't care if it stands or falls. He has no faith, no direction, no aim, no belief, neither in God nor in humanity. He cares neither whether society is transformed or not nor whether religion or irreligion prevails. He is not even irreligious. He is indifferent. He even goes to the mosque at times, just as he goes to the club or the movies. But everywhere he is only a spectator . . . . He never invests anything of himself—even to the extent of moist eyes at the death of a friend.[24]

In the era of two world wars, for more reflective Muslims, utopian myths about freedom and democracy have become discredited. It is not just "extremists" who have come to believe—rightly or wrongly—that modernist notions imply chaos as well as unbelief. Muslim impotence against so small a nation as the state of Israel made it clear that the strategy of Westernization no longer offered the way of victory, even though oil brought new riches.[25]

Whereas modernists have been prepared to regard *jihad* symbolically, fundamentalists will not make this "compromise" with modernity. To quote the Ayatollah Morteza Mutahhari: "Is it permissible for us to fight against that corrupt regime which props itself up with a putrid ideology that it uses like a chain around the necks of people to imprison them in a blind alley isolated from the call of truth; a regime which acts as a barrier against that call? . . . Or, in real terms, is it permissible for us to fight against that prison of repression or is it not? In the view of Islam this *is* permissible."[26] Yet, as the Iran-Iraq war seemed to demonstrate, *jihad* has become particularly impotent and self-defeating in the new global political developments in the postcolonial era in the Islamic world. Political issues, not just ideological ones, involve complex problems of power.

SCIENCE AND RELIGION

The relation between religious and scientific models has continued to play a central role in modernity. Lawrence emphasizes that on all levels of Muslim society there is a sense of exclusion when it comes to major concerns of the technological age.[27] Religion stands in ideological conflict with modern science.[28] Professor Abdus Salam, a Nobel Laureate in Physics (1979) and himself a practicing Muslim, charges that, among all major traditions and civilizations, science is the weakest in Islam.[29] Salam quotes Ibn Khaldun's

Muquddima (1332–1406): "We have heard, of late, that in the land of the Franks, and on the northern shores of the Mediterranean, there is a great civilization of philosophical science. . . . Allah knows better, what exists there. . . . But it is clear that the problems of physics are of no importance for us in our religious affairs. Therefore, we must leave them alone." Salam complains that Ibn Khaldun showed little curiosity or wistfulness. His words represent not only apathy but a drawing inward in isolation from science.[30]

Gustave E. von Grunebaum observed that the fatal weakness of Muslim science was that it was not integrated into the surrounding worldview, as it came to be subsequently in Western Europe.[31] Many rulers refused to support the sciences, and some even persecuted scholars who pursued their study. Today, in a more positive mood, Salam calls for a closer interrelation among science, morality, and religion. His question is specific:

> Why did creative Science die out in Islam? Starting around 1100CE, this decline was nearly complete by 1350CE. . . . No one knows for certain. . . . In my view, the demise of living science within the Islamic commonwealth was due more to internal causes—firstly of isolation of our scientific enterprise and secondly of discouragement to innovation (*taglid*) . . . the temper of the age had turned away from creative science, either to Sufism with its otherworldliness or to a lack of tolerance for taqlid and innovation in all fields of learning including the Sciences.[32]

Positively, as early as the eighteenth century, "fundamentalist" reformers had sought to reopen the gate of tradition, giving priority to the concept of *ijtihad*. The monotheistic message of the Qur'an was to be rethought, and Islam reenacted at its historical roots. This was a promising development. The revision envisaged in this period was even more drastic than those found in Christian fundamentalism. The term *ijtihad*, taken from the Muslim legal tradition, means "to exert one's intellectual powers to find answers to problems."[33]

EGYPT: AL-BANNA AND QUTB

The fundamentalist struggle against modernism in Islam has centered in three geographical and cultural areas in the Middle East, and the contemporary term *fundamentalist*, even though a modern one, is often applied to earlier periods of Islamic history. What has been the fundamentalist model, then and later? In the eighteenth century, the Wahabi "puritan" school arose in the Arabian peninsula. Championed by a regional prince who eventually conquered the entire peninsula with religious zeal, its paradigm today is dominant in Saudi Arabia, which controls the leading pilgrimage city of Islam, Mecca (which is closed to non-Muslims). It is one of a "fundamentalism from above." The Saudi's immense oil riches have given them worldwide power and influence, and they support generously their kind of fundamentalist Islam in other lands— even as they fear and oppose its Shi'ite Iranian version.

Egypt long has been the intellectual center of the faith; Al Alzar University, the Harvard of the Muslim world, is located in Cairo. Only a minority of Egyptian mosques are controlled by the government with which these mosques collaborate. The majority are private and not state supported. In the eyes of fundamentalists, the al-Alzar ulama have appeared as compromisers who have gone along with and sanctioned the status quo.

The influence exerted by the Muslim Brotherhood (like Gush Emunim later in Israel) has been much larger than might have been expected from the number of its immediate followers. It was organized by Hasan al-Banna, a former schoolteacher, in the period before the Second World War while the country was still occupied by the British. He attributed Muslim weakness in the face of English colonial power to internal failure and proposed a simple and stringent program based on conformity to the fundamentals of the religion. Al-Banna was not interested in intellectual issues as much as faithfulness to the basic teachings of the Qur'an. His puritanism and integrity of life soon attracted attention and gave him power.

The political setting in Egypt (as in most other Muslim areas) was very different from that in Europe or North America; parliamentary democracy was associated with colonialism and corruption. The Christian scholar Kenneth Cragg observes that, as against dishonesty and abuse of power, in Egypt the Muslim Brothers initially championed a thoroughness in piety and practice that no liberalism could equal, and their influence spread beyond its borders.[34] In a country in which parliamentary regimes were characteristically impotent and manipulated by political power, the fundamentalist strategy of resistance was straightforward and militant.

Protesting the continuing presence of British colonial rule in the pre–World War II era, al-Banna's program was not initially violent, even if it showed great zeal and exclusiveness. Its model has been labeled "theocracy" in Western thinking. Eventually, al-Banna and his followers came to be courted, and then resisted, by the palace while the country was still ruled by monarchy. The leaders of the nationalist revolution that eventually overthrew the Egyptian monarchy communicated with al-Banna and his associates. Soon, however, the new regime under Nasser turned to socialism and nationalism, cooperating with the Russians.

A leading opponent, Sayyid Qutb, was identified earlier in this chapter. Gilles Kepel argues that, as a martyr, Qutb became the royal road to the Islamicist movement, which became increasingly powerful in the seventies.[35] "Humanity today stands on the brink of the abyss," Qutb wrote. Both the West and the East are bankrupt in the domain of values. The present situation is not one of primitive pre-Islamic paganism but one of opposition to what has been forbidden in the revelation to the Prophet. Sovereignty has been removed from God. Qutb's use of the word *jahiliyya* was an innovation. Writing in a concentration camp, he concluded: "Any society that is not Muslim is jahiliyya . . . as is any society in which something other than God alone is worshipped. . . . Thus, we must include in this category all the societies that now exist on earth!" This was most distinctive in Qutb's model.[36] Al-Banna, the founder of the Muslim Brotherhood, never dreamed of accusing the society in which he lived of being non-Islamic. Qutb took a step that the ulama had hesitated to make throughout Muslim history, namely, excommunication of the ruling prince. The iniquitous ruling prince, Nasser, had the intellectual leader of the Muslim Brotherhood executed. There was no other figure like Qutb in its movement, and his ideas later inspired the assassins of Sadat. When Sadat became president, he gave the fundamentalist movement a place in public life again, a strategy that probably contributed to his assassination. Today, as the socialist pattern has proven to be a failure, revolutionary Islam espouses the centuries-long union of politics and religion.

RAHMAN'S RECONSTRUCTION

Fazlur Rahman, 1919–88, a Pakastani Muslim who taught in the United States during the last two decades of his lifetime, was looked to for leadership by many of his coreligionists.[37] A believing Muslim seeking reconstruction, not revolution or revival, he championed a very different contextual understanding of Islam and the Qur'an; his premise was that traditional interpretation needs to be significantly modified, because the Hadith material—the sayings of the Prophet outside of the Qur'an—is regarded as unreliable by modern critical scholars. In his own interpretation of Islam, Rahman accepted the verbal inspiration of the Qur'an but insisted that inspiration was not just mechanical. The Book came from the Prophet's heart and through him.

Rahman wrote in defense of his own reconstruction:

> The first essential step to relieve the vicious circle just mentioned is, for the Muslim, to distinguish clearly between normative Islam and historical Islam. . . . No amount of mechanical juxtaposition of old and new subjects and discipline can produce this kind of mind.[38]

In 1962 Rahman was appointed director of the Central Institute of Islamic Research in Pakistan. As part of his responsibilities, he was called upon to speak about problems of polygamy, divorce and inheritance laws, and finance: interest and banking in the newly formed country. In less than half a dozen years, pressures built up from fundamentalists, and in 1968 he was forced to resign as director.

Rahman wrote in criticism of fundamentalism:

> Neo-fundamentalism . . . seems to think it has a divine mission to shut down Islamic intellectual life. . . . But its assumption that Muslims can straighten out the practical world without serious intellectual effort, with the aid only of catchy slogans, is a dangerous mistake. Not only have neo-fundamentalists failed to seek new insights into Islam through broadening their intellectual horizons, they have even let go the richness of traditional learning.[39]

Critics still regard Rahman's contextual theology as important, even when they have disagreed with it. In contrast to the traditional view in Islamic law, Rahman argued that the Qur'anic view of God was a functional one. Moreover, he believed that the state obtains its warrant from the people. An egalitarian society, in his judgment, must allow institutions to change and make appropriate reforms.

THE TABLIGHI JAMAAT ALTERNATIVE

There are not only intellectual but also "grassroots" alternatives to Muslim theocracy. Tablighi Jamaat is described by Mumtaz Ahmad as a singular movement in the contemporary Muslim world.[40] A recent annual conference in Raiwind near Lahore, Pakistan, was attended by over one million persons from over ninety countries, he reports. The founder of the Tablighi Jamaat movement, Maulana Mohammad Ilyas (1885–1944), believed that true religious faith requires freedom from politics. Its politicization undermines its message. Ahmad describes his goal as being simply to help Muslims be good Muslims, irrespective of governmental polity. Of course, this is the antithesis of most of Muslim fundamentalism.

The Muslim peasants to whom Ilyas first preached remained partly Hinduized, even though they had converted to Islam. Ilyas's concern was to make their faith a living one. Resigning from a seminary position, he eventually took up residence in the old quarter of Delhi. From this center, he organized mobile units, usually of at least ten persons, and sent them into villages. Semieducated people were dispatched on missionary trips to give testimonies and preach. After Ilyas's death, thousands of such groups were organized under the direction of his son. Ahmad compares their direct and simple appeal to that of the eighteenth-century English Nonconformists, whose primary instrument also was itinerancy.

Ilyas was frail and intellectually unassuming, but his missionary zeal was untiring. Struck by an assailant whom he was trying to convert, he exclaimed: "You have done your job. Now let me do my job and listen to me for a while." Dying, he was asked about his condition, and he replied, "People out there are burning in the fire of ignorance and you are wasting your time here inquiring after my health!"

The Tablighi Jamaat movement's separation between the religious and the political is both clear and promising. It rejects the Iranian revolutionary spirit, describing Khomeini as an "archsectarian Shi'ite." It holds that what is most important is "food for the soul" and "spiritual nourishment," and its belief pattern is intended as strictly orthodox. Ahmad concludes that the Tablighi Jamaat movement embodies what Jaroslav Pelikan (writing of Christianity) calls "the affectional transposition of doctrine," rejecting doctrinal hair-splitting, legalism, and institutional forms of religion. Most of all, it makes clear that there are alternatives, and not just a single paradigm, in contemporary Islam.

The dominant Muslim revivalism often absolutizes the Islamic past—defensively—as against modern modes of life. From this premise, Muslim theocracies seek to impose an inclusive pattern on all citizens politically. A simple question needs to be asked in conclusion. Is Islam, in its essential character, fundamentalist? As it confronts modernity and experiences both short- and long-term crises, how is the Islamic paradigm to relate to its own past? Our conclusion is that the contemporary phenomenon is not just a consequence of modernity as an outer influence. Intrinsic dilemmas remain as Islamic law and the Hadith are held to be virtually equal in authority with the Qur'an. Issues of democracy and human rights are only complicated, not settled, by regarding Islam alone as the house of peace and all other communities as the house of war.

Paradigm theory can provide a basis for clarifying and evaluating these developments. It is a common mistake to compare a Muslim model, derived from an earlier (pre-Enlightenment) time frame, with a later and more modern pattern from Christianity—without reference to their very different settings. The historical evidence is that the Islamic paradigm is not intrinsically (and has not always been) fundamentalist.

Chapter 8

Hindu Fundamentalism

CONTEMPORARY ACTIVISM

Ayodhya, in Northern India, is alleged to have been the birthplace of the god Rama, the hero of the Hindu epic poem the *Ramayana*. For centuries the poem has been acted out during long evenings in Indian villages. More recently it has been broadcast on national television. In the fall of 1989, neighborhoods all over this huge country were making thousands of bricks and inscribing them with the names of their home states. They were to be sent to Ayodhya for the rebuilding of Rama's temple. Vishwa Hindu Parishad, the fundamentalist religious wing of the Rashtriya Swayamsevak Sangh, led the campaign for the temple project. *The New York Times* reported:

> Militant Hindus, ignoring historical scholarship and the doubts of moderate religious leaders, say that in 1528 the Mogul Emperor, Babar, built his mosque, the Babri Masjid, right over the spot where Rama was

born. They say he destroyed a Hindu temple, the Ram Janmabhoomi, in the process.[1]

The newspaper explained:

> In India, where lines still often blur between history and legend, reality and myth, or politics and religion, a dispute over sacred ground claimed by Muslims and Hindus is regarded as a powder keg.[2]

Thousands of persons were killed throughout India in the struggle that this controversial project entailed. In 1986, a court in nearby Faizabad had ordered that the gates of the mosque at Ayodhya be unlocked and its premises made available for Hindu worship. The reason was that it allegedly was standing at the location of an earlier Hindu temple. Fundamentalists were aroused and became active on both sides. Decades earlier, on the night of 22–23 December 1945, Hindu idols had been smuggled into the mosque's shrine, and the place had become desecrated for Muslims. Whereas the Hindu cult is practiced with dramatic statues of deities, the Muslim sanctuary is in the full sense iconoclastic. Hindu fundamentalists have insisted that the mosque be torn down and replaced by a temple. Early in the summer of 1992 two thousand Vishwa Hindu Parishad volunteers began laying a 21-by-9-meter concrete base foundation. When on December 6, 1992, rioters broke through police lines and destroyed the three-story mosque with pickaxes and crowbars, India erupted in religious warfare.[3]

Factual questions about the actual lives of particular divine personages have not been a concern for most Hindus. Historical interest in the relation between symbol and occurrence, doctrinal truth and falsehood, is in many respects a Western phenomenon. Most Hindus take it for granted that Rama and Krishna—both regarded as incarnations of the high god Vishnu—once lived on earth. Moreover, the distinction between the human and the divine is not as radical and sharp as in Western monotheisms. The question is about not a God "beyond the world," but the sacred and divine within it. Hindu traditionalists, on this premise, continue to resist secularity. Fundamentalists assert themselves in a paradoxically defensive but aggressive integralism that, as in the case of Ayodhya, has become politically radicalized.

TRADITIONS EAST AND WEST

Assuredly, the truly seminal Indian religious heritage encompasses a diversity of historical periods, with their different paradigms. The name *Hinduism* like the term *fundamentalism*, has been imported. The former is of Persian origin.

Originally, *Hindu* was applied by the Muslim invaders to identify what they found in India—a land of many rivers. *Hinduism* means literally "the belief of the people of India." To the present, India is a vast museum of the history of religion, and different Hindu models generally are not sorted out in the same way as in the West. To the visitor to India, an all-pervasive sense of the sacred seems to be expressed in an endless landscape of temples and holy places, and some Westerners have found its sense of hierophany, the manifestation of holy power, more vital than their own.

The distinctively Hindu relationship between myth, philosophy, and religious doctrine differs from the Western theisms. Indian philosophers speak of a plurality of worlds that are not unified in a single rational pattern. A variety of polytheistic, henotheistic, monotheistic, monistic, and pantheistic interpretations exist together, side by side. The German philosopher Hegel spoke of a vast undifferentiated symbolism in India, reflecting chaos more than meaning.[4] Most historians of religion, today, find this judgment to be too severe.

Without a founder, Hinduism is not a single religion in the same sense as is Christianity, Islam, or even Buddhism. The question of fundamentalism turns rather on the nature of mythos. Is there a rationale? "However muddled, contradictory or extravagent [the mythos may be], there is a fragment of a logos," Hans Küng has observed of the Hindu legacy. Küng is speaking against fundamentalism—not resolving all theological quandaries—when he writes: "Myths reveal deep structures of man and the world, space and time." He adds that they provide a direction for life as well as saving power, in short, that they are paradigms for living. To construe them as historical facts, or to impose dogmatic truths in their name, is to misunderstand their meaning. Küng warns against a kind of "medieval conservative mystification" that can only promote unbelief among the educated. If myths are preserved uncritically in an unmythical age, in his judgment, the real content of religion suffers, and faith can degenerate into superstition.[5] This, indeed, is the real danger in fundamentalism.

THE MYTHOS OF RELIGION IN INDIA

Spirit, not matter, has had priority in India. Philosophically, the Indian archetype is ascetic and idealistic as compared with, for example, Chinese or American realism (both of which have been, in the majority, more pragmatic). The Hindu mythos is exemplified in the symbol used to explain suffering and evil: the blind man carrying the lame man. Paradigmatically, the blind man represents nature and the lame man spirit. Life is a continual struggle in which even if nature finally seems to overcome spirit in death, spirit is not extinguished in its universal and cosmic dimensions. It endures even after an individual's lifetime and in the end is the only really Real; everything else is illusion. Ultimate salvation is not only liberation from the cycle of birth and rebirth but also final union with the spiritual One. To be sure, there are impersonal and more personalistic versions of deity and salvation; the latter is to be found in *bhakti* piety with its belief in incarnate savior gods.

India's many-sided religious past was researched empirically by Western archaeologists and linguistic scholars from the colonial period on. More recently, fundamentalists have appropriated their findings for their own nationalistic purposes. As we have already suggested, the Indian religious tradition has been seminal—so greatly so, that it is parent to a family of faiths. Jainism, Buddhism, and Sikhism all developed in the Hindu setting of the subcontinent.

Although the micromodels are plural and need to be distinguished in the more inclusive Hindu mythos, Western apocalyptic predictions, like notions of physical resurrection, seem too materialistic. From the Indian point of view, Western theistic views of history (such as premillenialism and fundamentalist versions of creation) foreshorten the historical time. The Indian outlook posits four great kalpas, or world ages, spanning millions and millions of years; humans are now living in the last and worst. It was in the Upanishadic period (600–200 B.C.E.) that the notions of birth and class were made determinant in Hindu philosophy.

David Bradley finds the predominant unifying conviction of religion in India to be that of reincarnation, of birth and rebirth in a series of lifetimes, a theme that came into prominence in the Upanishads.[6] How many gods are there? This question was asked orally by their authors long before it was set down in writing. The answer is that there seem to be many, but in reality all of the gods described mythologically (themselves subject to birth and rebirth) are finally only expressions of the ultimate Reality, the One behind the many.

Hindu apologists emphasize the inclusiveness of their religion. The path of *bhakti marga* (*marga* means "way") envisages salvation by faith. But salvation by works (*karma marga*) and salvation by philosophical insight (*jnana marga*) are also accepted. Christianity, less many-sided from the Hindu perspective, insists on *bhakti marga*. The Hindu outlook has been a "both/and" rather than an "either/or." Assuredly this puts the question of fundamentalism in a different setting than in the West.

Different levels are distinguished in the Hindu consciousness, as an idolatrous cultus and philosophical monism live side by side. The German scholar of Indian religion Heinrich von Stietencron observes:

> To be sure, we also find demythologizing in the Hindu religions . . . by means of karma, and consequently through degrees of religious knowledge or experience of God. At the highest level of such

knowledge or experience, we also reach the highest level of abstraction. But this does not make lower levels inconsequential. Without them, the ascent that leads in the end to salvation would never have begun.[7]

MOTHER INDIA

The new religious Right in India is not fundamentalist in the sense of being scripturalist. Norvin Hein writes: "Hindu theory upheld the Vedas [the early holy books] as superhuman, infallible, authoritative, but they [their defenders] had insufficient grasp of the circumstances of their origin to perceive what a literal interpretation would be."[8] Thomas J. Hopkins, also a specialist in Hinduism, points out that fundamentalism in the Indian setting places little emphasis on the transcendent goals set forth in classic esoteric texts such as the Upanishads. Indeed, Hopkins's claim is that religious nationalism has no real basis in the authoritative scriptures revealed as *scruti*, "spoken in the ears of men by the gods." One must look elsewhere to explain fundamentalist phenomena.[9]

Hopkins has concluded that the fundamentalist unifying mythos is a powerful image of India as the sacred motherland—Mother India—a goddess embodied in the land, rivers, and sacred places of the subcontinent. For millennia villagers have honored the goddess as the protector of the village domain as well as the representative of natural powers, both benign and malevolent. Eventually, her mythos was absorbed into the larger religious tradition and interwoven with local and regional shrines, rivers, and other sacred places into a pilgrimage network that essentially defined the territory of the holy land of India.

Hopkins points out that the concept of sacred territory was not primarily political: The name *India* had not yet come into usage, and there was no central ruling power. Political power and territorial controls were highly fluid. Kingdoms and their dynasties rose and fell. Symbolic unity instead was in the landscape of India, a territory defined by its holy places. Practically, the real binding force was the law (*dharma*, sanctioned by the Brahman priests), stories, rituals, deities, and especially household and temple *puja* (worship) practices.

In principle, religious exclusivism is based not primarily on creed or ritual, but on whether Mother India is acknowledged as one's sacred place. Often included in the effective mythical image is the goddess as *Shakti* or power. Even today there are places where the village goddess still is worshiped with blood sacrifices. Living blood from decapitated animals is poured directly on the earth and offered to an image of her depicting one of her various forms as the personification of natural powers. This is a tradition very different from that of the Vedic fire sacrifices, in which the smoke ascended heavenward; the blood flows downward.

The Hindu fundamentalist mythos honors the warrior tradition, today exemplified in disciplined cooperation and loyalty as well as physical training. The holy land must be kept pure by a dedicated band of manly warriors who follow the *dharma* of service and self-sacrifice. Hopkins emphasizes that this point of view runs counter to the more individualistic and transworldly goal of philosophical Upanishadic Hinduism. It does, however, have deep roots in Brahmanical texts on *dharma*.

Originally, the truth of *dharma*—law and structure—was set forth in the consensus of the elders of the local caste as moral and religious rules were enforced. The individual was enjoined to fulfill his or her role in life unselfishly and in particular to act without concern for the results of his action. Hopkins identifies fundamentalist roots in the teaching on family duty and kingship in the Dharma Shastras and in particular the Laws of Manu.

THE RASHTRIYA SWAYAMSEVAK SANGH MOVEMENT

The new religious Right in India is not limited to a single party or movement. The ideological and social forces at work are most evident in the growing merger between fundamentalism and nationalism in the activism of the Rashtriya Swayamsevak Sangh (RSS), founded in 1925 by Keshav Balirama Hedgewar. Hedgewar remained the authoritarian leader of the movement until his death in 1940. His successor, Madhav Sadashiv Golwalkar (d. 1973), continued this movement in the same style that Hedgewar had established. Appealing to an idealized mythical past, the RSS seeks to revivify and recreate Hindu self-consciousness. The loss of national loyalty is seen as being responsible for contemporary impotence and decadence. The RSS believes that religious observance has a strong effect on sociopolitical conditions, a view accepted in traditional Hindu metaphysics.

The revivalist religious goal is to recover the fundamental truth disclosed in an earlier era of revelation. Even today, RSS considers it to be imperative that a correct society adhere to the principles of *dharma*. A dynamic and more world-affirming view of *dharma karma* is championed by these fundamentalists, who seek to replace local loyalties by new ones now directed to the Hindu "nation." Some commentators see a new unified "Greater Hinduism" emerging that joins these forces with nationalism in reaction against the West as well as against indigenous religions.

Walter Anderson and Shindhat H. Damle, writing in *The Brotherhood in Saffron, the Rashtriya Swayamsevak*, describe how

> every morning at sunrise groups of men in military-style khaki gather outdoors before saffron flags in all parts of India to participate in a com-

mon set of rituals, physical exercises and lessons. For one hour each day in the year, they are taught to think of themselves as a family—a brotherhood—with a mission to transform Hindu society.[10]

By indoctrinating its followers, RSS seeks to inculcate self-control and identification with the group as well as religious zeal. Anderson and Damle write: "A system of myths, rites and symbols are intended to fuse the individual's identity to the larger Hindu community which the RSS claims to represent."[11] Cooperation and loyalty are expected. At the beginning, the RSS's aim was to develop a program that would give the moral, political, and intellectual strength necessary to achieve independence from Great Britain. After this goal had been reached after World War II (albeit not in the way that the RSS leadership had desired, that is, with the division of India and the separation of Pakistan), it then turned its attention to character and spiritual formation in the newly independent India.

For decades, the RSS leadership had distanced itself from politics—following a tradition that began with Hedgewar, who had given education and religion priority. It was not until the government actually banned the movement that the RSS turned to more direct political action, particularly through members active in affiliate organizations. It began training persons to work in the media and universities as well as in political parties themselves. As we noted, it is the Vishwa Hindu Parishad (the World Hindu Council), the religious and intellectual arm of the RSS, that has led the campaign to send bricks to Ayodhya, which has resulted in not only bitter controversy but violence and the loss of life.

Activists with an RSS background, united by their early *shakha* training, now work in a variety of activities and fields. The RSS training begins with preadolescents and becomes more explicitly ideological for adolescents. The purpose of such education is to develop a loyalty to country and religion that will remain with the individual throughout the rest of his or her lifetime, in short, that amounts to Hindu indoctrination. Leadership seeks to guide the way in which individuals work out the relation between themselves and society. Not everyone who begins training stays with the movement. Others, however, do develop lasting loyalties that significantly influence their future course in life. The RSS premise is that religious loyalty is necessary for individuals to achieve integrity and a sense of life purpose, especially in the midst of secularism and decadence. The strength and prosperity of the whole nation is seen as being dependent on this loyalty.

The RSS has increasingly gained new power and influence in the propagation of its mythos as it has challenged the establishment. Especially since the assassination of Mrs. Gandhi, the Indian middle class—the part of the population that has experienced modernization most of all—now increasingly finds fundamentalism a more tolerable alternative. Populist religious symbols are often used for reasons of political expediency. Earlier religious revival movements, the Arya Samaj and Brahamo Samaj, had denounced ritualism, idol worship, and various other external "obscurantist" observances of religion. Now *pujas* and processions are organized by fundamentalists in honor of a variety of gods and goddesses. The visible symbols of cult and mythology are promoted under RSS sponsorship.

The carefully designated RSS organizational structures are hierarchical. De jure authority is vested in the *karyavah*, or secretary, an older and respected person, but the young men, *mukhya shikshaks*, are the most active. For educational purposes, local *shakhas* are divided into four age groups: 6 or 7 to 10, 10 to 14, 14 to 28 and over 28. In addition to the local RSS office, there are city offices in the more populous areas, regional offices, and then state and central assemblies that meet once a year. The persons with the most power in the structure are known as *pracharaks*, and form a communication network outside of the official one. They have primary loyalty to the national RSS and are on loan from it. Generally well educated, they speak Hindi and English and are from upper-middle-class, urban backgrounds.

In the fundamentalist view, it is not politicians who represent the soul of the people; too often they lack real patriotism. The enlightened sage, the philosopher king, speaks for a higher authority beyond the ways of humanity as an interpreter of the national soul and higher law. The historian of Indian religion Heinrich Zimmer writes: "The perfected saint feels himself possessed by an illimited, far-reaching, all-pervading insight, which amounts actually to a faculty of omniscience."[12] Such saints are credited as having ex cathedra qualities of infallible intuition by Hedgewar and Golwalkar. These two leaders, after their deaths, were even spoken of as *avataras*, divine incarnations.

Although the RSS is not the only source of Hindu fundamentalist sentiment, there is little doubt that it is a leading one. There are other right-wing parties, and characteristically they fight among themselves. The RSS cause, in particular, needs to be seen not just as a sporadic response to grievances but as part of a long-term strategy. The RSS was outlawed during the emergency declared by Mrs. Gandhi, as it had been earlier following the assassination of Mahatma Gandhi. But seen in broader perspective it has played a role as new political parties have developed. Even Congress Party members have acknowledged that this movement has become "indispensable." Through a number of affiliates its influence is channeled in the press, on university campuses, and in political parties. However, by contrast, the hierarchically structured parent organization itself attempts to stay clear of politics whenever possible.

The new Hindu fundamentalist Right is not so much a rural phenomenon as a product of urban change. Communalism is a factor that figures most decisively in this development. Muslims, Sikhs, and Christians, albeit minorities, seem to threaten the Hindu majority—in the fundamentalist view. At the same time, a specific group of people, culturally, and a territory (Hindu sacred space) are given priority and special religious significance.

M. S. Golwalkar, the second RSS leader, clearly spelled out the goals of this fundamentalism: "The non-Hindu people in Hindustan must adopt the Hindu culture and religion, must learn to respect and hold in reverence Hindu religion, and must entertain no ideas but those of glorification of the Hindu race and culture . . . claiming no privileges . . . not even citizens' rights."[13] Embree reports that more recently Sankaracharya, a prestigious figure in Hindu orthodoxy, made public speeches in which he argued that ritual pollution and the idea of untouchability are scripturally sanctioned.[14] Although his view did not find wide support, it was not often challenged directly, either.

Christians and Muslims as well as the Westernized elite, fundamentalists charge, have values that form a gulf between them and the community of Hindus. This is evident in their ways of life, language, script, dress, and their festival calendars. Golwalkar observes: "They (Muslims) look to some foreign lands as their holy places. They call themselves 'Sheiks' and 'Syeds.' Sheiks and Syeds are certain clans in Arabia. How then did these people come to feel that they are their descendants? That is because they have cut off all their ancestral national moorings of this land and mentally merged themselves with the aggressors. They still think that they have come here only to conquer and establish their kingdoms."[15]

A well-known pacifist couplet runs: "Shower flowers on the enemy who pricks you with a thorn." The militant revision is: "He who pricks you with a thorn, pierce him in return with a spike and teach him a lesson he won't forget." Discipline and order as well as Hindu religious commitment are seen as more necessary for national survival than tolerance by fundamentalists, who point out that it was Hindu revivalism that began the drive for independence and was its primary source. Religious mythos should not be relinquished once the goal of freedom had been reached.

Fundamentalists were disgraced and even outlawed when Mahatma Gandhi was assassinated. Now there is a different ethos in their favor, and they are in prominence. It is a widespread Hindu judgment that the legal privilege that Muslims have claimed, for example, in family law, is significantly a cause of the crisis. Muslims, often forming a voting block, have gained political influence. Professor Rajendra Singh, as general secretary of the RSS, commented: "It looks very strange that India is the only country in the world where a majority [Hindus] is ruled by a minority and no one can be considered the

Defender of the Hindu faith."[16] The RSS seeks to unite Hindus ideologically, and this with the help of religious mythology. The problem is that their community is not at all one; indeed, Hindus seem to be almost endlessly divided.

THE HISTORICAL LEGACY

Fundamentalism, of course, must be evaluated against the religious history of the area. India is landlocked except for the mountain passes in the West. Following in its archetypal pattern, as we have noted, religious tradition has developed richly in a variety of models throughout its history while still maintaining its central mythos. A number of different paradigms from diverse periods live on. Fundamentalist sentiment looks to the popular epics, the *Mahabharata* and the *Ramayana*. Imbued with a warrior ethic and ideals of righteous rule, the epics emphasize protection of the people and preservation of the holy law. The stories of Rama, for example, like those about the god Krishna, exemplify activism and piety. The god Vishnu's role as the preserver of the social and cosmic orders also is widely affirmed. Indeed, the warrior kings, Krishna and Rama, are his incarnations. Not surprisingly, the means of arousing popular support are pilgrimages and renewal of sacred places, as at Ayodhya.

In the surge of the fundamentalist tide, the target is not so much the representatives of modernity as other religious groups; this is evident most of all in the increasing number of communal riots. Muslims and Christians as well as Sikhs are demonized. The situation is very different from earlier when liberal neo-Hindu leaders like Vivekananda, Aurobindo, and Gandhi, although nationalists, sought to purify the religion while at the same time claiming that the Hindu model was inclusive enough to include a place for all major faiths. Religious labels seemed only accidental to the reformers. Critics still see the present communal hostility as being caused partially by the complete inability of even these liberal Hindus to understand Muslims' and Christians' commitments to their own distinctive faiths and religious communities.[17] One reason is that the Hindu mythos, at the deepest level, is more radically individualistic, more concerned with transcending the social order, than Islam.

In the present agitation, centuries-old tensions between Hindus and Muslims, harking back to the Muslims' conquest of the subcontinent, are being intensified, becoming more explosive than ever, notwithstanding the division of the subcontinent between the Muslim theocratic state of Pakistan and the secular republic of India. When they conquered India, Muslims destroyed hundreds, indeed thousands, of statues of gods they regarded as idols. The invaders also razed hundreds of Hindu temples. Nevertheless, Muslims always remained a minority, and as rulers they were never able to overcome, much less destroy, the living Hindu mythos. Hinduism continued to be a vast social system more than a unified community, and on its own terms resisted Muslim rule.

Hinduism has still succeeded in preserving its culture. More recently, the Hindu outlook has served as a barrier against Marxism. The powerful role of caste and of the hereditary priesthood in Hindu defense against Buddhism in earlier centuries and later against Islam is not to be understated, in spite of all modern democratic sentiments. Fundamentalists today still champion an aristocratic paradigm, even though there is no one central ruling authority comparable to a pope or caliph. In the face of growing diversity, they seek unity on the basis of a common Hindu mythos. At Ayodhya, for example, various parties of the priesthood could not agree on procedures and defense of their faith. Some of them stood to lose constituencies if Rama's temple were reopened to Hindu worship.

MODERNIZATION

Early Hindu reform movements like the Brahmo Samaj and Arya Samaj were essentially movements against post-Vedic Hinduism of the type now championed by fundamentalists. A difficulty was that the early Indian nationalist movement could find no basis for political independence in earlier traditions of social *dharma*, popular temples, images, *puja*, devotionalism, and pilgrimage. Only in the nineteenth and early twentieth centuries did a few Hindu leaders (Bankim Chandra Chatterjee [1838–94], author of the national anthem, "Bande Matram"; Bal Gangadhar Tilak [1856–1920], and, most powerfully, Mahatma Gandhi [1869–1948]) begin to tap the resources of popular Hinduism in developing the foundations of a broad-based indigenous nationalist movement.[18] It needs to be recognized that what emerged was a new creation. Traditional Hinduism had no concept of nationhood in contrast to kingdoms, and it allowed no scope for political activism to ordinary citizens. What was now offered was a new Hindu mythos suitable to the nineteenth and twentieth centuries.

The philosophical-theological effort to make Hinduism more world affirming and open as well as activist is clear in the careers of Swami Vivekananda (1863–1902) and Aurobindo Ghose (1872–1950), neither of whom was a fundamentalist.[19] Aurobindo attempted to work out a synthesis of Hinduism and modern evolutionary thought. Both of these leaders reflected in the tradition of Advaita nondualist philosphy, drawing on the ideas of Shankara Archarya, the leading nondualist Vedanta thinker, who lived in the eighth and ninth centuries. Shankara's numerous commentaries on the Hindu scriptures have become classics, and he is still honored in his country today.

An important proposal for further revision of traditional views, made by Tilak even before India's independence, centered on what is perhaps the best-loved Hindu holy book, the *Bhagavad Gita*.[20] It was in fact a precursor of contemporary fundamentalism. In enunciating his view, Tilak dismissed the majority of earlier major commentaries on the Gita on the grounds that their emphasis on devotionalism and renunciation propagated a negative view of existence. Instead, he gave priority to the opening and closing passages of the Gita and its call for action. Today, one cannot simply accept Hinduism in the traditional sense: The individual must decide which duty is most appropriate.

A positive integration of Hindu religious thought in the twentieth century, no doubt, is to be found in the life and work of Mahatma Gandhi.[21] Gandhi read the New Testament and the *Bhagavad Gita* together and refused conversion to Christianity. Seeking to renew Hinduism ethically in the modern world—especially in his criticism of caste—he still affirmed the ultimate unity of God and the soul as he led his nation into independence.

Gandhi spoke of his own utopian vision as *Ramrajya*, the kingdom of the god, Rama, and envisaged it as the rule of truth and justice for all human beings. Reinterpreting traditional views of the popular Scripture the *Bhagavad Gita* in a nonfundamentalist way, he opposed hereditary untouchability. Of course, Muslims often saw the call for *Ramrajya* as Hindu imperialism.

Ghandi's great achievement was to secure India's freedom from the British Empire without bloodshed. *Ahimsa* (noninjury) was a doctrine emphasized in particular by Jainism and Buddhism, and Gandhi was influenced by it even as he interpreted his own heritage selectively. His use of *satyagraha*, "truth force," with the means of fasting and nonviolent protest to bring pressure against injustice, was a centuries-old Indian technique.[22] Gandhi accepted the Hindu claim that divinity lies deeply within every human person. Premising the unity of Brahman and Atman, God and the soul, he made this affirmation the basis for his fight against injustice and even caste.

Of course, fundamentalism is the antithesis of the beliefs championed by Gandhi. There were direct links and hostilities: Gandhi's assassin, Nathuram Godse, knew Hedgewar, the founder of the RSS, personally, and on occasion even traveled with him. Malik and Vajpeyi attribute the secularism of the new Indian republic more to Jawaharlal Nehru than to Gandhi.[23] Nehru premised humanism and secularism in his personal beliefs and social theory. In his judgment, science and nationalism would eventually overcome traditional religious communalism and obscurantism. This has yet to happen. By contrast, fundamentalism looks to the Hindu world that had emerged by early in the second millennium and persisted through both Muslim and British conquests.

Sarvepalli Radhakrishnan, the late philosopher president of India, interpreted tolerance and appreciation of other faiths—the spirit of Gandhi—as an essential component of Indian nationalist ideology.[24] Ainslie T. Embree in *Utopias in Conflict: Religion and Nationalism in Modern India*, does not agree with his analysis either practically or theoretically. Embree points out that religious fundamentalist and nationalist movements often interact as they face the future.[25] Together they are linked to a state of mind that is utopian, Embree emphasizes:

> Mircea Eliade has spoken of utopian thinking as characterized by "the desire to recover religious origins, and thus a primordial history," coupled with an emphasis on the renewal of old values and structures that testifies to "the hope of a radical *renovatio*."[26]

Embree is particularly skeptical of Hindu eclecticism:

> This emphasis on Hindu tolerance as a determining feature of Indian civilization cannot, I think, be taken as accurate reading of Indian civilization in earlier periods, but its significance lies in its use as a hermeneutic device to serve the special social and political circumstances of nineteenth-and twentieth-century India.[27]

Embree argues that Indian civilization is neither absorptive nor eclectic: Most remarkable is its endurance and the persistence of its style and patterns.[28] Embree's conclusion is that what is now called "Hinduism" is no more tolerant than Christianity or Islam and has borrowed less from the surrounding world in which it lives than they have.

EMBREE'S VIEW OF THE HINDU PARADIGM

Embree identifies five unquestioned assumptions that, reaffirmed by fundamentalists, still live on in the Hindu mythos. In short, they make up the basic archetype of classical Indian religious thought that fundamentalists now believe to be under attack.[29] Preserving its integrity over two and a half millennia, the paradigm already was beginning to become evident as early as 500 B.C.E. But the model is no more self-evident—simply "common sense"—than in any other setting when it is viewed in terms of the history of religions.

Hinduism, although claiming to be noncredal, is based on the following existential assumptions: (1) Time is not viewed as linear-progressive but as cyclical, repeating itself endlessly in cycles of vast duration, spanning thousands of millions of years. It has no beginning and end, and even the gods live and die in its endless cycles. (2) In this setting, Karma premises the return of the consequences of deeds in successive lifetimes. (3) Reincarnation is a parallel assumption, the birth and rebirth of individuals in successive lifetimes. (4) Dharma (an Indian term with various definitions): law, life pattern, and doctrine is central. (5) A claim for many levels of truth also is presupposed throughout the model.

Embree finds that the last premise, the Hindu notion of there being many levels of truth, is most alien to Western thought and assuredly bears significantly on the interpretation of myth. The question about the relation between myth and fact, doctrinal truth and falsehood, is in many respects more Western than Hindu. Heinrich von Stietencron observes:

> Westerners sometimes have the impression that myth constitutes a lower form of knowledge about God. They think it disguises more of the truth than it reveals, and hence religion must be demythologized. For the Hindu, by contrast, the myth veils the truth only when an ignorant person hears it, because he doesn't understand the language of the symbols. For the person with knowledge, it reveals more about God's nature and actions than mere abstract discourse can grasp, because it brings an element of dynamism into play. . . .
> God speaks to man at every level.[30]

Embree believes that *dharma* is the most socially significant of all the listed characteristics of the Hindu mythos. The term is understood by Hindus as signifying law, morality, or social usage—a set of values, attitudes, and conduct that are expected of a person in society. Conformity to *dharma* is a specific obligation imposed on each individual by life. "Better to do your own duty badly than another's well."[31] Class, of course, significantly determines one's *dharma;* it is hereditary and established by birth.

Hindu mythology remains alive among the folk piety of the masses that fundamentalists seek to mobilize. Today, Benares, the holiest of Hindu cities, by the Ganges River, honors above all others the Hindu god Shiva. Depicted in his cosmic dance as creator, sustainer, and destroyer of worlds, Shiva exemplifies its mythos. His dance (in contrast to Western historicized myths of the Exodus or Christian eschatology) symbolizes the cyclical character of time as well as the unreality and illusory character of the world (*maya*). The god is often depicted with a string of skulls around his neck; he is the destroyer of worlds as well as the creator and source of life. Religious mythology is not so much to be transcended as enjoyed; the world is the play of the gods.

Inspired by their own *dharma,* Hindus resisted Muslim cultural penetration and later the Europeans, the Portuguese, and then the British. Even though Hindus showed new openness to European civilization by the nineteenth century, Embree doubts that the Hindu mythos will be able to form a synthesis with modern science.[32] Fundamentalists, like their critics, Embree notes, lay claim to the Indian national goals of unity, social justice, political democracy, and secularism. However, they depart from modernism with respect to both means and ends. In short, their vision of the future, equally as utopian as that of the secular liberals, is a very different one.

Embree believes that fundamentalism's new power is not accidental.

> The advocates for traditional religious values are not merely defending the past, nor are they reactionary in a simplistic sense. They are, on the contrary, profoundly radical, for they, quite as much as the modernizers, have a vision of the future they intend to work for. They have their own program of change and a blueprint.[33]

There are practical as well as theoretical issues. Even with its traditional reliance on class distinctions, Hinduism has been more diverse—not one religion but a variety of religions. Ashok Singhal, the present leader of Vishwa Hindu Parishad (the World Hindu Assembly), explained during a visit to the United States that his movement is dedicated to unifying India's hundreds of sects: "There is no fighting among the sects; they live in harmony."[34] But they have never come together. In ten years, he predicts, Hindus will unify. Common Hindu principles and beliefs will make for unification. Then "they will be a force to be reckoned with in the world."[35]

Hopkins emphasizes that contemporary fundamentalism is significantly a response to the declining fortunes of earlier radical Hindu nationalist movements and an effort to preserve the cause in a more effective form. The continuity of symbols and mythos, as between earlier and later developments, is in an emphasis on a sacred motherland and the equation of disciplined manliness with religious virtue and concern to remove foreign intruders. The collection of symbols in the fundamentalist mythos is a relatively new creation in its present form. To be sure, the symbols all have roots, often deep roots in earlier life and thought, but their formation into a single religious-political mythos is more recent. Unlike Brahmo Samaj and Arya Samaj, earlier reform movements, the mythos as a whole had no clear scriptural foundation. In fact, it often appeals most of all to persons who have lost effective contact with the original meanings and sources of these symbols. Whether or not this is true of the leadership, it is the case with respect to the following on which mass support for fundamentalist movements depends.

Until the late 1970s, the major challenge to India's secular democracy came from linguistic movements and class conflict in the countryside and not from confessional politics. In the 1980s, Hinduism, once an "artifact of categorization," began to be a condition of national consciousness. What has been described as a "new Great Hinduism" began to emerge. Religious celebrations began to be more strident and militant, transcending localities and acquiring national dimensions. A consciousness of a more homogeneous religion crossed class and sect boundaries, enhanced by the electronic media. In the 1980s the government began to patronize Hinduism as it had not before. The Janata party, which defeated Mrs. Gandhi in 1977, had initiated this strategy, and Mrs. Gandhi continued it when she returned to office.

The reasons underlying change were not only fanatical or fundamentalist. Hinduism seemed to provide a satisfying worldview and social identity. In states where Hindus were a minority and Christians, Sikhs, and Muslims appeared to be a threat, Hinduism embodied cultural nationalism. However, there were dangers. Lloyd I. Rudolph and Susanne Hoeber Rudolph comment: "The lesson of partition that informed India's founding myth was that religious politics kills. What in India is called 'communalism' destroys civil society and the state."[36] India is a plural society today. Will it relearn the lesson of partition?

One of our questions has been whether the term *fundamentalism* applies to the diverse and pluralistic Hindu context. Does it still have relevance when taken from a Western monotheistic setting and introduced in the Eastern world? Today fundamentalist nationalists in India see mythos as being a greater unifying force than rational criticism. The key question continues to be how fundamentalist nationalists will relate to other parties in the secular republic. The short-term crisis is one of social order as well as economic development. The long-term crisis concerns the way in which a vast and diverse legacy (from the past history of religions—with its many-sided levels of insight and partic-ipation) will respond to the modern world. For it to be culturally relevant in the so-called postmodern era, how much must it be radically demythologized?

Chapter 9

Sikh Fundamentalism

THE COLLAPSE OF MODERATION

For a number of years, the dominant image in the minds of people of India will be that of a young Sikh spraying a group of people with an automatic, and killing women and children mercilessly. And along with it may appear the thought that few Sikhs condemn them.[1]

Fundamentalism is a fact of life. . . . The only safe statement that one can therefore make in regard to the next decade or two is that fundamentalism (whatever the term may include or exclude) will continue to be a force and shape the thinking of a substantial number of people, particularly in the younger age group.[2]

Late in the afternoon of Tuesday, 20 August 1985, a fifty-four-year-old Sikh with a long beard and gentle face walked into a temple near his home village of Singrur in India's Punjab. He bowed before the Sikh holy book, the

Granth Sahib, prayed, and then began to address his fellow worshipers. This man, Harchánd Singh Longowal, president of the Akali Dal, the Sikh's major political party, was known as being a moderate and not a fundamentalist. Speaking out against hatred and the use of force, he urged peace and new understanding between Hindus and Sikhs. Longowal, after long nonstop negotiations with Prime Minister Rajiv Gandhi, had signed an accord of peace and accommodation on 24 July.

Gandhi, the leader of the world's largest secular democracy, had been forced to confront the issue of fundamentalism. He came to power after his mother, who earlier had led the country, was assassinated by her Sikh bodyguards in revenge for an attack on the Sikh Golden Temple in Amritsar. As further violence threatened to build up, the new prime minister reversed the earlier intransigence of his mother's policy and proposed compromise. The moderate Sikhs, led by Longowal, responded positively. In return for new special privileges, they pledged to work for peace and coexistence under the constitution of a united India.[3]

Only a few moments after Sikh Longowal had begun speaking in the temple at Singrur, a young man seated in the front row pulled out a pistol and started firing. A teenage boy who reached over to stop the assailant was hit and killed. In the midst of the confusion, a man who at first appeared to be a bodyguard of the political leader rushed forward, shouting for order and urging everyone to remain calm. Then he turned and pumped several shots into Longowal, who died minutes later at a hospital. Religious fanaticism, already on the rampage throughout the Punjab, had won still another victory. Not only was a significant plan for peace and compromise between warring Sikhs and Hindus deprived of its most distinguished spokesman; moderates feared to speak out against the violence that had been inflamed by Sikh fundamentalist preacher, Jarnail Singh Bhindranwale.

Marty and Appleby, in *Fundamentalism Observed*, described Sikh fundamentalism—its traits and dynamics—as almost fitting their model of a "pure type." There is a people "fearing extinction under the conditions of a modernizing, westernizing, postcolonial, newly independent nation-state," and they "express their economic and political grievances through a communal reassertion of religious identity."[4] Under the leadership of a number of charismatic figures, a new "old Sikh identity" has been created from selective retrieval of traditional precepts and symbols, they observe. Political calculation has been an important accompanying consideration. Sikhism also provides an "almost pure type" for our pattern of paradigm analysis, as it offers a clear contrast between earlier and later paradigms. Moreover, these are not just rational abstractions but existential life patterns with mythological and ritual bases. Chronologically, the fundamentalist trend had become evident by 1978. Paul

Wallace observes that it had become a systematic campaign by 1981.[5] Repressed severely in 1984, it had regained momentum by 1985.

Today, the Sikh minority numbers only about eighteen million in a country fifty times as large. World-affirming and egalitarian, Sikhs have prospered economically more than the majority of Hindus and Muslims. Grudgingly granted only limited linguistic and geographical identity by the central government, Sikhs turned to religion as a rallying point for a new fundamentalist nationalism. Different from fundamentalism in the United States and more similar to that in the Middle East, Sikh fundamentalism has developed in a setting of religious communalism. Its spokespersons have made capital out of outstanding grievances—some only decades, and others centuries, old. By contrast, liberal-secular forces, commonly viewed as being socially marginal, appeared too impotent to stem the tide of communalism.

KHALISTAN AND THE SIEGE OF THE GOLDEN TEMPLE

Sikhs have been known as doers—farmers, carpenters, soldiers—all of which are well-known and admired popular images. Their distinctive religious heritage has at times been seen as representing a middle way between Islam and Hinduism. Founded by Guru Nanak (1469–1539), Sikhism did not replace either faith, and its continuing life was threatened by persecution by a variety of rulers. Why has Sikh fundamentalism become increasingly associated with violence in the late twentieth century? The answer is that Sikhs face new problems; earlier life models seem threatened. Proud of their long heritage of military prowess, many middle- and lower-class Sikhs have joined the struggle for their own separate nation, Khalistan. This became a real threat to the Republic of India once some members of the nationalist movement took to terrorism and stockpiling weapons.

Sikhs have excelled with both the plough and the sword. With their uncut hair and turbans, they are commonly described as being masculine and aggressive. The Punjab, where the majority of Sikhs live, became the food basket of India in the green revolution of the mid 1970s. Development of new strains of rice and wheat successfully produced high-yield crops to feed the nation. However, economic progress has not brought peace and order. Murder rates are higher in this part of India than elsewhere. Public order has disintegrated as the secular state established in the Indian constitution is opposed. Militant tales of Sikh history are recounted popularly even in comic books for children. In the Punjab, there is sufficient economic class division to promote unrest and even violence by landless laborers. Twenty-three percent of families own two-thirds of the land.

T. N. Madan compares the double-edged sword worn by male Sikhs to fundamentalism and their religious tradition. In his judgment Sikh fundamentalism is unlikely to abate in the near future. The room for reconciliation is very limited, because Sikh (and other) fundamentalists' definition of the relationship between religion and the state is diametrically opposite to that in the Indian Constitution.[6] Madan emphasizes that fundamentalism does not allow for dissent and the coexistence of multiple opinions. Instead, there is an attempt to enforce conformity on religious grounds. If Sikhs are not rulers, they must be rebels—a premise that is totalitarian.

The partition of the subcontinent into India and Pakistan in 1947 brought twelve million refugees into the Punjab. Hindus and Sikhs fought together in the region as allies in opposition to the Muslims. It is estimated that two hundred thousand persons lost their lives in hostilities in the area. Jeffrey remarks that this partition took by surprise the semiaristocratic Sikh families who had shared power with Hindus under British rule. There had been adjustments and remarkable economic growth after the English left, with new road and highway building projects. (One major roadway is named in honor of Guru Gobind Singh, the last in the line of the ten Sikh gurus.) Literacy has increased, so that today at least three out of five Sikhs can read. More than one hundred thousand of them attend colleges. Unfortunately, however, education as well as newspapers and magazines resulted in an increase, rather than a decrease, in communal tensions. It is not that Sikh traditions and history have remained unrecognized. Guru Gobind Singh's three-hundredth birthday was celebrated under government sponsorship in 1967. Two years later, the five-hundredth anniversary of the birthday of Guru Nanak was celebrated.

In recent decades, the growing phenomenon of Sikh fundamentalism has presented a difficult dilemma for Indian government leaders. Should state power be used to suppress its fanaticism, or should officials ignore it or seek compromise with it? None of these strategies has proved effective. Unable to ignore the Sikh military buildup at the Golden Temple in Amritsar, Prime Minister Indira Gandhi on 5–6 June 1984 ordered the army to storm the building. Unfortunately, it was not only the militants' bastion, but the religion's most sacred shrine. Over two thousand persons were killed. Longowal was among the moderates who surrendered to the Indian army.

Mrs. Gandhi tried a military solution, purging the extremists from the Golden Temple with "a surgical operation." Actually, in a few hours she sowed new and even more intense hatred, triggering a tragic series of events that led to her own assassination by two of her Sikh bodyguards on 31 October. In reprisal, Hindus in New Delhi as well as other cities went on a rampage, beating up and killing Sikhs, burning their shops and vehicles. The fury lasted for four days and nights, and often there was very little police protection for its victims. In what became politically instigated violence, Hindus killed at least twenty-seven hundred people, seeking to teach the Sikhs a lesson.

Both Sikhs and Hindus no longer live in a self-contained world. Fundamentalist terror in all instances was the antithesis of religious teachings in both faiths, those of Mahatma Gandhi as well as those of the Sikh founder, Guru Nanak. Why did Mrs. Gandhi act in the way she did? Had she not read T. S. Eliot's play about the murder of Thomas á Becket by henchmen of Henry II? The conflict between the secular and the religious orders has been a dramatic theme in Western literature for centuries.

Fundamentalist Sikhs seek not only recognition of their own distinctive identity and rights. Since 1981, they have also increasingly called for full independence in their own independent state of Khalistan. They argue that it is only in this setting that Sikhs can find a congenial environment and political milieu. The constitution of India provides not only for individual freedom of religion but also for protection of minorities. Sikh fundamentalists highlight the latter in a triumphalist demand reflecting earlier precedent: "The community of baptized Sikhs will rule." During more than half a century, beginning a few years after the United States' Declaration of Independence, from 1780 to 1839, Ranjit Singh and his heirs presided over their own Sikh nation. Unlike in the present fundamentalist initiative, other religions shared in the power structures in the spirit of tolerance. Indeed, its borders extended far beyond the area of the present Punjab where the majority of Sikhs now reside. Finally conquered by the British, the Sikhs remained loyal during the Mutiny of 1857 and were rewarded with a special role in society as trusted soldiers throughout the empire.

Of course, conditions changed radically when the British departed; preference was no longer given to them. When independence came to the subcontinent, following the Second World War, it was, as I have noted, the secular Republic of India that provided a homeland for millions of Sikh refugees who did not wish to live under Muslim rule in Pakistan. At the time of the attack on the Golden Temple, the president of India was a Sikh. Unfortunately, the polity of separation of religion and the state in a secular democracy lacked ideological appeal, in particular to the extreme Right. Fundamentalist leadership began a self-destructive campaign of terror in which thousands of innocent victims were killed. The course of events led young people to despair about their future.

Madan's argument that the Sikh tradition does not form a single whole, as fundamentalists claim, is a crucial one.[7] In the past, a number of sources of Sikhism have been called on, and several definitions offered, about what makes someone a Sikh. More recently, Sikh cultural elites, fearing assimilation into a syncretistic Hindu society, have retreated within their own community, narrowing group identity. M. J. Akbar, in *India: The Siege Within*, comments that in terms of the later definition of Sikh purity, as it has been defined by fundamentalists, the first nine guru teacher leaders of the religion would have been impure.[8] The "pure Sikh" identity combines a number of different and even contradictory elements from the past in its ideology and practices. The widely traveled reporter Georgie Anne Geyer describes the development: "I began to see that Khomeinism was not unique at all," she writes:

> What led to the Freudian death of Indira Gandhi, "India's mother," and perhaps began to presage the long-prophesied and feared (by Mahatma Gandhi among many others) disintegration of the Indian subcontinent was actually quite typical of conditions that foster backward-looking movements. First, secularized life-styles had been spreading among the young Sikhs. More and more young men were shaving off their sacred beards and refusing to wear the Sikh turbans.
>
> In trying to salvage their interests in a time of changes, the traditional clergy reacted by trying to ignite a new fundamentalism. However, their efforts—and even those of the once-radical Independence party, the Akali Dal—were soon overshadowed by ultraradical Sikhs led by the ferocious Jarnail Singh Bhindranwale. When he and his men took over the sacred Golden Temple, they transformed it into a sanctuary for murderers and terrorists who thought they would be untouchable within its precincts.[9]

THE SIKH LIFESTYLE

Sikh males are easily identified. Since the beginning of the eighteenth century, Sikh militancy has been symbolized by a distinct style of dress. The beard and hair remain uncut, and the latter is worn in a topknot. A two-edged dagger is carried by men of the religious community who have undergone initiation with "the baptism of the sword." The initiation was instigated by Gobind Singh, the last of a line of ten guru teachers.

The present historical question is how a religion that continues to teach that the ultimate purpose of life is union with God through his indwelling in the human soul, could become a source of violence far beyond what one might expect from its numbers. As in the case of Shi'ite Muslims, martyrdom can promote militancy. The ninth guru, Tegh Bahadur, 1622–75, who ruled from 1664 until his death, was executed by the Muslim emperor. It was his son, Gobind Singh, who initiated "the baptism of the sword." Known as "the Lion," in 1699 he called an assembly of Sikh warriors and asked for five volunteers willing to die for their faith. God had demanded a blood sacrifice, he said. Four times the guru entered his tent and then emerged with a bloody sword. The fifth time he brought out all the warriors, still alive. A goat had been substituted for human sacrifice.

The tenth and last guru instituted the ceremony that continues to the present. Each warrior was given nectar and responded, "The khalsa (community of the pure) is of God, the victory is to God." From Gobind Singh's time, Sikh males have been identified not only by their holy book but by the five Ks (a title taken from their original names in the Sikh tradition): long hair worn in a topknot with an uncut beard; the wearing of a comb; wearing of a steel bracelet; short pants and the carrying of a double-edged sword or dagger, by men, or a single-edged one, by women.

After all of Gobind Singh's sons had been killed, he commanded that following his death the religion's holy book, the Granth Sahib, and not a living guru, should be the authority. The Scripture—which includes materials from other religions—is revered in worship; it is fanned and carried in procession rather than a representation of deity. Today, the Sikh holy book is the focal point of Sikh worship, as the living presence of the ten gurus and the Word of God.[10]

Initially, the defense of Sikh communal identity was aimed at persecuting Muslim emperors. During British rule and more recently, the Sikhs have opposed the assimilation forced on them by the Hindu majority. When the Sikh empire fell and was replaced by British rule in 1846, Sikhs in masses turned to Hinduism. But their religious identity was largely saved by British patronage and support. Members of the religion were recruited for the army and took their oath using the distinguishing marks of Sikh identity. In 1890, the viceroy, Lord Lansdowne, declared the government to be sympathetic to the Sikh religion.

In communal defense, the Singh Sabha movement was founded at Amritsar in 1873 and at Lahore in 1879, having it as its purpose to arouse the love of religion among its members and to propagate the true Sikh religion. Sikhs built schools and orphanages and established archives. Their organization protected them not only against Christian missionaries but against the conversionist Hindu Arya Samaj, a movement that had penetrated to the Punjab in 1877. In spite of all of this, Sikhs and Hindus often shared cultural life until the present fundamentalist crisis. Many Hindu families encouraged their oldest sons to become Sikhs. Fundamentalism on both sides, of course, challenges this arrangement.

The Shiromani Gurdwara Prabandkah Committee (SGPC), founded in November 1920, along with the Akali Dal, the "Band of Immortals," sought to recover and purify Sikh temples, known as *gurdwaras*. Hindu ritual had been mingled with Sikh practice at the time of the Sikh kingdom. A respected ruler like Ranjit Singh not only honored the Hindu Brahman priests, but at his death the rite of *sati* was performed by royalty. Against such eclecticism as well as the threat of assimilation, the Singh Sabha Movement grew in strength during the later period of British rule.

The Sikhs no doubt had problems in controlling their own religious establishment. The offices of temple custodian (*mahant*) and priests (*pujara*) had fallen into the hands of unbaptized sects of Hindus. The Sikh reform program was to purge idols and dismiss alien priests. Sikhism was strengthened, but the task was not accomplished without struggle—one that, in contrast to the present, remained nonviolent. Thousands of Sikhs were arrested, beaten, whipped, and jailed when they took up the cause of reform. Gandhi praised their refusal of violence enthusiastically. Finally, the Gurdwara Reform Act of 1925, which was passed through the state parliament with the support of Muslim and Hindu repesentatives, turned over the places of worship to the control of the SGPC.

THE HOLY BATTLE OF THE TURBAN AGAINST THE CAP

Today, Sikh fundamentalists assert their identity more violently in terms of "the holy battle of the turban against the cap." Such slogans refer, of course, to the turban which men wear over their own Samson-like unshorn hair, comparing it to the cap that covers the shaved skull of the Hindu. Even if only a limited number of ascetic Hindus shave their heads, to the Sikh militants the turban seems to stand tall and majestic on the top of their own heads. By contrast, the cap lies squat on the Hindus. "How can a cap have dominion over the turban?" they ask. "When has the turban ever bowed to a cap?"

Such symbols were used by the fiery fanatic and preacher, Jarnail Singh Bhindranwale. He invoked the words of Guru Gobind: "When the struggle reaches the decisive phase may I die fighting in its midst."[11] It was indeed Bhindranwale's fate to die in the battle for the Golden Temple. At first encouraged by the central government against more moderate leaders, he was one of the most outspoken advocates of a national homeland. His message:

> It is a matter of keeping the unshorn hair, the beard, and the sword-belt. The Sikhs are a separate nation. Some say we are separate already. If so, then why say we are second-class citizens? that the Sikhs are historically separate even the cap-people have admitted. But if Bhindranwale proclaims this, they say that what he wants is Khalistan. We have endured enough slavery over the past thirty-six years. Now, no matter how many years may roll, we must be freed.[12]

By his opponents, Bhindranwale came to be regarded as the Ayatollah Khomeini of the seccessionist movement in the Punjab. He gained widespread popular support, speaking to the masses with rustic simplicity. "You cannot have courage without reading gurbani [the sayings of the gurus, i.e., the Scripture]."[13] "Young men: with folded hands, I beseech you. . . . Until we enter our home, until we have swords on us, shorts on our bodies, Guru's word on our tongues, and the double-edged sword in our hands, we shall get beatings. It is now up to you to decide . . . the decision is in your hands."[14]

"A Sikh should be a true Sikh," Bhindranwale proclaimed. "The most important thing for me is Amrit Prachar [the preaching of purity]. If a true Sikh drinks, he should be burnt alive."[15] Fundamentalism and extreme nationalism were combined in his mission. Born in a Jat family, he did not come from the Sikh elite. With only five years of primary school education, he received his religious training in a *taksal*, a seminary-like institution. In time he became the head of one such *taksal*. He instigated violence when the Nirankara sect of Sikhs attempted to hold its annual convention in Amritsar. The Nirankaras are considered heretical by other Sikhs because, unlike other Sikhs, they believe in a living guru, and they have made additions to the Sikh holy book, the Granth Sahib. Bhindranwale marched at the head of a procession protesting the meeting. In the riot that followed, twelve of his followers and three Nirankaras were killed. Subsequently, he was alleged to have helped organize the Delhi murder of the leader of the Nirankaras, Baba Gurbachanhan Singh.

American anthropologist Murray Leaf writes:

> There does not seem to be any doubt that Bhindranwale was the main organizer of a terrorist campaign that was responsible for the murder of several hundred innocent Hindus and that in publicly wearing arms and defiantly proclaiming his willingness to use them he was making himself a target for retribution. Moreover, by setting up his headquarters in the Golden Temple he was in effect daring the authorities to violate the temple in order to capture him. Neither the people of Punjab nor the precepts of the Sikh religion condone murder.[16]

"We ourselves are ruining Sikhism," Bhindranwale argued. "The Sikhs have never been so humiliated, the Hindus are trying to enslave us. Prepare for war." "They are perpetrating atrocities on us, exterminating our youth, burning our Holy Book, and insulting our turbans. . . . There is no need to get a licence for arms." "For every village you should keep one motorcycle, three young baptized Sikhs and three revolvers."[17] Bhindranwale emphasized that peaceful means are not to be found in any part of the Sikh scriptures—a judgment lacking real foundation.

In its early development, the Sikh outlook provided a way of life that was never readily accepted in Indian society. Worshipers shared a common meal in what is called "the kitchen of the Guru." The notion of class impurity was opposed. Nanak's concern for social justice—cutting across religious lines—suggests a way out of some contemporary dilemmas. Claiming a special divine call, Nanak had said: "Take up arms that will harm no one; let your coat of mail be understanding; convert your enemies into friends; fight with valor but with no weapon but the word of God."[18] Once when he was in ecstasy, at the age of thirty, he had the experience of having been given a cup of nectar to drink in the presence of the One true and living Deity and given the charge: "Go thou and repeat my Name; cause others to repeat it."[19]

> Nanak, without the indwelling Name of God one endures suffering throughout the four ages [of the universe]. What a terrible separation it is to be separated from God and what a blissful union to be united with him.[20]

In keeping with the founder's teachings, Sikhs are to pray silently each day:

> There is but one God whose name is True, the Creator, devoid of fear and enmity, immortal, unborn, self-existent, great and bountiful. The True One was in the beginning, the True One was in the primal age. The True One is, was, O Nanak, and the True One also shall be.[21]

A legend from the later tradition of the *Janam-Sakhis* tells how Nanak accepted the hospitality of a poor Hindu carpenter rather than that of a rich Muslim official. When the founder was asked why, he squeezed the carpenter's coarse bread; milk appeared. Then he squeezed the bread of a rich man and drops of blood came forth. Nanak's example and teachings can be appealed to against contemporary violence, and his teachings still serve as the main doctrines of Sikh belief.

The period of the founder, the late fifteenth and early sixteenth centuries, was, in fact, a violent time. Nonetheless, Nanak was a man of peace. Sikh tradition recounts that he was captured when the Lodi sultanate was conquered by Babur in 1526; according to the legend, he was recognized for his unique religious role and released.

History was not always so kind to his successors. The emperor Akbar practiced tolerance, but his successor, Jahangir, in 1605 summoned the ruling Sikh guru to his court. His demand was that all passages opposed to Hinduism and Islam be expunged from the Sikh holy book. When Guru Arjun refused, he was tortured and died a martyr's death, which has been described graphically in Sikh literature.[22] The long tradition of Sikh martyrdom is a source of inspiration to the present. Sikh fundamentalists, like those in a variety of other religions, assume a militant, literalistic stance and oppose any critical investigation of the religious past. Of course, from a broader perspective, the very diverse historical manifestations within one religion become evident. A static model can no longer be presupposed. W. H. McLeod's research, for example, opens the possibility of reinterpretation, even as biblical higher criticism opens up new perspectives and problems in the case of Judaism and Christianity. What at first appears to be a dangerous "unpacking" of the traditions of the past can in the end give them living vitality. McLeod writes:

> The orthodox Sikh interpretation insists upon the notion of complete accord, not merely with the teachings but also with the actual intention of the first Guru; whereas some other commentators have suggested radical divergence from those teachings.[23]

Such complete accord is in fact an artificial harmonization.

The founder accepted that God is called by various names: *Hari, Ram, Gopal, Allah, Khuda,* and *Sahib.* There was no anthropomorphic (fundamentalist) literalism in his view. Deity was conceived by him in spiritual terms and without a fundamentalist view of creation. The Granth Sahib recounts that for countless ages there was only undivided darkness, without heaven or earth, just *hakam,* the infinite order of deity. In his primal form, God is devoid of all attributes, absolute and unconditioned. But God did endow himself with attributes that made him accessible to the human mind.

Sikhs employ the term *maya* to describe the world, but their usage of the term is not the same as in Hinduism. It means less illusion than delusion, untruth, and separation from God. They symbolize it by reference to *anjan,* the black salve for the eyes that in northern India stands for darkness and untruth. The Granth Sahib likens the sinfulness of unsanctified human beings to headless persons, wanderers, and vagrants. Self-centered and self-willed, the latter fail to discern the divine order. "As the oceans are filled with water, so immense is my sinfulness. Be merciful, show a measure of Thy grace that this sinking stone may cross over."[24]

Today, Sikhs of all types evoke their past history. Generally they identify at least three major periods in the history of their faith. McLeod, the leading Western scholar on Sikhism, accepts this periodization but describes it as being a useful oversimplification.[25] Major changes in the religion were brought about by the decisions of ruling gurus: the first was when the founder, Nanak, a mystic and man of peace, established a line of teachers, appointing his own successor. A second watershed was in 1503–4 when the fifth guru, Arjun, attempting to preserve the religion's identity, ordered the official compilation of its Scriptures.

The third watershed came in in 1699 when Guru Gobind Singh founded the Khalsa, the elite militant order of the so-called five Ks. Instigating the baptism of the sword, he enjoined male Sikhs not to cut their hair or foreskins. He attempted to establish a physical identity that would not allow them to deny their faith and would breed courage. Gobind merged divinity with the sword, calling the latter "pure steel." The Sikhs would be transformed from jackals into lions and obtain political power (kingdom) in this world and spiritual bliss hereafter. "God subdues enemies, so does the sword; therefore the sword is God, and God is the sword." The change of life model, not just of an intellectual pattern, is clear.

McLeod describes the background of this major change of religious mythos with respect to deity as well as ethics initiated by Gobind Singh. In 1634 the guru decided to move his followers from the plains to the Sivalik Hills, seeking protection against Mughal hostility. Elements of the hill culture penetrated the Sikh religious consciousness:

> God for Guru Gobind Singh, was personified by steel and worshipped in the form of the sword. For him, the characteristic name of God was *sarab-loh*, the "All-Steel", and it is no accident that in the preparation for Sikh baptism the baptismal water is stirred with a two-edged sword. In his writings and in those which were produced at his court we find constant references to the mighty exploits of the Mother Goddess, one of the most notable being his own *Chandi ki Var.*[26]

Historically, the change of model initiated by the last guru proved successful, bringing political rule (in a premodern era). Whether it can do so any longer stands to be seen in the dispute about fundamentalism. The militancy that led to the invasion of the Golden Temple at Amritsar, of course, is a simplistic and dangerous alternative.

THE CASE FOR DIALOGUE

It would be a great mistake to regard all Sikhs as in principle necessarily fundamentalist, in view of recent terrorism and violence. But the dilemma posed by historical events is at least threefold. First, how are Sikhs to live in a modern secular state such as the Republic of India? Are they to oppose it, seeking the restoration of their own independent nation as it existed before British conquest? What are the possibilities and limitations of this strategy? Second, what is right, in view of the contrasting models of tolerance and militancy within the Sikh tradition itself? How can Sikhs defend themselves against discrimination and majority dominance in today's secular polity and pluralism? Third, how are the differences in outlook between the early and later leaders and their models—its ten gurus—to be appraised by their followers? To what extent can teachings from different eras be integrated to provide a critical historical understanding as opposed to the traditional devotional one? Clearly, fundamentalism in the Sikh setting provides no answers. On the contrary, it only deepens long-standing personal and political dilemmas.

It has been argued that the fundamentalist strategy is in principle antireligious.[27] It is premised on a position that stands in opposition to the national constitution. Madan finds that instead of religion's providing the value premises of politics, as Mahatma Gandhi had advocated, it serves to further political ends. In short, it no longer is the essence and guide of life in all spheres, but a sign of distinction between politically organized comunities. Fundamentalists now argue that Sikhs need an environment and political system more congenial to their religious needs.

In this context there is more religious fervor and political passion than theological concern or intellectual vigor. Strong emotions are evoked, not rational argument. Scripture is read, but there is little or no discourse about it. The assassination of Mrs. Gandhi is seen as righteous retribution for attacks on Sikh honor. Longowal, who compromised with Mrs. Gandhi's son, is regarded as a betrayer.

As opposed to fundamentalist separatism, federalism is seen as the only negotiable political solution.[28] The revivalism of Bhindranwale has gained momentum through the romanticism of overseas Sikhs, who send in more than $200 million each year. Bhindranwale compiled a list of names of people whom he said had betrayed Sikhism and circulated it on cassette tapes. When there was public protest about his encouragement of training in the use of firearms, he replied that it was part of the Sikh tradition and not a sin.

Bhindranwale's success was mainly based on his ability to create powerful political symbols. More theatrical than Longowal and better able to deal with the press, he championed his own vision of Sikh history. Bhindranwale was arrested but never tried for his involvement in the November 1981 murder of Jagat Narain. When he surrendered to authorities at Chowk Mehta, a crowd of over fifty thousand assembled, including the presidents of Akali Dal and the SGPC. Fortunately, there is also the Sikh tradition of passive resistance. As late as August 1982, moderate Akali Dal party Sikhs practiced it in protest against Mrs. Gandhi's arbitrary measures. Offering themselves for arrest, they crowded thirty thousand persons into the Punjab's jails, whose capacity was only seven thousand.

Jeffrey concludes that events in the Punjab have shown how much "the ferment of modernization" can generate ethnic conflict, religious revival, and even secession.[29] But there are also new possibilities. Citizens have a new opportunity and potential to cooperate and create institutions that can really serve their own needs. If they are really dedicated, they can transform the Indian state and make it work for themselves rather than against them.

As it turned out, Longowal was more powerful dead then alive; he is now seen as a hero of both the Akali Dal and Indian unity. One must hope that his influence will be more lasting than that of Bhindranwale. Seeking a political victory, the Akali Dal party advertised: "Vote so that he may live forever in thought and in deed . . . A man of God . . . A man of peace . . . Sant Longowal died for the rebirth of Punjab. Vote for a Government that would keep alive his ideals."[30]

Chapter 10

Buddhist Fundamentalism

MYTHOS

Is it appropriate to apply the designation *fundamentalism* in a Buddhist setting? Be that as it may, Buddhism, as a religion without God, raises crucial questions about mythos. Apologists for Theravada, the school predominant in Southeast Asia, often allege that their outlook is unmythological and can be confirmed empirically on the basis of experience.[1] Of course, in its Mahayana (the northern "Greater Vehicle") forms, Buddhism has brought forth a wide variety of symbolism and mythologies in its different schools. In terms of the history of religion, Buddhism certainly has its own distinctive paradigm: "All is sorrow, pain and suffering. All is change, impermanence and unreality."[2] This is the first of its Four Noble Truths. The religion expresses a deep sense of the transiency of life, its brokenness, and concludes that nothing abides. Positively, the Buddhist model has been described as a profoundly spiritual view of the universe without any permanent reality.

Gautama Buddha, the founder of the religion, who lived in the sixth century B.C.E., rejected all speculation concerning the beginning of the world or about life after death—as expressed in philosophies or in myths.[3] Generally speaking, Buddhism is identified by its "three jewels": the Dharma, the Buddhist teaching; the Sangha, the teaching order; and the Buddha himself. Still, historically Buddhism has tolerated and even encouraged a wide variety of symbolism, at least in some schools, but in the end mythology is "transcended" by the ultimate nothingness or emptiness (the latter is a Mahayanist term) that is Nirvana. When salvation finally is obtained—when the boat has reached the other side—to use a Buddhist figure—the religion then can be discarded. The Dharma, the Sangha, and even the Buddha are no longer needed.

Buddhists speak of Nirvana as being beyond description. What can such symbolism signify? Our problem is one of understanding sympathetically from within (as much as possible) a religion whose paradigm and message are very different from that of the faiths based on belief in God. The Buddhist "Gospel," timeless as it may ultimately be, initially became known through Gautama Buddha's experience of Enlightenment. The religion has had a more boundless view of time than Judaism, Christianity, or Islam and is less historically oriented. The laws of karma and reincarnation, birth and rebirth, are presupposed. Western monotheisms have required a complete break with past religious life and practice—in particular, the end of idolatry—when they have made converts. Buddhism, by contrast, has intermingled with native cultures, appropriating much of their religious symbolism, just as it has exported its more ultimate insights concerning Enlightenment. In Japan, Shinto gods at times were equated with Buddhas or Bodhisattvas, Buddhas-to-be.

In the end, all is insignificant compared to the ultimate experience of Nirvana exemplified by the Buddha. The historical Buddha is not important in the same way as the historical Jesus. Indeed, there has been not just the Buddha, Gautama, appearing on earth in his human body in the sixth century B.C.E., but a whole succession of Buddhas—Enlightened Beings. There has been at least one for each world age. In some respects the Buddhist outlook is comparable with Gnosticism in the West. The Buddha body is described as threefold: a body of earthly appearance, a glorified body known to the heavenly beings, and an ultimate body beyond all representation.

Buddhism has been philosophically rich and productive. Still, the religion is not first of all logos, but more existential, something much more akin to what has been called "mysticism," perhaps for lack of any other name. Nagarjuna, the classic philosopher of Mahayana, spoke of the nothingness of nothingness of nothingness, and so on.[4] At first glance, his exposition seems to be a reflection of nihilism. His philosophy was based on the experience of "absolute" emptiness or nothingness in Enlightenment. What makes it difficult is that the problem is not just to identify and understand the ultimate. There is also the difficulty of describing the spiritual quality of salvation when it is identified as "emptiness"; the term is particularly Mahayanist. In their less eclectic traditions, southern Thervadists have claimed an equally radical demythologizing thrust: They only meditate and do not pray. Buddha is revered but not honored as divine.

Can Buddhist "negative theology," then, be described as the "ultimate demythologizing"? This no doubt was what the founder had in mind with respect to the Hindu ideas of deity and caste distinction. Gautama's religious quest is summed up visually in Buddhist temples by pictures of his chariot ride. As he drove along the way in his chariot, he first saw an aged man, decrepit and leaning on a staff. Then as he rode on, he passed a diseased person, a corpse, and finally a monk decently clad. Shocked by the exigencies of life, Gautama renounced the world and set out in quest of salvation, leaving his wife and child in the middle of the night. After years of ascetic discipline, he finally attained the release and peace Buddhists identify as Enlightenment. They have been perennially inspired by this momentous occasion, and monks long have debated its mode and description.

There are historical issues to consider at the outset of any contemporary appropriation. Traditionally, Theravada Buddhists have claimed to continue the original teaching set forth by Gautama Buddha in the sixth century B.C.E. Today, it is clear that literary analysis of source materials makes historical questions much more complicated. Some Mahayana documents seem to be earlier than the Theravada sources. Researchers have concluded that the Theravada Scriptures were not taken originally from the founder but are a scholastic presentation of his teachings. To be sure, his teachings were the object of meditation in monastic communities. One may ask whether Gautama's insights, with respect to Nirvana, for example, were definitive enough to be preserved in any other way.

The traditions that have been mediated from the age of the Buddha are multiple, and their interpretation depends in part on how the Mahayanist revolution, which we will describe subsequently, is understood. Mahayana can be seen as a revolution against a "fundamentalism" that appeared very early in the history of the religion, or as a "modernist" modification of its legacy in such a way as to threaten its identity. Neither designation is fully appropriate. We will begin with Thai Buddhism in considering the role of revivalism and fundamentalism in the Buddhist tradition.

BUDDHIST FUNDAMENTALIST PHENOMENA

Donald K. Swearer, writing in *Fundamentalisms Observed,* identifies two Theravada Buddhist fundamentalist movements in Thailand along with fundamentalist phenomena in Sri Lanka (Ceylon).[5] Characteristically, nationalism and religious revivalism have appeared together at the same time. Opposing accommodation to modernity, they are both absolutistic and aggressive—in short, fundamentalist—Swearer concludes. They represent not only a reassertion of a religiously grounded communal identity, but a new apologetic interpretation of the Buddhist mythos.[6]

The two Buddhist centers in Thailand have been described as follows: Lay members, robed in white, mix with saffron-robed monks on the the grounds of Wat Dhammakaya, the new temple at Prathum Thani, a forty-five-minute drive by car from Bangkok. Evidently the pattern of devotion is not the usual one. In the meeting hall of the temple, the visitor notes that there is only a single Buddha image. Because the movement is looked on favorably by the regime, high state officials can be seen visiting the temple. Registered with the state in 1978, the Wat Dhammakaya practice has its own models of ordination and leadership, but is not fully separated from other forms of Buddhism. Swearer views it as sectarian as well as fundamentalist-revivalist.[7] Today, its adherents are estimated at over a million persons. Its simplistic message is carried nationally on radio and television.

On first appearances, at least, Thai Buddhism appears both culturally deep and at the same time tolerant. Western ideas are welcomed more than elsewhere and assimilated into the Thai Buddhist synthesis. At the same time, the state uses the religion and its institutions to help control the country, a very old Buddhist tradition. Efforts are made to discourage unrest. Prophetic critics who have attacked the status quo in the name of the religion have not been free from threat and arrest. Sociologically as well as religiously, fundamentalist groups like the Wat Dhammakaya party are interested most of all in preserving the integrity of faith and community life in face of the "Great Western Transmutation" and its secularizing influence. However, there is not the drastic and overt revolt against the West as in Islamic fundamentalism.

Personal religious experience is emphasized in a pattern that in a number of respects seems more like Pietism than dogmatic fundamentalism. In their training sessions for laypersons, the Wat Dhammakaya clergy employ long-standing tantric and yogic forms of meditation, teaching the samatha trance-producing form of Buddhism to large groups. Charismatic figures lead a journey to a new way of life that appeals to young people—as Western evangelists do in a different setting. The goal is insight beyond all rational concepts—in short, salvation, Nirvana.

A second Thai movement, Santi Asoka, is sociologically more overtly sectarian, and Phra Bodhiraksa, its founder-leader, is outspoken, taking issue with contemporary life and culture. He has done this so strongly that he has been defrocked by the Thai government. Today, his strategy continues to be one of taking risks, speaking bluntly, and protesting against defilements of lay-persons and monks. The tradition of the movement he founded is still not un-qualifiedly antigovernment. Santi Asoka members include the popularly elected governor of Bangkok, Chamlong Srimuang, who is known as an uncorrupted politician.

The movement's antirationalist, anti-intellectual, and even antiritualistic tendencies have been traced back to the traditions of earlier "forest monks."[8] Its revolutionary-reforming intent is evident as one enters an assembly hall. No Buddha images are present. Nor is holy water offered by priests in the Santi Asoka ritual. The intention is to banish the magical and superstitious along with the meaningless aspects of ritual. The movement's puritanism in some re-spects even resembles Wahabi Muslim fundamentalism.

In his own distinctive symbolism, Bodhiraksa, the founder, wears the white robe associated with Brahman priests as well as unordained "homeless" religious practitioners (rather than the saffron robe of Buddhist monks). He was born in 1934 and his personal religious experience in 1970 remains central: In that year, he sensed an illumination—a brightness, openness, and detachment that could not be explained in human terms—an experience on which he bases his own authority. Opposing the country's ethically tolerant, relativistic ethos, he is not just a moralist but a religious figure. In fundamentalist fashion, Phra Bodhiraksa criticizes motion pictures and television, as well as smoking and drinking, and calls for radical transformation of Thai belief and practice. The central issue is thus how Buddhism will be related to the modern world. A number of the violent features of other fundamentalisms seem to be lacking in his movement, possibly due to Buddhism's sense of compassion.

More than Islam or Judaism, Buddhism is a religion of the twice-born, requiring negation before affirmation. Although it initially was without myth-ical concepts of a God or gods, its "ultimate Emptiness," Nirvana, has been compared functionally with deity by some ecumenically minded interpreters. The Santi Asoka movement seeks to "return to roots," to an original situation perceived as being primordial and ideal: a condition of unity, certainty, and purity. At the same time, critics find its teachings simplistic and absolutistic; in short, it lacks the depth of classical Buddhism.[9]

Buddhist fundamentalism in Ceylon, by contrast, has been more directly sponsored "from above" by the popularly elected government, in disregard of any separation of religion from the state. There have been a variety of levels of Buddhist life on the island, some intellectually sophisticated and others unre-flective and primitive. A large folk piety has supported the growth of funda-mentalist civil religion. Anti-Western leadership often has come from monks who are hostile to the modern world in general as well as to the West in particular.

Ceylon was given independence from the British Empire following the Second World War. The Sri Lanka Freedom Party was organized by S. W. R. D. Bandaranaike in 1951 and came to power five years later. Taking a stand different from the tolerant one of Mahatma Gandhi in India, Bandaranaike had a platform that was both chauvinistic and racist (directed, in particular, against the large Tamil Hindu community). Supported by the United Monks' Front, he proclaimed that he was ready to restore Buddhism to its rightful place as the state religion. The twenty-fifth hundredth anniversary of the birth of Gautama Buddha was celebrated with national sponsorship. But under Buddhist fundamentalist rule, the island did not prosper and has become instead a place of violence and terror.

The Buddhist community does not hold a monopoly. The population in Ceylon is only three-fourths Sinhalese, and there is a large (Hindu) Tamil minority. Mythology enters the political scene as revivalism looks to a heroic past. The national chronicle contains accounts of the original settlement of the Sinhalese on the island as well as their victory over Tamil invaders. In short, it records a millennia-old antithesis. Even as Bandaranaike proclaimed a new Buddhist era, he did not move with enough speed and resolution to satisfy the Monks' Front, and he was assassinated by one of its secretaries in the fall of 1959. His wife, Sirimavo Bandaranaike, took his place as ruler. In the summer of 1963, violence broke out against the minority community in Colombo. Shops and homes were destroyed and burned, political prisoners killed. Decades later, resistance was still led by the Tamil "Liberation Tigers." It had not come to an end even after nearly three years of Indian army occupation intended to restore public order.

The violence is said to be justified popularly by Buddhists as the playing out of a religious scenario, a ritualized reenactment of the drama of good and evil.[10] Buddhist symbols are given a narrowly particularistic meaning and become subservient to a search for national identity. Swearer's conclusion is that there is a simplistic transformation of a one-dimensional and univocal earlier worldview. Unfortunately, a rich past is put at the mercy of the fundamentalist ideology of a militantly chauvinistic Buddhism. The outlook is one of not so much a sectarian individualistic fundamentalism as a religiously sanctified nationalism.

EVALUATION: WHAT IS BUDDHIST FUNDAMENTALISM?

In the West, fundamentalism often is equated with biblicism. It needs to be noted that the Buddhist Scriptures are longer and larger than the Jewish and Christian collections. It has already been noted that there are problems in ascertaining sources as between different Buddhist traditions. Generally speaking, the view of Scripture here is different from in the Western theisms. There is much less critical concern about authorship; indeed it is at times nonexistent. Not only do the earliest still-extant sources date from a period two to three hundred years after Gautama's lifetime, the writers of Scripture do not depend on a historical relation to the founder in the same way as in the New Testament or the Qur'an. But various parties or schools often do take one Scripture as normative for their doctrine and teaching.

In the last analysis, the differences among Buddhist schools are much greater than among Christian denominations. Buddhism underwent revolutionary change in the Mahayanist (Greater Vehicle) movement, which began about the same time as the founding of Christianity in the West. The Mahayanists had their own new, inclusive interests in terms of cult and philosophy. Buddhism also underwent significant cultural transformation when it was carried from India to China and Japan as well as other areas such as Burma and Tibet. Mahayana became dominant in northern regions. Some historical accounts identify Mantrayana, the leading school in Tibet, as a third major form of Buddhism.

Early Buddhism was psychological and positivistic. Later Mahayana schools, by contrast, developed numerous philosophies and expanded in cultus. An older, nonsymbolic tradition (the Theravada) had become too negative in its view of salvation and Nirvana, the ultimate, Mahayanists believed. A more extensive cultus (in appearance often polytheistic, with a multitude of Buddhas), and a new and more altruistic model of sainthood, the Bodhisattva ideal, emerged. As in the case of the Christian salvation described in the Gospel of John, Nirvana in this setting is not just otherworldly but real in the present. For the Mahayanist, it is not only a distant goal. Even at present, Samsara, the world of change, can be seen through to Nirvana. In the Zen model, for example, Enlightenment is to be realized immediately, even here and now. In the mythological terms of popular religion, there is a variety of heavens and hells that individuals may pass through before ultimate salvation; none are permanent.

Hopkins emphasizes the Buddhist fundamentalists actually do not place much importance on texts.[11] In this, they differ significantly from Western scriptural fundamentalists. It is not just that their Scriptures are more extensive and diverse than those of Western traditions. Practically, the otherworldly monastic/ascetic thrust of Buddhism at the upper meditative-philosophical level has characteristically been balanced by concerns for the social-political order that supports the Buddhist establishment; this trend is still reflected in Theravada fundamentalism. Hopkins's claim is that religious nationalism has no real basis in the most authoritative Scriptures.

He finds that with a religious ideology wedded to nationalism or communal politics, fundamentalists seldom reflect the more inclusive and sophisticated views of salvation developed by mainstream philosophers. Even though they may emphasize transworldly salvation as the ultimate goal, their chosen role is to serve as more this-worldly defenders of the faith and guardians of salvation. The fundamentalist symbolism is one of an army of faithful warriors, or a purified community that will restore an idealized or imagined past by purging the present world of whatever stands in the way of this goal.

Hopkins points out that the differences between the Theravada and Mahayana schools of Buddhism are reflected in their respective fundamentalisms: The monastically-led nationalistic fundamentalism in Southeast Asia has its background in the traditionally close connection between the Sangha, the monastic order among Theravadans, and their ruling kings. Up to modern times this relationship created a Buddhist stake in the political order. For Theravada Buddhist fundamentalists, the mythical ideal is a political realm like that of Asoka that supports Buddhist values and a purified Sangha that will restore the nation's spiritual health. For millennia, Buddhism relied on ties with the king and government. Reference to the myth of King Asoka, the Indian monarch who championed the religion, has been almost as powerful as the mythology of the Buddha in areas such as Sri Lanka.

MAHAYANA MYTHOLOGY

In the Mahayanist schools a number of doctrines developed as corollaries to its expanded mythical framework. The many-sided teachings of the school include a variety of submodels (microparadigms): salvation by faith and salvation by works. For example, the Bodhisattva Amida—a Buddha-to-be and not a historical figure (rather, one may say, a mythical one)—vowed to help all of humankind before entering Nirvana himself. To this end, he founded an Eastern paradise to which human beings could retreat and rest before seeking further Enlightenment. Subsequently, the conviction developed that faith in Amida's grace, instead of meditation or good works, could bring salvation. The individual need only invoke the Bodhisattva's name at the moment of death, trusting in him, to receive salvation. In popular forms of Buddhism, the paradise that he founded at times became an end in itself.

Of course, there are a number of parallels in the history of religion. One is dealing with not factual history but vehicles of salvation. Chan (in China) or Zen (in Japan) Buddhism is iconoclastic and seeks instant Enlightenment without recourse to written books. At the other end of the spectrum are schools of a more inclusive nature.

Some of the intolerance and militancy evident in Theravada fundamentalism has been carried over into Mahayana in the fundamentalism of Soka

Gakkai in Japan. This so-called New Religion looks to the teachings of Nichiren, a thirteenth-century saint and leader. The difference from Theravada was that, from the outset, Nichiren's outlook was nationalistic but antiestablishment. His teachings were oriented toward laypersons more than the monastic order, seeking to bring them worldly prosperity through personal faith and practice, even while at the same time purifying the nation.

The Mahayanist goal in this setting is not the restoration of a mythical past but rather the transformation of the present world into the cosmic Buddha realm. The Mahayanist premise, very different from the Theravadan, is that this world is the ultimate Buddha realm in its essential reality and is thus the only place where spiritual and material satisfaction can be achieved. For Mahayana Buddhists there is no essential difference between what are designated as "Samsara" and "Nirvana," the present world of change and the "Ultimate." Both are at the same time emptiness and the Buddha nature. These claims are set forth in simplistic populist form today in fundamentalist settings.

JAPANESE FUNDAMENTALISM—SOKA GAKKAI NICHIREN BUDDHISM

Mahayana Buddhists are not always eclectic. A fundamentalist pattern can be identified in Soka Gakkai, a so-called Japanese New Religion in the tradition of Nichiren Buddhism. Its leaders have developed their own analysis of past Buddhist models and ages—all directed to their own school's last stage. Characteristically, Soka Gakkai, more than most other forms of Buddhism, shows a sense of history and even eschatology and is radically intolerant.

Soka Gakkai has made millions of converts, and within its realm of influence there is, in fact, Buddhist fundamentalism. A brief reference to Japanese national history since the Meiji Restoration is required, to clarify the setting. In less than a century, the island kingdom passed from feudalism to the modern world and then to the postmodern world. In World War II, the Japanese battle spirit was popularly inspired by what is identified as Shinto fundamentalism, belief in a living divine emperor.[12] With the country's defeat, this form of fundamentalism collapsed. Now another fundamentalism, that of a "New Religion," has emerged in its place as a populist phenomenon.

American occupation in Japan resulted in significant secularization, against which the so-called New Religions reacted. Actually, there were hundreds of them, but only a few had a significant number of followers. Most of their ritual and symbolism is eclectic, preserving old Japanese traditions in a new setting. In short, the Japanese did not accept the religion of their conquerors after World War II. A whole new group of "cults," often combining

Shinto, Buddhist, and even Hindu and Christian traditions, have become a major force in the country. A postmodern retrogression to archaic religious symbolism—literalistic, simplistic, and populist—is evident. Although part of this development can be described as fundamentalist in a number of respects, none of the New Religions is as intolerant as Soka Gakkai.

The New Religions have drawn most of their followers from the ranks of the new urban proletariat. Many of these religions have had "living founders" who from trance states have conveyed insights of the Japanese tradition— Shinto and Buddhist—in a modified but contemporary form.[13] Leaders have addressed simply and practically the exigencies of the new postwar situation, often in very literalist religious terms. Politicians have patronized a number of them, notably Soka Gakkai, in the same way as American presidents have associated with television evangelists.

Similarities between the new religious Right in the United States and in Japan are not hard to identify. Both have charismatic founders or leaders and conduct their programs with modern tools such as computers. The Japanese movements, like their counterparts in American popular religion, are almost without exception anticommunist. A variety of figures in the New Religions rival even outdo Pat Robertson and Oral Roberts in faith healings and religious ecstasy.

Beneath the bewilderment of the postwar period, violent revolution was brewing in Japan among liberated tenant farmers as well as industrial workers. Communists and socialists had been released from prison, and there was a widespread interest in the writings of Marx and Engels. In a situation in which economic exploitation seemed very real, the New Religions helped to turn the tide away from Marxism.

Nichiren Buddhism teaches belief in a savior, faith, and paradise, and practices a simple prayer of faith in the "Name" that is not found in early Buddhism. The parallels with American fundamentalism are at least threefold: nationalism, a sense of "these latter days," and authority centered on a particular Scripture. Doctrines are eclectic and at the same time simple. The New Religions' founders claim to have unusual spiritual power in divination, sorcery, and faith healing. Not originating from aristocratic backgrounds, they can relate to the everyday problems of their followers.[14]

Along with other such leaders, the founders of Soka Gakkai were imprisoned during World War II. After they were released after the country's defeat, their goal became the total conversion of Japan. After converting millions of persons, like the leaders of the Moral Majority, they sought to achieve political influence through a somewhat separate wing, Komeito. Nichiren Buddhism traces its origin back to the thirteenth century, a time of crisis in Japan. The Mongol invasion threatened Japan from the mainland of Asia. Although Nichiren claimed "orthodoxy" in the tradition of the Tendai school of Buddhism, historians often credit him with actually inaugurating a new movement.

The populist appeal of Nichiren's own life is not to be underestimated. The saint's biography is reported to have been the most widely read book in the occupation period after World War II. The extremely powerful message of the Lotus Sutra, the canonical basis of Nichiren doctrine, is set forth in fundamentalist terms.[15]

The Buddhist Lotus Sutra embodies the mythos.[16] Called *Hokekyo* in Japanese, historical criticism has made it clear that this sutra could not have come from Gautama himself, as the followers of Tendai and Nichiren schools claim. Still, there is evidence that it was written before 250 C.E. The setting for this "living Buddha's" final teaching is Vulture Peak. Multitudes of Bodhisattvas pour out of chasms in the earth. Nichiren is identified with Jogyo Bosatsu, who leads them. It is this Bodhisattva who appears in the period of complete despair, the period of the End of the Dharma, to provide new encouragement.

Nichiren believed that while some persons could be persuaded by tolerant methods, a show of intolerance was necessary for others in order to convert them to the truth. He used the term *shakubuku* to define the mode of missionary activity that he taught his followers; it means literally "to destroy and conquer." So long forgotten that only a few Japanese remembered its original meaning, it was revived by Soka Gakkai. Today, the movement's leaders seek a more conciliatory and socially accepted image.

Soka Gakkai's dramatic and literalist symbolism has an eschatological dimension. When, at last, prophecy proves true and Nichiren Buddhism is accepted by the Japanese nation, an appropriately built platform will be the site of elaborate ceremony and celebration. Under Komeito, the political arm of Soka Gakkai, millions of persons have become active and involved in elections, and this in all probability is not a passing phenomenon even in a society of rapid change. Buddhism is simplified in the Soka Gakkai's few tenets for missionary purposes. It is widely observed by critics that members of Soka Gakkai are not generally disturbed by a day-to-day confrontation with moral choices. Their religion is seen as a key to happiness that magically opens doors that have previously been locked.[17] Promising success and happiness in their eudaemonistic version of salvation, they are attacked as simplistic and reductionistic by their enemies on every side.

Nichiren's thirteenth-century militant teachings were inspired by his belief that he himself was a Buddha reincarnate. At a time when Japan was threatened by invasion from the mainland, he spoke out so uncompromisingly for political and religious reform that he was sentenced to death. Tradition reports that miraculously, after he had been taken to the execution ground and the executioner had raised his sword, a light fell from heaven and saved his life. Most of all, his followers in Soka Gakkai have been inspired by his zeal to save others.

The phenomenal growth that Soka Gakkai experienced following World War II has slowed down, if not stagnated. Its mood is now one of consolidation, and its leader, Diasaku Ikeda, has traveled throughout the world seeking international recognition. He is praised by his admirers for teaching common people to read the map of life in a new dimension and with a new landscape. Of course, it would be a positive development if fundamentalist leaders elsewhere reached out similarly in accommodation.

CONCLUSION

Comparison of Buddhist and Christian fundamentalism raises basic questions about distinctions of language. Buddhism denies substantial being and timeless truth. Are religions like Christianity and Buddhism encountering similar realities? Both Buddhism and Christianity have existential and soteriological concerns, each calling initially for renunciation. Of course, the recognition of a variety of historical models in both religions (as in the writings of the Japanese scholar Hajime Nakamura, for example), provides a new approach to issues between nonfundamentalists.[18] Buddhism as an answer to the evil of suffering slowly developed its mythology and cult following the death of the founder. This probably was necessary, for it to have power as a religion.

Buddhist apologists claim that theistic notions "substantialize" symbolism and mythical language about the Ultimate. To speak of "truth" and, even more, of "reality" may reflect a Western prejudgment. With respect to religious experience in both East and West, it needs to be recognized that a negative theology must precede a positive one. Fundamentalists generally do not make this premise. It may in part be due to their attempt to return to primordial myth. Buddhism and Christianity both premise a negative theology (and self-denial) preceding positive insight. They both have demythologized—in the prophetic traditions and in mystical traditions, respectively—but there also has been remythologizing.

Buddhism and Christianity, both late developments in the history of religion, followed Hinduism and Judaism chronologically. In principle, neither Buddhism nor Christianity is a simply nationalistic faith. Both have criticized their "parent religions." By contrast, Japanese fundamentalism, like fundamentalism in the United States, is nationalistic, exclusivistic, and in a sense messianic. The crucial question in both settings is what aspect of their respective traditions (Buddhist or Christian) will find expression throughout the larger life of the religion. In short, to what extent will fundamentalism be, or not be, dominant.

Buddhism—for the most part—presents its own kind of problems with respect to fundamentalism, as it is without belief in God. At the same time, fundamentalist-type phenomena appear suggesting that more than simply questions about theism are at issue. Of course, the Mahayana revolution and the richness, as well as the ambiguity, it brought to Buddhism complicate issues of fundamentalism. Buddhists finally cannot avoid confrontation with the modern world. As a religious and social system, their faith is making adjustments to it. In evaluation of ideologies and developments, the fundamentalist paradigm needs to be distinguished from traditionalism. Paradoxically, part of the religion's present vitality seems to lie in the fundamentalist revolt against modernism. The critical issue is whether a religious dynamic becomes static and myths are no longer growing and creative. Fundamentalism is not excluded simply by being a Buddhist.

Chapter 11

Conclusion

NIETZSCHE'S CLAIM FOR "THE DEATH OF GOD"

It seemed to be "a sign of the times" that in the era of the Vietnam War an attempt was made to revive Nietzsche's appraisal of the future.[1] "God is dead!" he had proclaimed. Critics who did not necessarily share his atheistic conviction nonetheless believed that his nihilism illustrated the cultural and religious situation. Viewed from the larger and longer perspective of history— rather than apologetics or sectarianism—it was clear that the sacred had become defunct, Nietzsche believed.

The strength of Nietzsche's exposition lies not only in an existential attack on idealistic philosophy, but also in its highly symbolic mythical language. In his *Thus Spake Zarathustra*, Nietzsche drew a dramatic vision of a new age, proclaiming it from the mouth of the ancient monotheistic prophet Zarathustra (Zoroaster), who lived in Persia centuries before the Christian era.[2] Nietzsche, recognizing the importance of myth, did not mean literally that God really had died—only that a particular symbolism had.

In earlier periods, symbols of deity had been a powerful force, transforming individual life and initiating a new era, the so-called Christian era. Now, even in the Europe of his time, rightly or wrongly, Nietzsche judged that symbols of the sacred had become impotent. The death of belief in God (even though concepts remained) had left a great vacuum. Nietzsche made it clear—in his attack on Enlightenment rationalism, for example—that an archetypal mythical model or paradigm was at issue.

The crisis is not just one of ideas or philosophy, but one touching the deepest level and dynamic of culture. Dilemmas reach to the holy even as it lives on. The bottom line of Nietzsche's conviction is that archetypal symbolism, like the life and death of the sacred, cannot be ignored. He would have found today's fundamentalism strange indeed, but he would have understood that a sense of the holy continues even in new and unexpected forms. Of course, Nietzsche's skepticism and rejection of faith claims were directed most of all against the Christian mythos. But it was not directed against one religion alone. Is fundamentalism—taking mythos literally but with radical seriousness—the refutation of Nietzsche's position?

David J. Krieger, in *The New Universalism, Foundations for a Global Theology*, notes that the age of "the flight of the gods" seems to be coming to an end.[3] "Everywhere there are signs of a reawakened awareness of the sacred. The question is not how to make contact with the sacred, but rather to mediate and synthesize its many conflicting manifestations."

Krieger speaks of the borderlessness of contemporary life and thought. Older philosophies and language games have become impotent. There is no simple universal metalanguage between different realms of discourse, for example, as between philosophy and theology. In this chaotic setting, fundamentalism has emerged, and the reasons for its rise ought not to be minimized. Krieger even reflects that it can be a valuable, if not necessary, moment of definition, because its advocates set limits and take a stance. In this he sees a positive contribution. But the continuing question is still whether the setting will be one of dialogue and not become simply defensive and static. Will it be open to the whole history of religion? The fundamentalist-modernist antithesis cannot be appraised properly when it is approached only from an apologetic stance that makes secularism the chief target. This will perpetuate old problems, Krieger insists.

GROWTH AND DEVELOPMENT OF FUNDAMENTALISM

Much has changed since the name *fundamentalism* was coined in the United States in the early 1920s.[4] This label was used to identify a literalist millennial low-church movement that continues to the present. Revivalist and biblicist, it began in the northern part of the country. In its post–World War II resurgence, it was concentrated more in the South and West and became less theological and more populist. The television revolution gave its evangelists a new "bully" pulpit.[5]

The fundamentalist movement has now also become politicized. With a growing emphasis on folk piety, it is in part charismatic Pentecostal with regard to leadership (Robertson, Roberts, and Swaggart). Various models of the new religious Right are appearing all over the world, East and West, bringing about change in areas of social flux. Most recently, they are being championed in formerly Communist Eastern Europe by fundamentalist missionaries.

Today, with revivalism in all of the major religions, fundamentalist spokespersons call for re-Christianization, re-Islamization, re-Judaization, or re-Hinduization. Moreover, movements of the new religious Right are linked to the history of religion by their perennial appeal to a primordial reality from the past. Although no single word encompasses all of the phenomena of the growing popular piety, the term *fundamentalism* continues to be used popularly in description, for lack of a more convenient one.[6] Claiming timeless absolutes, fundamentalist interpretation of religious symbols is literal and univocal. Millennialism, a mythical pattern of long standing, is usually present in it. Expectation of a utopian golden age, ushered in by special providential action, takes a variety of forms cross-culturally.

The distinguishing feature of all fundamentalisms has been their defensiveness against modernity.[7] All major religions—Hindu or Buddhist, Jewish, Christian, or Muslim—have premised a paradigmatic kerygma, a preaching or message, given in revelation or inspiration. Its absolutization in fundamentalism is not limited to a single faith. Scriptures embody a religion's major symbolic paradigm, relating other, less essential materials to it. Historically, it is important to note that a variety of theological subparadigms cross confessional lines: Incarnation and monotheism, law and grace, redemption and everlasting life are not limited to a single religion. Incarnation of deity, for example, is affirmed in Christianity and Hinduism but not in Judaism or Islam.

The historian of religions Wilfred Cantfield Smith has pointed out that, throughout most of the past, religions lived in self-contained communities in different parts of the world.[8] The traditions of a particular faith were taken for granted. In consequence, their adherents were not as conscious of other outlooks as they are today. Since the Second World War, in particular, the transportation and communication revolutions have brought adherents of different traditions together. Religious belief systems and practices are not limited by a particular geographical setting as much as before. Religious models and points of view, fundamentalist and modernist, overlap.

In the United States and Western Europe, Christians, Muslims, Jews, Hindus, and Buddhists often live side by side in the larger urban centers, and their children attend the same public schools. In such a situation, strict cultural separatism no longer is possible. Nevertheless, religious subcultures often seek to preserve the exclusiveness of their own particular outlooks. Communal strife—for instance, between Jews and Arabs, Hindus and Muslims—has led to terrifying violence in the Middle East and India. Still, in the long run, dialogue—voluntary and involuntary—has become inevitable in a new technological age. The difficulty is that fundamentalism cuts off the exchange of ideas, both within a particular religion and between religions.

FUNDAMENTALISM AND COMMUNISM

Religious fundamentalism has grown up and developed in a period in which Communism and its forced denial of mystery has loomed as an overpowering threat. Now, there has been a major crisis at the end of the twentieth century in the collapse of the Marxist social order in Eastern Europe. Indeed, the term *fundamentalism* has also been applied to late-twentieth-century Communism, with the recognition that its ideology had become decadent and was turned into a pseudoreligion.[9] Writing decades ago, Arthur Koestler was perceptive when he wrote of the (Communist) "God that failed" in his *Darkness at Noon*.[10] Very abruptly, a major persecution of religion has come to an end. An atheistic, Marxist-based obscurantism has collapsed, but religiously oriented fundamentalisms have not. Communist oppression favored an integralist and often reactionary religious paradigm as it attempted to confine faith to the sanctuary. Now, former domains in Eastern Europe are a missionary field for Christian fundamentalists.

Marxist visions of a universal secularity have faded, while fundamentalism continues to hold sway on other continents even more than in Europe. It is clear, for example, that the Muslim fundamentalist revolution has proved more enduring than the Marxist one. The same can be said of other religious fundamentalisms. It is still too early to say what the long-term consequences will be. Victory against Communist atheism has been motivated widely by nationalism and an emotional longing for freedom—strong enough to break up the Soviet empire. A religious remnant of believers remained vital enough to play a decisive role in the 1989 "people's revolutions" in Eastern Europe. Still-existing religious communities had sheltered civil society in face of totalitarianism. But it is evident that determined religious conviction, especially when joined with nationalism, can have negative social consequences, in intolerance and militancy, as well as liberating positive ones.

Often linked to folk piety, fundamentalisms have given their followers rituals for daily life—symbols expressed in communal myths and rites.[11] It is clear that they have a much deeper existential base than is evidenced in the doctrinal debates they have engendered. Reference to mythos is necessary for understanding the phenomena engendered by this conviction. Mythos includes narrative and not abstract ideas alone. As primordial, it is not just an intellectual reference that can be reproduced analytically in advance of its expression in history. Its narrative illumines the paradoxes of life situations, for example, as between freedom and destiny, the human and the divine. In principle, it is not just speculative but also reflects what Pascal identified as "reasons of the heart."[12]

THE UNITED STATES' PATTERN AS EXAMPLE

The French commentator Gilles Kepel points out that the fundamentalist revolution often has taken up where the Communist revolution has left off in failure.[13] This seems to be the case not only in Muslim and Jewish milieu, but in Protestant growth areas as well, such as Latin America and Korea. Rightwing patterns developed in the United States are repeated abroad—theme and variation—in new settings.

The development of fundamentalism in the United States in the era of the First World War gives significant clues about larger worldwide religious trends. The nation, having developed its own distinctive ideology of freedom in the Revolutionary and Civil wars, had been protected throughout the nineteenth century by two great oceans. Fundamentalism developed in a time in which soldiers of the country fought "to make the world safe for democracy" and the political and cultural landscape was rapidly changing.[14] By the Second World War, the change of mythos (and paradigm) reflected not only the new perspectives that emerged with evolution and biblical criticism but the worldwide crisis of ideology evident in Nazism and Communism. Fundamentalists, like the Americans of the earlier Evangelical Empire, had not looked first of all to Europe, even though their traditions initially came from that continent. What broke down was faith in Europe and Western civilization, especially as it was identified with an accompanying growth of secularism.

Fundamentalism was a "new answer" to chaos and meaninglessness. The moral crisis of European civilization, along with the end of colonialism in the world at large, gave its advocates an opportunity in varied geographical settings. All major religions generated restorationist revivalist models, generally with simplification of earlier beliefs and teachings. A response to modernism, fundamentalism in non-Western settings arose defensively, especially among groups with some Western-style education. They had begun to enter the new world generated by technology and science, but did not come to terms with it positively.

The Western press and academics have become interested in the fundamentalist revolution in the last decades of the twentieth century.[15] It is sometimes acknowledged by reporters as well as social scientists researching fundamentalism that they themselves are "outsiders" with their own nonreligious premises.[16] Methodologically, this may be a necessary reaction to an intolerant dogmatism. Not surprisingly, Muslim and Hindu conservatives go on the defensive, criticizing Western studies of their religions and cultures as artificial constructions. Even though it is obvious that secular analysis has offered a necessary and valuable critique, by itself alone it is often epistemologically ambiguous and too dependent on cultural setting. A history-of-religion approach opens more doors, focusing on the existential concerns of fundamentalism as well.

It is the meeting of one kerygma and its mythos with another (including pseudoreligious ones such as Communism) in the contemporary world that evokes fundamentalist aggressiveness, especially when the setting is one in which there is the threat of secularity. In Hindu and Buddhist as well as Islamic settings, fundamentalist reaction against the modern world has taken the form of an attack against the West. Strong polemic against a continuing cultural colonialism is common, but other issues are at stake as well. Traditional sacred canopies are challenged not only by science and technology but by Enlightenment ideology and the Great Western Transmutation (a term taken in the first chapter from Hodgson's analysis). All major religions have to face the problem of entering the modern world, and continue to do so. Fundamentalists refuse to accept this situation and see most of all a growing nihilism; unbelief seems rampant in a new culture propagated by the mass media.

The fundamentalist response, more often than not, has been a renewed theocratic claim as well as involvement in politics. It has had persistent premillennialist overtones. Modernists and religious liberals optimistically had viewed history under the symbol of progress on the pattern of an army marching (almost automatically) forward. But this paradigm no longer finds as much popular support as before, after the chaos and suffering of two world wars. More pessimistic fundamentalist (literalistic) eschatological expectations often have taken its place. Continuing life in time appears as perennially equidistant from eternity. This is the pattern in which most traditional religions have seen it, with their mythos of "last judgment."

THE REMAINING ENLIGHTENMENT LEGACY

Reacting against a dogmatic confessionalism that had led to religious warfare, the Enlightenment championed the separation of church and state. Centering more on science than on religious tradition, its demythologizing posed an inclusive challenge to the scriptural paradigms of major religions. Historically, the legacy of the Enlightenment remains an indispensable protest against obscurantism and superstition. Not surprisingly, its influence spread worldwide. But its champions generally did not recognize their own historicity or the symbolic grid they were applying with respect to both nature and events—in universal terms. Now Enlightenment rationalism has faltered and declined, in face of such diverse outlooks as Darwinism and existentialism, for example. A growing popular nihilism along with the Communist persecution of religion in diverse ways have contributed to the rising power of fundamentalism.

Viewed retrospectively, the Enlightenment claim for universal ideas and values was not as culturally undetermined as was believed. Hans Blumenberg argues that a categorical ethical imperative can be appropriated in support of both religious warfare and humanistically oriented civilization. *Jihad*, for example, has been envisaged as a divine command.[17] When Enlightenment rationalism spread out beyond Europe into the colonial world, its underlying convictions were already being questioned widely. Confronted by the reality of the survival of the fittest, the Enlightenment ethic as formulated by Kant in the categorical imperative had lost its universality.

Still, today, in contrast with fundamentalism, the lasting importance and relevance of Enlightenment criticism remains clear. The case of Eliade, in exile from his native country, Romania, is an example. Following the debacle of Nazism and Communism, he was not prepared to abandon the Enlightenment pluralism so necessary to civilized life.[18] However, this much Eliade had in common with fundamentalists: He did accept the critique of the Enlightenment rationalist mythos to a certain extent and called for a return to roots. Recognition of religion as primordial and as the seedbed of culture would offer the basis for a new and more profound humanism, he believed. A continuing sense of the sacred, perennially expressed in myth and ritual but too much forgotten in secularization, illumines human community and the cosmos. It is not just a matter of personal private experience. Secular myths—an echo of earlier ones about the gods—are not powerful enough to sustain humanity.

NEW BASES FOR CRITICISM AND EVALUATION

If all of reality could be encompassed by the human mind and mastered in human knowledge—a widespread goal in the Enlightenment—all reference to any existential mythos would be rendered outmoded, as Comte understood, writing from less rationalistic premises. What Paul Tillich described more existentially as "myth"—historical symbol—would be rendered unnecessary.[19] But life and events are not so simply described. It is impossible to know the course of history in advance, since historical development always includes the indeterminate of human freedom. The English historian Herbert Butterfield uses the metaphor of music playing to indicate its open and very fragile character.[20] If freedom is an "uncaused cause," as Kant suggested, then there may remain realities, even in everyday life, that are better described in "existential" and even mythical terms and not abstractly.[21]

Today (in the late twentieth century), as secularity seems to be declining in influence, it is not certain what will appear in the place of this paradigm. Eliade's premise that humans have always (from the beginning) had a capacity for mythos may offer the basis for a kind of natural theology developed on a primordial affirmation of the sacred. He believed, at least, that it could serve as the basis for a new humanistic civilization. The Christian theologian Küng asserts a somewhat similar premise.[22] Again looking to the Enlightenment, he stresses that a religious outlook that in the name of the sacred proves to be inhuman cannot be true. Küng knows that historically a sense of the holy often has evoked intolerance and persecution as well as community and altruism— phenomena that continue to characterize fundamentalism in various places.

In short, Küng's antifundamentalist appeal for a dialogue between major world religions is not based on an uncritical judgment that they have displayed unequivocal goodness and virtue in the past. He believes that dialogue is necessary for human survival in the contemporary world. "No peace in the world without peace among world religions," he asserts.[23] Küng has found, moreover, that such dialogue can be creative and even exciting. His analysis provides ample justification for examining fundamentalism in cross-cultural perspective. What the new religious Right does not understand, in its own self-containedness, is that believers really cannot know their own religion today without positive knowledge of other religions. As Marty and Appleby show in their study *Fundamentalisms Compared*, one fundamentalism can be understood better by comparing it with another.

The revisionism of the Protestant theologian Friedrich Schleiermacher, formulated at the beginning of the nineteenth century, remains more relevant than may first appear to be the case.[24] His contribution was one of historicizing Christianity: It could no longer be defended as timeless truth, he believed. Schleiermacher described religion in general as a feeling of absolute dependence and a sense and taste for the infinite. The existentialists have pointed out that human beings have had a radical and perennial sense of contingency, finitude, and powerlessness as they confront fate. The fear of death reaches deeper than any secularity. On the other hand, humanity has a sense of the reality of something "beyond," be it God or Nirvana, a dimension that is not simply of this world.

RECONSTRUCTION

Still the question remains as to what is primordial. In Islam, for example, it is argued that all persons were originally Muslims until they were perverted by other teachings. Buddha through his Enlightenment was said to be able to see back through successive lifetimes to the "beginning." Actually, there is no simply demythologized or unmythical beginning. In the dialectic of confrontation with the holy, symbols produce further symbolism. But from time to time, the growth of myths is interrupted and redirected by practical considerations in the lives of communities as well as individuals—geography, war, famine, defeat, and victory. Fundamentalism has been identified as a reactionary revolution in a time of social crisis, and, of course, it works against a dialogue among religions.

As opposed to absolutism, it needs to be emphasized that the history of religion includes both demythologizing and remythologizing. Symbol systems are not just abstract, impersonal, or heaven-made, as it were. Demythologizing is indeed necessary but not enough; remythologizing is called for in recognition of a "reality" that transcends the subject-object antithesis and, as Tillich insisted, can be understood only symbolically.[25]

Religions in most cases have not been completely new in substance; instead, they build on existing foundations, transforming and "converting" already-given symbols into new patterns.[26] In this setting, it becomes clear that fundamentalist barriers to dialogue are arbitrary. The Israelites borrowed from the Babylonians, Assyrians, and Persians as well as the Canaanites; the Christians from the Jews, taking over the whole of "the Old Testament"; the Muslims from the Jews and Christians. Hinduism and Buddhism have continued to influence each other throughout the centuries. Sikhism was innovative but also drew on earlier traditions.

H. Richard Niebuhr, in his book *The Meaning of Revelation*, did not use the term *mythos* or emphasize symbolism.[27] Indebted to the earlier interpretations of Ritschl and Troeltsch, he described revelation nonpropositionally and existentially. For Niebuhr, prophetic monotheism is the essence of revelation; mysticism is less definite. He sees revelation as correcting the sinful images (substitute: *myths*) that develop in different religious traditions over time. Such a judgment comes from the center of the religious experience, he believed. Even though his main interest was not interreligious dialogue, he nonetheless showed that, more often than not, religious symbolism has been idolatrous, as it has made human beings themselves the center of the universe. Such idolatry cuts off ultimate openness to deity.

Niebuhr is correct that, in terms of the history of religion, traditions need to be criticized more radically than Eliade implies. Perennially, the egoistic, sinful images that so often corrupt their symbolism (mythos) need to be converted. Religion is not absolute, but to be "seen through" to God (or Nirvana, for Buddhists). When criticism of both theology and culture is inhibited by fundamentalist absolutism, a reified mythos easily becomes a threat in the modern world, theocracy being an example. At worst, it is practically dangerous. If civilization is blown up and destroyed by modern arms, it may well be fundamentalists rather than secularists that bring about a "nonreligious eschaton."

For centuries, indeed millennia, major religions have lived in hostility with each other. Muslim-Hindu and Sikh-Hindu violence has not diminished with the end of colonialism, but continues to grow. The Muslim-Christian pattern long has been one of holy war and crusades. Christians have persecuted Jews, a pattern that continued under Nazi paganism. Today, more positively, a Christianity conscious of its background in Judaism, or of Buddhism and Hinduism, need not lose its identity. Knowledgeable about the monotheism of Islam and/or Judaism (as against its own popular tendencies toward tritheism), it will be richer.

TILLICH'S THEOLOGY OF MYTH AND SYMBOL

For Krieger, Tillich's theology still provides a relevant critique that offers a way out of dilemmas.[28] (He notes that Tillich taught a joint seminar with Eliade at the University of Chicago during the last years of his life.) Tillich was attacking the fundamentalist-modernist antithesis when he wrote in *The Future of Religion:* "Therefore, as theologians, we have to break through two barriers against a free approach to the history of religions: the orthodox-exclusive one and the secular-rejective one."[29] From Krieger's point of view, fundamentalism's greatest error has been to make secularism its target. Its exclusivism literalizes religious symbolism rather than allowing it to develop its own living dynamic and power. Moreover, Krieger is sure that the health and integrity of modern secularism has been overstated. Tillich's criticism was that both positions, fundamentalism and secularism, presuppose continuity, unity, sameness, and totality and deny radical otherness.

To his great credit, Tillich (who had read Nietzsche carefully again) raised the question of the relation of faith and reason. Defending secular criticism, he acknowledged that philosophy has certain authentic claims over-religion. But rather than endorsing a simply secular view, he was sure that as soon as philosophical inquiry attains it "real" object, it loses its identity. Instead, it becomes theology, a response to revelation. Tillich's premise was not that religious beliefs have become relativized, but that religious conviction has become pluralized. His concern in this setting was not simply with Christianity. The contemporary situation is radically pluralistic and cannot be escaped by a "calculated return to naiveté"; this is a "delusive step." The only way forward is the inner overcoming of antithesis.

Tillich understood that "the history of religions in its essential nature does not exist alongside the history of culture. The sacred does not lie beside the secular, but in its depths."[30] The sacred—as creative ground—has the power to "convert" and transform the secular by critical judgment and under-standing. But religion can have this role "only if it is at the same time a judg-ment on itself, a judgment which must use the secular as a tool of one's own religious self-criticism."[31] In this setting, appraisal of different paradigms in re-ligion is not only possible but necessary. Myth criticizes myth.

Tillich had written earlier in *The Dynamics of Faith*:

> Myths are always present in every act of faith, because the lan-guage of faith is the symbol. They are also attacked, criticized and tran-scended in each of the great religions of mankind. . . . [32]
>
> There is no substitute for the use of symbols and myths: they are the language of faith. The radical criticism of myth is due to the fact that the primitive mythological consciousness resists the attempt to interpret the myth of myth. . . . The resistance against demytholigization ex-presses itself in "literalism." . . . [33]
>
> Symbols of faith cannot be replaced by other symbols, such as ar-tistic ones, and they cannot be removed by scientific criticism. They have a genuine standing in the human mind, just as science and art have. Their symbolic character is their truth and their power. Nothing less than sym-bols and myths can express our ultimate concern.[34]

We have agreed with Tillich and Eliade that religious mythos is a major dynamic of culture. The sacred outlasts the secular and is more creative. Reli-gious symbolism is not simply antithetical to the modern world. As Tillich ar-gued, it arises from "the depths of being." One of our main claims has been that in such evaluations, paradigm and temporal context can be most instrumental. The long-term problem of how major religious traditions and their respective models relate to each other has been greatly illumined (indeed in a revolutionary way) by modern research in the history of religion. The meeting of one symbolism with another, religious and/or secular (the latter is sometimes called a "pseudomythos") continues to the present. Even in modernity (contrary to a simply secularist view) there is not only demythologizing but subsequently a dynamic of remythologizing.

Notes

1. THE PROBLEMATIC

1. Lionel Caplan, ed., *Studies in Religious Fundamentalism* (Albany: State University of New York Press, 1987), pp. vii, 1.

2. Bruce B. Lawrence, *Defenders of God: The Fundamentalist Revolt Against the Modern Age* (San Francisco: Harper & Row, 1989), p. ix.

3. Ibid., p. 6.

4. Thomas Meyer, ed., *Fundamentalismus in der modernen Welt* (Frankfurt am Main: Suhrkamp, 1989). Cf. Martin Stoehr, "Fundamentalismus—protestantische Beobachtungen," p. 238, in this Meyer volume.

5. Ibid.

6. Lawrence, *Defenders of God*, p. 6.

7. Robert Frykenberg, "On the Comparative Study of Fundamentalist Movements: An Approach to Conceptual Clarity and Definition," unpublished paper. Cf. Robert Frykenberg, and Pauline Kolenda, *Studies of South India, An Anthology of Recent Research and Scholarship* (Madras:, New Era Publications, and New Delhi: American Institute of Indian Studies, 1985).

8. George M. Marsden, *Fundamentalism and American Culture: The Shaping of Twentieth Century Evangelicalism, 1870–1925* (New York: Oxford University Press, 1981), p. 204; idem, *Understanding Fundamentalism and Evangelicalism* (Grand Rapids, Mich.: Eerdmans, 1991), p. 9 et seq.

9. Cf. Emmanuel Sivan, *Interpretations of Islam: Past and Present* (Princeton, N.J.: Darwin Press, 1985).

10. H. L. Mencken, *Prejudices: Fifth Series*, first published in New York, 1926. Quoted in Marsden, *Fundamentalism and American Culture*, p. 188.

11. Ibid., p. 187.

12. Ibid.

13. H. L. Mencken, *Philosophy of Friedrich Nietzsche*, Kennikat Press reprint of 1908 edition, p. 138. Cited by Gary Wills, *Under God, Religion and American Politics* (New York: Simon & Schuster, 1990), p. 102.

14. Wills, *Under God*, pp. 99, 106–7.

15. Auguste Comte, *Auguste Comte and Positivism, the Essential Writings*, ed. Gertrude Lenzen (New York: Harper & Row, 1970).

16. *Cf.*, Langdon Gilkey, "The Creationist Issue: A Theologian's View," in *Cosmology and Theology (Concilium)*, ed., David Tracy and Nicholas Lash (New York, Seabury, 1983); *Creation on Trial, Evolution and God at Little Rock* (Minneapolis: Winston Press, 1985).

17. Frykenberg, "Fundamentalist Movements."

18. Nancy Tatom Ammerman, *Bible Believers: Fundamentalists in the Modern World* (New Brunswick, N.J.: Rutgers University Press, 1987), pp. 16, 88.

19. Ibid., p. 7.

20. Ibid., pp. 41–42.

21. Ibid., p. 47.

22. Ibid., p. 51. Cited from Peter Berger, *The Sacred Canopy* (New York: Doubleday, 1969), pp. 26–27.

23. Ammerman, *Bible Believers*, p. 61.

24. Ibid., p. 102.

25. Berger, *The Sacred Canopy*, pp. 55–58.

26. Lawrence, *Defenders of God*.

27. Ian S. Lustick, *Jewish Fundamentalism in Israel: For the Land and the Lord* (New York: Council on Foreign Relations, 1988), p. 6.

28. Jerry Falwell, *The Fundamentalist Phenomenon: The Resurgence of Conservative Christianity* (Garden City, N.Y.: Doubleday, 1981), p. 11.

29. Cf. James Davison Hunter, "Fundamentalism in Its Global Contours," *The Fundamentalist Phenomenon*, ed. Norman J. Cohen (Grand Rapids, Mich.: Eerdmans, 1990), p. 63.

30. T. N. Madan, "Fundamentalism and the Sikh Religious Tradition," in *Fundamentalisms Observed*, ed. Martin Marty and R. Scott Appleby (Chicago: University of Chicago Press, 1991), p. 619 et seq.

31. Oberoi presented his outlook in a paper given at the University of Chicago research group. Cf. Madan, "Fundamentalism," p. 606.

32. Cf. Bruce Lawrence, "The Fundamentalist Response to Islam's Decline," in *Islam in the Modern World*, The 1983 Paine Lectures in Religion, ed. Jill Raitt, (Columbia: University of Missouri, 1983), pp. 11–40.

33. Marty and Appleby, *Fundamentalisms Observed*, pp. 605–6.

34. Crawford Elder, *Appropriating Hegel* (Aberdeen, Scotland: Aberdeen University Press, 1980).

2. AMERICAN FUNDAMENTALISM

1. Lowell D. Streiker, *The Gospel Time Bomb: Ultrafundamentalism and the Future of America* (Buffalo, N.Y.: Prometheus Books, 1984).

2. Ibid., p. 79.

3. Eric W. Gritsch, *Born Againism, Perspectives on a Movement* (Philadelphia: Fortress Press, 1982), p. 10.

4. Ibid., p. 53.

5. Ibid.

6. Quoted in James C. Helfey, *The Truth in Crisis: The Controversy in the Southern Baptist Convention* (Dallas: Criterion Publications, 1986), p. 53.

7. Quoted in ibid., p. 49.

8. Ibid., p. 50.

9. Ibid.

10. Gritsch, *Born Againism*, p. 13.

11. Hal Lindsey, *The Late Great Planet Earth* (New York: Bantam, 1983).

12. Marsden, *Fundamentalism and American Culture*, pp. 46, 70.

13. II Thessalonians 3:10. Cf. Clyde L. Manschreck, *History of Christianity in the World* (Englewood Cliffs, N.J.: Prentice-Hall, 1985) pp. 12, 26.

14. Albert Schweitzer, *The Quest for the Historical Jesus* (New York: Macmillan, 1959).

15. Hans Küng, *Theology for the Third Millennium* (New York: Doubleday, 1988). Küng develops his paradigm theory in this book. Lawrence, *Defenders of God*, p. 1.

16. James Barr, *Fundamentalism* (Philadelphia: Westminster, 1970).

17. Caplan, *Religious Fundamentalism*, pp. 53–56, 198.

18. Hans Küng and David Tracy, ed. tr. Margaret Koehl, *Paradigm Change in Theology* (Edinburgh, Scotland: T. & T. Clark, 1989).

19. Falwell, *The Fundamentalist Phenomenon*, p. 8.

20. Cf. Niels C. Nielsen, Jr., "Buddhism and Christianity, Advancing the Dialogue," *The Christian Century,* 25 April 1984, pp. 433–35. Both Nakamura and Küng were keynote speakers at the Second Conference on East-West Religions in Honolulu, Hawaii, 3–10 January 1985.

21. Hans Küng, *Christianity and World Religions, Paths to Dialogue with Islam, Hinduism and Buddhism* (Garden City, N.Y.: Doubleday, 1986); idem, *Das Judentum* (Munich: Piper, 1991).

22. Pablo A. Deiros, "Protestant Fundamentalism in Latin America," in Marty and Appleby, *Fundamentalisms Observed*, pp. 142–96.

23. Ibid., p. 144.

24. Ibid., p. 181.

25. David Stoll, "A Protestant Reformation in Latin America?" *The Christian Century,* 17 January 1990, p. 45. Cited in Deiros, "Protestant Fundamentalism," p. 181.

26. David Martin, *Tongues of Fire: The Explosion of Protestantism in Latin America* (Oxford: Basil Blackwell, 1990).

27. Deiros, "Protestant Fundamentalism," p. 160 et seq.

28. Ibid.

29. H. Richard Niebuhr, *Christ and Culture* (New York: Harper, 1951).

30. Lawrence, *Defenders of God*, p. 8.

31. Marshall Berman, *All That Is Solid Melts Into Air: The Experience of Modernity* (New York: Simon and Schuster, 1982), p. 345. Quoted in Lawrence, *Defenders of God*, p. 1.

32. Lawrence, *Defenders of God*, p. x.

33. Ibid.

34. Küng, *Theology for the Third Millennium*.

3. MYTHOS IN THE HISTORY OF RELIGION

1. Cf. Mircea Eliade, *A History of Religious Ideas*, tr. Willard R. Trask (Chicago: University of Chicago Press, 1978–1985). Eliade was speaking to a group of colleagues from the American Society for the Study of Religion.

2. Lynn Pool, *One Passion, Two Loves: The Story of Heinrich and Sophia Schliemann, Discoverers of Troy* (New York: Crowell, 1960).

3. Cecil Roth, *Historical Background of the Dead Sea Scrolls* (New York: Philosophical Library, 1959).

3. Mircea Eliade, *The Nature of Religion* (New York: Harcourt Brace Jovanovich, 1959), p. 229.

5. Ibid.

6. Cf. Stanley L. Jaki, *The Road of Science and the Ways of God* (Chicago: University of Chicago Press, 1978).

7. James Frazer, *The Golden Bough* (London: Macmillan, 1900).

8. Mircea Eliade, *Shamanism: Archaic Teachings of Ecstasy,* tr. Willard R. Trask (New York: Pantheon, 1964); *Yoga, Immortality, and Freedom,* tr. Willard R. Trask (New York: Pantheon, 1958).

9. Mircea Eliade, *Sacred and Profane* (New York: Harper & Row, 1961), pp. 68, 121 et seq.

10. Mircea Eliade, *Birth and Rebirth,* tr. Willard R. Trask, (New York: Harper & Row, 1958), pp. x–xi.

11. Thomas J. J. Altizer, *Mircea Eliade and the Dialectic of the Sacred* (Philadelphia: Westminster, 1963).

12. Guilford Dudley, III, *Mircea Eliade and his Critics* (Philadelphia: Temple University Press, 1977), p. 120.

13. Carsten Colpe and Heike Papenthin, ed. *Religioser Fundamentalismus— unversichtbare Glaubensbasis oder ideologiscsher Strukturfehler?* (Berlin: Alektor Verlag, 1989), p. 7 et seq.

14. Joseph Campbell, *The Hero with a Thousand Faces* (New York: Pantheon, 1949).

15. Ernst Cassierer, *Philosophy of Symbolic Forms,* tr. Karl Manheim, v. 2 (New Haven: Yale University Press, 1953–57).

16. Cf. C. Levi-Strauss, *Myths and Meaning* (New York: Schocken, 1979).

17. Kurt Hübner, *Die Wahrheit des Mythos* (Munich: Beck, 1985), p. 57 et seq.

18. Rudolph Otto, *The Idea of the Holy* (London: Oxford University Press, 1950).

19. Mircea Eliade, "Archaic Myths and Historical Man," *Philosophy of Religion,* ed. Norbert O. Schedler, (New York: Macmillan, 1974), pp. 60–70; cited in Jack Carloye, "Myths as Religious Explanations," *Journal of American Academy of Religion,* June 1980, p. 176. David G. Bradley has pointed out the continuing relevance of the theme of creation in terms of repeated new beginnings throughout the history of religion.

20. Eliade, *Sacred and Profane*, p. 118.

21. Mircea Eliade, *Myth of Eternal Return*, tr. Willard R. Trask (New York: Pantheon Books, 1954), p. 34.

22. Paul Ricoeur, *Symbolism of Evil* (New York: Harper & Row, 1967).

23. Theodoor Marius van Leeuwen, *The Surplus of Meaning: Ontology and Eschatology in the Philosophy of Paul Ricoeur* (Amsterdam: Rodophi, 1981), p. 135.

24. Eliade, *Shamanism*.

25. Leonard J. Biallas, *Myths, Gods, Heroes, and Saviors* (Mystic, Conn.: Twenty-Third, 1986), p. 23.

26. Karl Jaspers, *Origin and Goal of History* (New Haven: Yale University Press, 1953).

27. Biallas, *Myths, Gods, Heroes, and Saviors*.

28. Eliade, *Myth of Eternal Return*, p. 92.

4. THE AMERICAN PARADIGM

1. Meyer, *Fundamentalismus in der modernen Welt*.

2. *New York Times*, 24 August 1984, section 1, p. 1.

3. Gary Wills, "Nelle's Boy, Ronald Reagan and the Disciples of Christ," *The Christian Century*, 12 November 1986, pp. 1004, 1006.

4. Francis Schaeffer, *A Christian Manifesto* (Westchester, Ill.: Crossway Books, 1982).

5. Martin Marty, Forward to Donald G. Mathews, *Religion in the Old South* (Chicago: University of Chicago Press, 1977), p. xi.

6. Albert J. Raboteau, "Afro-American Religion: An Overview," *Encyclopedia of Religion* (New York: Macmillan, 1987), vol. 1, p. 99.

7. Mathews, Religion in the Old South, p. 84.

8. James Turner, *Without God, Without Creed: The Origins of Unbelief in America* (Baltimore: Johns Hopkins University Press, 1985).

9. Cf. Stephen Toulmin, *The Return to Cosmology, Post-modern Science and the Theology of Nature* (Berkeley: University of California Press, 1982), p. 162.

10. Turner, *Without God*, p. 263 et seq.

11. Richard P. McBrien, *Caesar's Coin* (New York: Macmillan, 1987), p. 42 et seq.

12. Robert Bellah, "Toward Clarity in the Midst of Conflict," *Christianity and Crisis*, 29 October 1984, p. 391. Robert Bellah, "Civil Religion in America," *Religion in America*, ed. Robert H. Bellah and William G. McLoughlin, (Boston: Houghton Mifflin, 1968), pp. 3–23.

13. Alexis de Tocqueville, *Democracy in America*, tr. Henry Reeve, vol. 1 (New York: Knopf, 1946), p. 308.

14. Ibid., pp. 305–6.

15. Carl Becker, *The Heavenly City of Eighteenth Century Philosophers* (New Haven: Yale University Press, 1932).

16. Hans Küng, *Does God Exist? An Answer for Today* (Garden City, N.Y.: Doubleday, 1980), p. 123.

17. Loren Eiseley, *Darwin's Century: Evolution and the Men Who Discovered It* (New York: Doubleday, 1958), pp. 17–18.

18. George Marsden, *Understanding Fundamentalism and Evangelicalism*, p. 164 et seq.

19. Wills, *Under God*, p. 16.

20. Turner, *Without God*, p. 114 et seq.

21. Ibid., p. 179.

22. William A. Hutchison, *The Modernist Impulse in American Protestantism* (New York, Oxford, 1982).

23. Turner, *Without God*, p. 198.

5. THE CASE FOR MYTHOS

1. Paul Tillich, *Dynamics of Faith* (New York: Harper and Row, 1957), p. 48 et seq.

2. Hendrikus Berkhof, *Christian Faith*, tr. Sierd Woudstra (Grand Rapids, Mich.: Eerdmans, 1986), pp. 18, 75.

3. Karl Jaspers and Rudolf Bultmann, *Myth and Christianity* (New York: Noonday Press, 1958), p. 16.

4. Cf. Kurt Hübner, *Die Wahrheit des Mythos*.

5. Ibid., p. 29.

6. Ibid., p. 21.

7. Cf. Hans Werner Bartsch, ed. *Kerygma and Myth*, tr. Reginald H. Fuller (London: Society for the Propagation of Christian Knowledge), 1953.

8. Jaspers, *Origin and Goal of History.*

9. Comte, *Comte and Positivism.*

10. Bartsch, *Kerygma and Myth.*

11. F. W. Schelling, *Philosophie der Mythologie,* p. 248; cited in Ernst Cassierer, *The Philosophy of Symbolic Forms,* vol. 2, p. 248.

12. Karl Jaspers, *Origin and Goal of History.*

13. Schelling, *Philosophie der Mythologie,* p. 52; cited in Cassierer, *Philosophy of Symbolic Forms,* p. 21.

14. Northrop Frye, *The Great Code* (New York: Harcourt Brace Jovanovich, 1982).

15. Eliade, *Sacred and Profane,* p. 223.

16. Hübner, *Die Wahrheit des Mythos,* pp. 59–60.

17. Karl Jaspers, *Die Grossen Philosophen* (Munich: Piper, 1957), p. 250 et seq.

18. Cf. Eliade, *A History of Religious Ideas,* vol. 1, p. 259.

19. Mircea Eliade, *Myth and Reality,* tr. Willard R. Trask (New York: Harper & Row, 1963), p. 162 et seq.

20. Hans Blumenberg, *Work on Myth,* tr. Robert M. Wallace (Cambridge: MIT Press, 1985).

21. J. J. Bachofen, *Der Mythos von Orient und Okzident* (Munich: 1926). Quoted in Helmut Thielicke, "A Restatement of the New Testament Mythology," in Bartsch, *Kerygma and Myth,* p. 159.

22. Thielicke, "A Restatement of the New Testament Mythology," p. 153.

23. Ibid., p. 141.

24. Ibid.

25. Hübner, *Die Wahrheit des Mythos,* p. 324 et seq.

26. van Leeuwen, *The Surplus of Meaning,* p. 146.

27. Ibid.

28. Frye, *The Great Code.*

29. Ibid., p. 63.

30. Ibid.

31. Ibid., p. 55.

32. Ibid.

33. Leszek Kolakowski, *The Presence of Myth*, tr. Adam Czerniawski (Chicago: University of Chicago Press, 1981).

34. Ibid., p. 95.

35. Ibid., p. 19 et seq.

36. Ibid., p. 61 et seq.

37. Ibid., p. 130.

38. Ibid., p. 64.

6. JEWISH FUNDAMENTALISM

1. Lustick, *Jewish Fundamentalism in Israel*, p. 2.

2. Ibid., p. 57 et seq.

3. Lawrence, *Defenders of God*, p. 123.

4. Ibid., p. 122.

5. Lustick, *Jewish Fundamentalism in Israel*, p. 35.

6. Lawrence, *Defenders of God*, p. 137.

7. David J. Schnall, "Religion and Political Dissent in Israel, The Case of Gush Emunim," in Richard T. Antoun and Mary Elaine Hegland, ed. *Religious Resurgence, Contemporary Cases in Islam, Christianity and Judaism* (Syracuse, N.Y.: Syracuse University Press, 1987), p. 169 et seq. Cf. also, David J. Schnall, *Radical Dissent in Contemporary Israeli Politics: Cracks in the Wall* (New York: Praeger, 1979), pp. 142–54.

8. Cf. Gideon Aran, "Jewish Zionist Fundamentalism: The Bloc of the Faithful in Israel," in Marty and Appleby, *Fundamentalisms Observed*, p. 319.

9. Ibid., p. 319.

10. Cf. Lustick, *Jewish Fundamentalism in Israel*, p. 95.

11. Cf. ibid., p. 42.

12. Ibid.

13. Charles S. Liebman, "Responses to Jewish Civil Religion," in *Civil Religion in Israel*, ed. Don Yeliva Eviezer, (Berkeley: University of California Press, 1983), p. 149 et seq. Cf. also, "The Religious Component in Israeli Ultra-Nationalism," *The Jerusalem Quarterly*, no. 41 (1987), pp. 127–44.

14. Liebman, "Responses to Jewish Civil Religion," p. 204.

15. Cf. Aran, "Jewish Zionist Fundamentalism," p. 297.

16. Lawrence, *Defenders of God*, p. 123.

17. Ibid., p. 120.

18. Ibid., p. 122.

19. Jacob Neusner, *The Way of Torah, An Introduction to Judaism* (Belmont, Calif.: Wadsworth, 1988), p. 145. Neusner, writing in *Concilium* (Summer 1992), discourages the use of the term *fundamentalism* in a Jewish context.

20. Robert Gordis, "A Dynamic Halakhah: Principles and Procedures of Jewish Law," *Judaism*, vol. 29, no. 1 (Winter) 1980, p. 85.

21. Louis Jacobs, "The Talmud as the Final Authority," *Judaism*, vol. 29, no. 1 (Winter) 1980, pp. 45–48.

22. J. David Bleich, "Halakah as an Absolute," *Judaism*, vol. 29, no. 1 (Winter) 1980, p. 30.

23. Neusner, *The Way of Torah*.

24. Ibid., p. xii.

25. Ibid., p. 42.

26. Ibid., p. 43.

27. Cf. ibid., p. xvi.

28. Ibid., p. 43.

29. Ibid.

30. Ibid.

31. Ibid., p. 3.

32. Ibid., p. 44.

33. Ibid., p. 155.

34. Cf. Liebman, "Responses to Jewish Civil Religion," p. 199.

35. Lawrence, *Defenders of God*, p. 137.

36. Lustick, *Jewish Fundamentalism in Israel*, p. 29 et seq.

37. Ibid.

38. Ibid.

39. Liebman, "Responses to Jewish Civil Religion," p. 198.

40. Ibid.

41. Lustick, *Jewish Fundamentalism in Israel*, p. 37.

42. Ibid., p. 34.

43. Ibid., p. 31.

44. Ibid.

45. Cf. Lawrence, *Defenders of God*, p. 148.

46. Ibid., p. 134.

47. David Newman, "Gush Emunim between Fundamentalism and Pragmatism," *The Jerusalem Quarterly*, no. 39 (1986), p. 32 et seq.

48. Ibid.

49. Cf. Lustick, *Jewish Fundamentalism in Israel*, p. 141 et seq.; Aran, "Jewish Zionist Fundamentalism," p. 328.

50. Aran, "Jewish Zionist Fundamentalism," p. 326.

51. Ibid., p. 323.

52. Ibid., p. 329.

53. Ibid.

54. Ibid.

55. Ibid., p. 333.

56. Gilles Kepel, *Die Rache Gottes, Radikale Moslems, Christen und Juden auf dem Vormarsch* (Munich: Piper, 1991), 276 et seq.

57. Aran, "Jewish Zionist Fundamentalism," p. 332.

7. MUSLIM FUNDAMENTALISM

1. Robin B. Wright, *Sacred Rage, The Crusade of Modern Islam* (New York: Simon & Schuster, 1985), p. 27.

2. Lawrence, *Defenders of God*, p. 196.

3. Ibid., p. 219.

4. Howard LaFranchi, "School Girls in Veils Spark Debates," *Christian Science Monitor,* 30 October 1989, p. 6.

5. Lawrence, *Defenders of God,* p. 200.

6. Youssef M. Choueiri, *Islamic Fundamentalism* (London: Pinter, 1990), p. 13.

7. Ruhollah Khomeini, *Writings and Declarations of Imam Khomeini,* tr. Hamid Algar (Berkeley: Mizan Press, 1981).

8. Robert Bellah, *Beyond Belief: Essays in a Post-Traditional World* (New York: Harper, 1978), pp. 146–67.

9. Ibid., p. 160.

10. Ibid., p. 149.

11. Ibid., p. 65.

12. John O. Voll, "Fundamentalism in the Sunni Arab World," in Marty and Appleby, *Fundamentalisms Observed,* p. 347 et seq.

13. Bellah, *Beyond Belief,* 153.

14. Ibid., 147.

15. Ibid.

16. Yvonne Yazbeck Haddad, *Contemporary Islam and the Challenge of History* (Albany: State University of New York Press, 1980), pp. 47–50.

17. Ibid.

18. Ibid.

19. Lawrence, *Defenders of God,* p. 48.

20. Malise Ruthven, *Islam in the World* (New York: Oxford University Press, 1984), p. 289.

21. Ibid., p. 237 et seq.

22. Lawrence, *Defenders of God,* p. 216.

23. Ibid., p. 214.

24. Jahal Al-i Ahmad, *Occidentosis, A Plague from the West* (Berkeley: Mizan Press, 1984), p. 94.

25. Ruthven, *Islam in the World,* p. 314 et seq.

26. Quoted in Lawrence, *Defenders of God,* p. 188.

27. Lawrence, *Defenders of God*, p. 193, 236.

28. Cf. Gustave E. Von Grunebaum, "Relations of Philosophy and Science: A General View," in *Essays on Islamic Philosophy and Science*, ed. George F. Hourani, (Albany: State University of New York, Press, 1961), pp. 1–4.

29. Quoted in "Islam and Science, Concordance or Conflict," *The Review of Religions*, vol. 72, no. 9, p. 39.

30. Ibid., pp. 34–46.

31. Ibid.

32. Ibid.

33. Gilles Kepel, *The Prophet and Pharaoh, Muslim Extremism in Egypt*, tr. Jon Rothschild (London: Al Saqi Books, 1985), p. 79.

34. Kenneth Cragg, *Counsels in Contemporary Islam* (Edinburgh: Edinburgh University Press, 1965), p. 110 et seq.

35. Kepel, *Prophet and Pharoah*, p. 37 et seq.

36. Ibid.

37. Fazlur Rahman, *Islam and Modernity, Transformation of an Intellectual Tradition* (Chicago: University of Chicago Press, 1982), p. 141.

38. Ibid., p. 137.

39. Ibid.

40. Marty and Appleby, *Fundamentalisms Observed*, pp. 510–24.

8. HINDU FUNDAMENTALISM

1. Barbara Crossette, "For a Holy Place, Unholy Fury Rages," *New York Times*, Friday, 27 October 1989, p. 6.

2. Ibid.

3. Ross Atkin, "Violence Erupts in India," *The Christian Science Monitor*, December 8, 1992, p. 2.

4. Cf. Burleigh Taylor Wilkens, *Hegel's Philosophy of History* (Ithaca, N.Y.: Cornell University Press, 1974).

5. Cf. Hans Küng, Josef van Ess, Heinrich von Stietencron, and Heinz Bechert, *Christianity and the World Religions, Paths of Dialogue with Islam, Hinduism, and Buddhism* (Garden City, N.Y.: Doubleday, 1986), p. 270.

6. David G. Bradley, "Prophet, Guru, Sage: Three Paradigms of the Hierophant," *Proceedings of the XVth Congress of the International Association for the History of Religion,* Netley S. A., Australia: Wakefield Press, 1966), pp. 17–23.

7. Heinrich von Stietencron, "Religious Practice: Rite, Myth and Meditation," Küng et al., *Christianity and World Religions,* pp. 254–55.

8. Norvin Hein, in commentary on this manuscript. Cf. Niels C. Nielsen, Jr., ed., *Religions of the World* (New York: St. Martin's Press, 1988). Hein is the author of the chapter on Hinduism in *Religions of the World,* pp. 106–99.

9. Professor Thomas J. Hopkins reviewed this chapter on Hinduism and added this explanation and comment to it. Cf. Hopkins, *The Hindu Religious Tradition* (Encino, Calif.: Dickinson, 1971).

10. Walter Anderson and Shindhar H. Damle, *The Brotherhood in Saffron, The Rashtriya Swayamsevak Sangh and Hindu Revivalism* (Boulder, Colo.: Westview Press, 1987), p. 1.

11. Ibid., p. 6.

12. Heinrich Zimmer, *Philosophies of India* (New York: Pantheon, 1951). Quoted in Anderson and Damle, *The Brotherhood in Saffron,* p. 353.

13. Anderson and Damle, *The Brotherhood in Saffron,* p. 71 et seq.

14. Cf. Ainslie T. Embree, *Utopias in Conflict, Religion and Nationalism in Modern India* (Berkeley: University of California Press, 1990).

15. Anderson and Damle, *Brotherhood in Saffron,* p. 73.

16. Cf. Yogendra K. Malik and Dhirendra K. Vajpeyi, "The Rise of Hindu Militancy, India's Secular Democracy at Risk," *Asian Survey,* v. 29, no. 3 (March 1989), p. 318.

17. Ibid.

18. This is Hopkins's comment. Cf. footnote 9 of this chapter.

19. Anderson and Damle, *Brotherhood in Saffron,* p. 13 et seq.

20. Ibid.

21. Ibid., p. 19.

22. Ibid.

23. Malik and Valpeyl, "Rise of Hindu Militancy."

24. S. Savepalli Radhakrishnan, *The Hindu View of Life* (London: George Allen & Unwin, 1961).

25. Embree, *Utopias in Conflict.*

26. Ibid., p. 13.

27. Ibid., p. 20.

28. Ibid., p. 6.

29. Ibid., p. 26 et seq.

30. Heinrich von Stietencron, "Religious Practice: Rite, Myth, and Meditation," in Küng et al., *Christianity and the World Religions,* p. 254.

31. *Bhagavad Gita* III 35. Cited in Embree, *Utopias in Conflict,* p. 29.

32. Embree, *Utopias in Conflict,* p. 37.

33. Ibid., p. 41.

34. Richard Vara, "Hindu Leader Aims at Unity for Sects," *Houston Chronicle,* Saturday, 31 August 1991, p. 3E.

35. Ibid.

36. Lloyd I. Rudolph and Susanne Hoeber Rudolph, "Confessional Politics, Secularism and Centerism in India," in *Fundamentalism, Revivalists and Violence in South Asia,* ed. James Warner Bjorkman, (Riverdale, Md.: Riverdale, 1988), pp. 75–87.

9. SIKH FUNDAMENTALISM

1. Comment of K. F. Rustamji, a retired police official, cited in T. N. Madan, "The Double-Edged Sword: Fundamentalism and the Sikh Religious Tradition," Marty and Appleby, *Fundamentalisms Observed,* op. cit., p. 620.

2. Comment of Amrik Singh, a Sikh intellectual, cited in ibid., p. 621.

3. Pranay Gupte, "The Punjab: Torn by Terror," *New York Times Magazine,* 8 September 1985, p. 68.

4. Marty and Appleby, *Fundamentalisms Observed,* pp. 833–35.

5. Paul Wallace, "The Dilemma of Sikh Revivalism: Identity vs. Political Power," in *Fundamentalism, Revivalists and Violence in South Asia,* ed. James Warner Bjorkman (Riverdale, Md.: Riverdale, 1988), p. 58.

6. Madan, *Double-Edged Sword,* p. 622.

7. Ibid., p. 599 et seq.

8. M. J. Akbar, *India: The Siege Within* (Harmondsworth, Middlesex: Penguin, 1985), p. 187.

9. Georgie Ann Geyer, "When the Future Becomes the Past," in *Beyond Reagan, The Politics of Upheaval,* ed. Paul Duke, (New York: Wagner Books, 1986), p. 290.

10. Cf. Niels C. Nielsen, Jr., *Religions of the World,* p. 366.

11. Quoted in Madan, "Double-Edged Sword," p. 619.

12. Quoted in Akbar, *India,* p. 187.

13. Quoted in Madan, "Double-Edged Sword," p. 598.

14. Ibid., p. 600.

15. Quoted in Akbar, *India,* p. 188.

16. Murray J. Leaf, "The Punjab Crisis," *Asian Survey,* vol. 25, no. 5 (1985). Quoted in Madan, "Double-Edged Sword," p. 597.

17. Quoted in ibid., p. 601.

18. Ibid., p. 602.

19. Quoted in Nielsen, *Religions of the World,* p. 362.

20. Ibid., p. 363.

21. Ibid., p. 362.

22. Ibid., p. 366.

23. W. H. McLeod, *The Evolution of the Sikh Community* (Oxford: Clarendon Press, 1976), p. 3. McLeod's writings include *Guru Nanak and the Sikh Revolution* (Oxford: Clarendon Press, 1976), and *Early Sikh Tradition, A Study of the Janam-sakhis* (Oxford: Clarendon Press, 1980).

24. Gauri 17, Adi Granth, p. 416. Quoted in McLeod, *Guru Nanak and the Sikh Religion,* p. 148.

25. McLeod, *Evolution of the Sikh Community.*

26. Ibid., p. 13.

27. Madan, "Double-Edged Sword," p. 609.

28. Tobbin Jeffrey, *What's Happening to India Today, Punjab, Ethnic Conflict, Mrs. Gandhi's Death and the Test for Federalism* (London: Macmillan, 1986), p. 18.

29. Ibid., p. 205.

30. Ibid., p. 207.

10. BUDDHIST FUNDAMENTALISM

1. Nielsen, *Religions of the World*, p. 203 et seq.

2. Ibid., p. 206.

3. Donald K. Swearer, "Fundamentalist Movements in Theravada Buddhism," Marty and Appleby, *Fundamentalisms Observed*, p. 628 et seq.

4. Mircea Eliade, *A History of Religious Ideas*, vol. 2, p. 222 et seq.

5. Swearer, "Fundamentalist Movements" in *Fundamentalisms Observed*, p. 647.

6. Ibid., p. 656 et seq.

7. Ibid., p. 667 et seq.

8. Ibid., p. 668.

9. Ibid., p. 677.

10. Ibid., p. 647 et seq.

11. Hopkins's comments are from his review of the manuscript of this book before its publication.

12. Winston Davis, "Fundamentalism in Japan: Religious and Political," Marty and Appleby, *Fundamentalisms Observed*, p. 782 et seq.

13. Niels C. Nielsen, Jr., "Religion and Philosophy in Contemporary Japan," *The Rice Institute Pamphlet*, Houston, Texas, vol. 43, no. 4 (January, 1957).

14. H. Neill McFarland, *The Rush Hour of the Gods, A Study of New Religious Movements in Japan* (New York: Macmillan, 1967).

15. Noah H. Brannen, *Soka Gakkai, Japan's Militant Buddhists* (Richmond, Va.: John Knox Press, 1968), p. 65 et seq.

16. Ibid.

17. Niels C. Nielsen, Jr., "Buddhism and Christianity."

18. Cf. Hagime Nakamura, *Ways of Thinking of Eastern Peoples: India, China, Tibet, Japan* (Honolulu, Hawaii: East-West Center Press, 1964).

11. CONCLUSION

1. Cf. Radoslav Tsanoff, *The Great Philosophers* (New York: Harper, 1953), p. 558 et seq.

2. *Ibid.*

3. David J. Krieger, *The New Universalism, Foundations for a Global Theology* (Maryknoll, N.Y.: Orbis, 1991), p. 1.

4. Ernest R. Sandeen, *Origins of Fundamentalism, Toward a Historical Interpretation* (Philadelphia: Fortress Press, 1968).

5. John Pollock, *Billy Graham* (New York: McGraw-Hill, 1966), p. 240.

6. Marty and Appleby, *Fundamentalisms Observed*, p. 814.

7. Lawrence, *Defenders of God*, p. 54 et seq.

8. Wilfred Cantfield Smith, *The Meaning and End of Religion* (New York: Macmillan, 1962).

9. Cf. Niels Nielsen, *Revolutions in Eastern Europe, The Religious Roots* (Maryknoll, N.Y.: Orbis, 1991).

10. Arthur Koestler, *Darkness at Noon*, tr. Daphne Hardy (New York: Macmillan, 1941).

11. Cf. Riffat Hassan, "The Burgeoning of Islamic Fundamentalism: Toward an Understanding of the Phenomenon," in *The Fundamentalist Phenomenon*, Norman J. Cohen, ed. (Grand Rapids, Mich.: Eerdmans, 1990), pp. 151–71. Hassan writes defensively as a Muslim.

12. Tsanoff, *The Great Philosophers*, p. 304.

13. Gilles Kepel, *Die Rache Gottes*, p. 32 et seq.

14. George H. Marsden, *Understanding Fundamentalism and Evangelicalism* (Grand Rapids, Mich.: Eerdmans, 1991), p. 9 et seq.

15. Cf. Marty and Appleby, *Fundamentalisms Observed*, pp. vii, 814 et seq.

16. Ibid.

17. Hans Blumenberg, *Work on Myth*.

18. Cf. Eliade, *Sacred and Profane*, p. 229.

19. Tillich, *Dynamics of Faith*, p. 49 et seq.

20. Herbert Butterfield, *Christianity and History* (London: Collins, 1941).

21. Cf. Tsanoff, *The Great Philosophers*, pp. 452 et seq.

22. Hans Küng, *Theology for the Third Millennium*.

23. Ibid.

24. Tsanoff, *The Great Philosophers*, 472 et seq.

25. Paul Tillich, *Systematic Theology* (Chicago: University of Chicago Press, 1967), vol. 1, p. 172.

26. Eliade, *A History of Religious Ideas*, vol. 1, p. xiv.

27. H. Richard Niebuhr, *The Meaning of Revelation* (New York: Macmillan, 1970).

28. Cf. Krieger, *The New Universalism*, p. 37 et seq. Paul Tillich, "The Significance of the History of Religions for Systematic Theology," in *The Future of Religions*, ed. J. C. Braür (New York: Harper and Row, 1966), p. 83.

29. Tillich, "The Significance of the History of Religions," pp. 82–83.

30. Ibid.

31. Ibid.

32. Tillich, *Dynamics of Faith*, p. 49.

33. Ibid., p. 51.

34. Ibid., p. 53.

Index

A

B